HIStory or OUR Story

Before You Were Called 'Negro' Who Were You?

You Are Who You Were!!

"You shall KNOW **The Truth** and **THE TRUTH** shall <u>Make</u> You FREE"
John 8:32

By: 'Shemuel' Sam Taylor King III

Second Edition

First, I want to thank the Most High, the One and True Living God for opening my mind. Secondly, YOU MUST HAVE AND REFER TO A BIBLE WHEN READING THIS BOOK! <u>I REPEAT</u> YOU MUST HAVE A BIBLE TO FULLY COMPREHEND THIS BOOK! The purpose of me writing this book is to help open the eyes of my people to who they really are, and what the Bible really teaches. <u>The eyes do not see what the mind does not consider</u>. If you are able to read this book from cover to cover, the contents restore the so called 'black man and woman' to his/her true History, Culture, Language, Nationality, and God. We are supposed to stand on the shoulders of those who came before us to help build up the next generation. How can we, when we don't know who came before us? <u>We are who we were</u>. You are who you were! That's why it's so important to know your history. I have taken much time and have conducted extensive research to uncover information that was meant to be kept hidden from our minds. We, so called '<u>blacks'</u>, in North America, come from royalty and our history is exceedingly rich. You will be absolutely amazed at what really belongs to us. Throughout this text, I provide definitions of old English words in the King James Version (KJV), the New King James Version (NKJV), and the American Standard Version (ASV) that we don't use regularly today. This methodology was adopted in order to bring better clarification and understanding as to what the Word of God is actually saying. If you read this book cover to cover, I <u>GUARANTEE</u>, you will learn a <u>minimum</u> of 75% more about history than you already knew at the time you began reading this book. The trumpet is sounding and if you are a child of the Kingdom, then you will hear His voice. Israel –IS -REAL-ER than you may think. REAL EYES REALIZE REAL LIES!

Black man, you are like a Beautiful Rose that leads the world to believe
That you're a weed
Why do you concede to negative imagery
And yes the world believes exactly what it sees
And the tragedy is that you say times have changed
But you changed for the worst to me
When will you bring some positivity to the things that you do, hear and see
And bring the UNITY in CommUNITY

-Sam and Paula King-

With No UNITY, there is NO COMMUNITY.

© Blurb 2015
Sam King retains copyright to this book. All rights reserved. No portion of this book may be reproduced in any form except for brief quotation in reviews without the written permission from the author of the body of work.

© Blurb 2015
Editor: Dr. Paula King
'Shemuel' Sam Taylor King III retains the copyright to this book. All rights reserved.

HIStory or OUR Story

Thought Provoking Questions This Book Answers:

Black history, what do you know about black history? Let me ask you a question. Prior to the trans-Atlantic slave trade in the 1600's, what was YOUR nationality? What did you call yourself? Some may say African. Well, Africa is a continent and there are over 47 different countries in Africa. Which country do YOU come from? What language did YOU speak prior to the 1600's? There are over 1,500 different dialects being spoken in Africa, pick one. What clothing did YOU wear? Was it high heels and stilettos? Was it skinny jeans and wrist bands? What food did YOU eat? Hamburgers and hot dogs? French fries and spaghetti O's? What religion did YOU partake in? Was it Christianity or Catholicism? Who was YOUR God? What was His Name? How did YOU worship Him? Most of you have no idea of the answers to any of these questions? You have no recollection of any of your history prior to the trans-Atlantic slave trade. Now is that a coincidence or by random chance? I don't think so. Have you ever asked yourself, why is it that in the public school system that every time the subject of black history is taught it always begins in the 1600's and with slavery? Why is that? Doesn't that raise some antennas and spark inquiry? Why is it that the public school system is so committed to relegating black history solely to the past 396 years? Why is that? Is it because there is some deficiency in historical data? Or maybe it's because there is no black history at all, prior to the 1600's? Maybe black people just poofed out of thin air, sporadically landed on slave ships and said "hey, we got a new species here"; and start importing and exporting us all around the world? Maybe that's what happened? The question arises, what is the drawback on this history? Why does it keep being withheld? What's the big idea about it? Why is it being held hostage, that's the question? Why can't it be expounded on, one hundred years prior to the 1600s? Three hundred years, five hundred years, one thousand years, why is that information not being revealed? What's the big secret? What's the mysticism about it?
What you're going to come to realize is that your identity is THE BIGGEST KEPT SECRET ON THE PLANET EARTH!!

Oh you thought NASA and the space station and the secret missions being conducted by them, were the biggest kept secrets on earth? No, this is BIGGER than that! You thought that the government, the C.I.A. and the F.B.I. were hiding information about UFO's, Planet X, Nibiru, and aliens, you thought that was the biggest kept secret? No, this is bigger than that. The elite confederate have spent billions of dollars and constructed an innumerable amount of psychological strategy to insure that you never receive and acquire this information. Well now, the "secret" is out. You are about to receive pertinent information from some of the most reputable biblical scholars, historians, and archaeologists. They all know something that you don't know!

And that is

YOUR IDENTITY!!

Thought Provoking Questions This Book Questions:

Have you ever thought within yourself that something is not right, that there must be more to our history?

The Trans-Atlantic Slave trade was the biggest slave trade in human history. With all of the futuristic prophecies warning us of future tragedies such as wars, famines, and earthquakes, why would God not mention the biggest slave trade in human history somewhere in the Bible?

Why is it that in America, in the African-American communities, the ratio of males to females is grossly disproportionate, with females out numbering the males significantly?

Why do so called African-Americans make up the majority of the prison population in America, but are considered minorities in the overall American population?

Why is it that according to the National Black Church Initiative (NBCI), which is a coalition of 34,000 churches, they say "the black woman makes up generously 78% of the black church". In order to combat this epidemic, for the past seven years, the NBCI has a "bring the black men back to the church" campaign. Have you ever thought about why the black man is missing from today's church?

Have you ever thought about why African American children statistically lead all other demographics in being born out of wedlock in single-parent homes?

What does the saying really mean: "If you want to hide something from black people, put it in a book"?

Cool Quotes:

Eyes are useless when the mind is blind.

Until the lion has his historian, the hunter will always be the hero.

Don't dig your grave with your own knife and fork.

The mind cannot teach what it does not know.

What does it profit a man to gain all the material things on this earth, and to lose the consciousness of who he is ??
How you can you understand "HalleluYah" when you dont know who YaH Is ???

Table of Contents

1. We Come From Greatness
2. Our Covenant Agreement with The Most High
3. Our Nation's 'Pinnacle'
4. The Hellenization of the Hebrews
5. The Warning From On High
6. Our Fall As A Nation
7. Columbus Discovered America- OR DID HE?
8. The Greatest Cover-Up of All Time
9. Origins of our so called 'American Traditions'
10. We Did It, They Hid It
11. The Residual Slave Mentality
12. Know Thy Enemy
13. The Recovery Of His People
14. The Two Witnesses of Revelation Explained
15. Be Patient
16. World War III and The Final Judgment
17. The Regeneration
18. A Message To Our Men
19. A Message To Our Women
20. A Love Letter To The Righteous From Dr. Paula King

About the Author

Greetings Family,

My name given at birth was Sam King. My spiritual born again name is Shemuel ben Yahsrael, meaning "Shemuel son of Israel". Shemuel is the Hebrew name of Samuel. I refer to myself as a "son of Israel" because I am a descendant of the man once named Israel. I **DO NOT** believe that a personal name change is in **ANY WAY** a requirement for salvation. It was a personal thing for me. I wanted to relinquish the European slave name passed down to me, and take a Hebrew name of my forefathers. When African Americans ask me my name, I want them to hear something from their original culture. Right now, the names of African Americans are German, English, Italian, and Latin derivatives which are not reflective of their pedigree. The first thing you learn about a person when you meet them is their name. Their name usually reveals something about their image and culture. If you hear the name Lui Wang or Phi Nguyen, you might picture either a **Chinese, Vietnamese, Japanese,** or **Korean** individual. When you hear the names Hauwa Balami, Omotola Atkintunde or Afam Odili, you more than likely will picture native **Africans**. If you hear the names Heidi White, Katie Clark, Allison Switzerland, Jake Price, or Dustin Hunter, you probably envision Caucasian Americans. Unfortunately today, when you hear a lot of African American names, our true history, culture and nativity are not reflected. You don't hear names like Shela'moh, Mat-i-yahu, Sari-yah or Yah-pha anymore like you should. Instead, a lot of our African American names, today, resemble Caucasian Americans' names, which we are not. We carry names such as Michael Thurman, Brad Myers, or Eric White, all of which have no ancestral or cultural roots in our heritage.

In the scriptures, name changes occurred often. God changed Abram's name to Abraham, Jacob to Israel and Sarai to Sarah to cite a few. The name change often denoted a change in destiny or course of action. Well for me, my calling has mandated a change in the course of all my prior actions. Not only that, but with a name is a past, a reputation, habits, identity, and a meaning. The meaning of my Gentile given name is 'sun child' or 'bright sun'. My Hebrew name Shemuel means 'El listens' or 'God listens'. Not only is the meaning of the name important, it's also culturally accurate.

When my ancestors came to the Americas they all came with names from their homeland, but the Europeans re-named them and thus it is so this day. If a Chinese person were to say his name was "Patrick Murphy", you would look at him like he's insane because Murphy is an Irish name. A Chinese man has no connection whatsoever with the name "Murphy". If it doesn't look proper for a person who is Chinese to be walking around named Murphy, Jones, Johnson or Smith, I think it's just as improper for a black person, or the so-called "negro" to walk around with these names. During slavery, the same **slavemaster who owned us put his last name on us to denote that we were his property.** So when you see a negro today who's named "Johnson", if you go back in his history you'll find it was either his great-grandfather or one of his forefathers who was owned by a white man named Johnson. If his surname is "Henry", his grandfather was owned by a white man that was named Henry. The real names of our people were destroyed during slavery.

HIStory or OUR Story

Proverbs 22:1-2
A GOOD NAME is to be chosen <u>than great riches</u>, and favor is better than silver or gold. The rich and the poor meet together in the grave; the Most High is the maker of them all.

Ecclesiastes 7:1
A GOOD NAME is better than precious ointment..

Proverbs 10:7
THE MEMORY of the righteous is a blessing, but **THE NAME** of the wicked will rot.

As you can see in **Proverbs 10:7**, a **name**, **history/memory** and **legacy** are all interconnected. **THE NAME** and **THE MEMORY** of a thing are related. If you destroy the name, you destroy the memory. If you destroy the memory, you destroy its history.

I have been in this truth now for eight years and I tell you it is an ever learning process. So much has been taken from us 'so called' blacks in America that it would make your head spin. I started out as the average Christian from ages 5 to 18. During my first year in college, I saw the movie "The Passion of the Christ" and re-dedicated my life to God. During most of my earlier years I attended church, but did not read the Bible as often as I should've. After watching "The Passion of The Christ", one thing I knew for sure was that there is only one Bible and over 100 different denominations. Something is gravely wrong with that! So, I set out to seek the truth. I didn't immediately run to the church or ask people questions. It's a good thing! For it is written, "If the blind leads the blind, both fall into a ditch" (**Matthew 15:14**). I did not want someone to give me a context killer. which is a lie or baseless opinion. If you have an incorrect context, you will have an incorrect conclusion. So if the lenses you use are faulty, then the view will be faulty. I wanted everything to come from the Bible and straight into my mind without being twisted or coerced. I also read other religious texts such as the Quran. I studied Hinduism and Buddhism along the way in my search for the truth. My quest pointed me back to the Bible, in which I ultimately stayed. I took college courses on the old and new testament as well as an 'Introduction to Religions' class to expand my awareness. I took separate classes on the Greek and Hebrew languages because the Old Testament was written in Hebrew and the New Testament has mostly been translated from the Greek. I wanted to obtain a greater understanding of the text being written because a lot gets lost between translations. After many years of doing public speaking in other forums, the Most High has revealed to me that the time has come for me to use the same platforms to advance the Truth. Through blood, sweat, tears, and countless hours of studying and devotion, I am able to present you with this body of facts. Deal with it as you may, but finally it is here. I feel that this is my greatest life's work and my greatest contribution to this world so far--for me to be able to extend the olive branch of truth to my people! I believe you only become a fool when you think you know everything.

1 Corinthians 3:18
"Let no man deceive himself. If any man among you seems to be wise in this world, <u>let him become a fool</u>, **THAT HE MAY BE WISE**"

Explanation of Terms

In this book, the correct names are restored to us concerning our true nationality, God, Christ, and the patriarchs of the Bible. For example I do not use erroneous terminology, such as 'the Lord' when referring to the name of the Most High, but I call Him by His True name Yahuah pronounced (**yah-oo-ah**) (see page 407-408). Most of the characters, even Christ, have been "**GIVEN**" Latin, Roman and English names. They were "**GIVEN**" names to best relate them to the ruling class at that time in history. In the beginning, God had dominion over Adam and his wife so he "**GAVE**" them a name: "Adam" (**Genesis 5:1-2**). After that God made Adam to rule and have dominion over all of the fish, birds, cattle, and every living thing (**Genesis 1: 28**). Because of this endowed authority, Adam also "**GAVE**" names to all the cattle, birds, and beasts (**Genesis 2:20**). The 'dominant' always re-names the dominated; for example: Kunta Kente was "**GIVEN**" the slave name "Toby". When Dani'EL was held captive in ancient Babylon he was "**GIVEN**" a slave name "Bel-te-shaz'zar". Hana'niYAH was "**GIVEN**" the slave name "Sha'drach", Misha'EL was "**GIVEN**" a slave name "Me'shach, and Aza'riYAH was "**GIVEN**" the slave name "Abed'Nego"; (**Daniel 1: 3-7**). Notice that in **Daniel 1:7,** it says that they were "**GIVEN**" names, meaning their original names were NOT transliterated. The definition of "transliterate" is: to write or print (a letter or word) using the closest corresponding letters of a different alphabet or language providing the closest phonetic sound. Notice in the following scripture, **2 Kings 24:17,** scripture does NOT say that MattaniYah's name was transliterated but **CHANGED**!! Additionally, all of these Israelites were named after God, with names ending in either 'Yah' or 'El'. Once their names were "**CHANGED**", they no longer had Yah's name on them (just like any father normally will name his children after himself) (**Numbers 6:27**). Instead of being named after Yahuah they were given names that glorified Babylonian gods instead (**Daniel 4:8**).

Here are some references:

The correct transliteration for the Most High is YAHUAH, meaning "Yah who exists"

The correct transliteration for the Proper Name of the Messiyah is Yahushua, meaning "Yah who saves"

The correct transliteration for the Proper Name Jacob is Yah'kob, meaning "Wrestle with Yah"

The correct transliteration for the Proper Name Abram is Avram, meaning "many"

The correct transliteration for the Proper Name Abraham is Avraham, meaning "father of many"

The correct transliteration for the Proper Name Mary is Miriam, meaning "Beloved"

The correct transliteration for the Proper Name Moses is Musa, meaning "Drawn"

The correct transliteration for the word Messiah is Messi'yah, meaning "Yah anointed"

The correct transliteration for the Proper Name Jerusalem is Yahrushalom, meaning "Yah place of peace"

The correct transliteration for the Proper Name John is Yah'onon, meaning "Yah is gracious"

The correct transliteration for the Proper Name Matthew is Mati'yahu, meaning "Gift of Yah"

The correct transliteration for the Proper Name Saul is Sha'ul, meaning "asked for"

The correct transliteration for the Proper Name Elijah is Eli'yahu, meaning "Yah my Power"

The correct transliteration for the Proper Name Adam is Adamah, meaning "earth/ground"

The correct transliteration for the Proper Name Jeremiah is Yirmi'yahu, meaning "Yah has uplifted"

The correct transliteration for the Proper Name Isaiah is Yesha'yahu, meaning "Yah is salvation"

The correct transliteration for the Proper Name Zechariah is Zekara'yah, meaning "Yah remembers"

The correct transliteration for the Proper Name Obadiah is Ovadi'yah, meaning "Servant of Yah"

The correct transliteration for the Proper Name Hosea is Hoshe'yah, meaning "Yah delivers"

The correct transliteration for the Proper Name Nehemiah is Nehami'yah, meaning "Yah comforts"

The correct transliteration for the Proper Name Zephaniah is Zephani'Yah, meaning "Yah hides"

The correct translation for the word God is Elohim, meaning "Power". Elohim is often abbreviated El.

The correct translation for the name El Shaddai is "El Almighty"

The correct transliteration for the Proper Name Israel is Yisra'el, meaning "Prevail with power"

The Proper Name Dani'el is already correct; it means "El is my judge"

The correct transliteration for the Proper Name Ezekiel is Yezeqi'el, meaning "El strengthens"

The Proper Name Gabri'el is already correct, it means "El my strength"

The correct transliteration for the Proper Name Micha'el is Mikai'el, meaning "El-like"

The correct transliteration for the Proper Name Joel is Yah'el, meaning "El is Yah"

The correct transliteration for the Proper Name Samuel is Shemu'el, meaning "El hears"

The correct transliteration for the Proper Name Abijah is Abi'yah, meaning "Yah my father"

The correct transliteration for the Proper Name Adonijah is Adoni'yah, meaning "Yah my master"

The correct transliteration for the Proper Name Amariah is Amari'yah, meaning "Yah spoke"

The correct transliteration for the Proper Name Athaliah is Athali'yah, meaning "Yah afflicted"

The correct transliteration for the Proper Name Bithiah is Bithi'yah, meaning "Daughter of Yah"

The correct transliteration for the Proper Name Gedaliah is Gedal'yah, meaning "Yah is great"

The correct transliteration for the Proper Name Gemariah is Gemar'yah, meaning "Yah accomplished"

The correct transliteration for the Proper Name Hanaiah is Hana'yah, meaning "Yah is gracious"

The correct transliteration for the Proper Name Hezekiah is Hezek'yah, meaning "Yah strengthens"

The correct transliteration for the Proper Name Jehosaphat is Yahusaphat, meaning "Yah has judged"

The correct transliteration for the Proper Name Judah is Yahudah, meaning "Yah praises"

The correct transliteration for the Proper Name Nethaniah is Nethan'yah, meaning "Yah has given"

The correct transliteration for the Proper Name Jesse is Yi'shai, meaning "Gift"

The correct transliteration for the Proper Name Hodiah is Hod'yah, meaning "Yah's majesty"

The correct transliteration for the Proper Name Seraiah is Sera'yah, meaning "Yah is ruler"

The correct transliteration for the Proper Name Tobiah is Tobi'yah, meaning "Yah is good"

The correct transliteration for the Proper Name Uriah is Uri'yah, meaning "Yah my light"

The correct transliteration for the Proper Name Uzziah is Uzz'yah, meaning "Yah is my power"

The correct transliteration for the Proper Name Zebediah is Zebed'yah, meaning "Yah bestowed"

The correct transliteration for the Proper Name Zedekiah is Zedek'yah, meaning "Yah's justice"

The correct transliteration for the Proper Name Neriah is Nera'yah, meaning "Yah's lamp"

The correct transliteration for the Proper Name Moriah is Mor'yah, meaning "Yah seen"

The correct transliteration for the Proper Name Malachi is Malak'ai, meaning "My Messenger"

The correct translation for the word Cumbaya is Kumba'yah, meaning "Come by here Yah"

The correct translation for the word Hallelujah is HalleluYah, meaning "Praise Yah"

HIStory or OUR Story   Chapter 1

We Come From Greatness: Mansa Musa

The **myth** has been perpetuated far too long that we 'so called' black people in America were 'rescued' by the Europeans. White America has told us that they 'saved' us and that we were 'uncivilized' swinging from trees with bones in our noses. We were taught that we were heathens, unintelligent and primitive, all of which is untrue. You've probably never heard of him, but **Mansa Musa,** a black man**,** is the richest person in recorded history. The 14th century emperor from West Africa was worth a **staggering $400 billion**, after adjusting for inflation, as calculated by Celebrity Net Worth. To put that number into perspective the Net Worth's calculations mean Musa's fortune far surpassed that of the current richest man in the world, Bill Gates (as of January 21, 2015). According to Forbes, **Gates' net worth is $76 billion**. Mansa Musa died sometime in the 1330s. He left behind an empire filled with palaces and mosques, some of which still stand today (Encyclopedia Britannica). But the emperor really turned historic heads for the over-the-top extravagances of his 1324 pilgrimage to Mecca. The trip, which he embarked upon during the 17th year of the monarch's reign, was hosted by the leaders of both Mecca and Cairo and apparently was so brilliant, it almost put Africa's sun to shame (Encyclopedia Britannica). Musa's wealth was a result of his country's vast natural resources. The West African nation was responsible for more than half of the world's salt and gold supply, according to Net Worth. Research also reveals that the fortune was also fleeting. When you read the story of Helm (Solomon) the Hebrew Yahsraelite, he too was extremely wealthy.

HIStory or OUR Story   **Chapter 1**

We Come From Greatness: Our Early Contributions To The World

The so called 'Black African' was the first human on the planet. At that time, there was one big land mass called Pangaea. Out of Pangaea, the original southern continent, or land mass, from which Africa was made was called Gondwana. Africans were the first humans on this planet 200,000 years ago. They were in East Africa in the Nile Valley region. Genesis gives a road map of the land of Eden and where it was geographically by its rivers the Gihon, Tigris, Euphrates, and the Pishon river.
It was not until 170,000 years later , which was only 30,000 ago that the first white person came into existence in the Caucasus Mountain area.

- **Africans** created the first language in the West African country now called Ghana. That language is Twi and Khui.
- **Air Conditioning Concept** 3000 BC- The Egyptians (who are correctly called the Kemites) poured water in shallow clay trays that were placed on beds of straw. This was done at night so that, during the natural evening temperature drop, evaporation would cause a cooling effect in the rooms where the trays were located.
- **Amen** 2500 BC- This word, which Christians now use at the end of their prayers, was originally spelled Amun and it means "the hidden one." It was the last name of the highest Egyptian (Kemetic) deity. In fact, around 1360 BC, the Egyptian (Kemetic) ruler Seti The Great was worshipped as the god Amun. When the Hebrew Yahsraelites were slaves in Egypt they they later adopted the word and changed its meaning. Today the word amen, which is a common ending to prayers, comes from the Hebrew word *emunah;* it's in effect a way of saying "I believe what was said is true."
- **Geometry** Tacokoma 1500 BC (circa) Tacokoma, like Tishome who invented calculus and Ahmes who invented algebra, was a brilliant Egyptian (Kemetic) mathematician.
- **Handshake** 2800 BC -This contact between two persons signified the conferring of power from a god to an earthly Egyptian (Kemetic) ruler. As a matter of fact, in the so-called hieroglyphic (correctly called medu netcher) picture writings, the verb "to give" is drawn as an extended hand. This is where the European named Michelangelo got his idea for the Sistine Chapel drawing.
- **Toothbrush** 3000 BC -In order to clean and strengthen their teeth, the Egyptians (Kemites) used a chew stick, which was a pencil-sized twig with one end frayed to a soft, fibrous condition.
- **Toothpaste** 2000 BC -The Egyptians (Kemites) made toothpaste from powdered pumice stone and strong wine vinegar that they brushed onto a chew stick. This was much different from the early Roman toothpaste that was made from human *URINE*, which the Romans also used as a mouth wash. In fact, Roman physicians around 100 AD claimed that brushing with urine whitened teeth and fixed them more firmly in the sockets. And wealthy Roman women paid dearly for foreign urine, especially Portuguese urine.
- **Wedding Ring** 2800 BC To the Egyptians (Kemites), a circle, which has no beginning and no end, signified eternity, just as marriage signifies an eternal bond.

If I were to write a book on everything the black African contributed to history, the pages could not contain the information, so I'll stop right here.

HIStory or OUR Story   Chapter 1

Just some facts that we as a people were not taught that we should know about the world around us. The original humans were called the 'Aborigines'. The Aborigines were a people. The etymology of the word "aborigine" reveals that the prefix "ab" means "origin, as in original. The first man or original man was ABstracted from God himself. An analysis of the word "Human" yields "Hue-man". The word Hue means color, so you have the Hue (colored) man. The word Humus means soil or a dark organic material. Dust we are and to the dust we return upon death. We believe that the first hue-(colored) man was made from the brown earth as the bible says that he was. To take away color from a thing is to denature it. White is the recessive side of black. White comes from black, black does not come from white. You can dilute black to create white, but you cannot dilute white and create black, this is a fact. Mendel's law even states that light eyes and skin are recessive.

We have been taught to hate black or brown, but we must remember that in the beginning even the bible says there was '**Darkness**' upon the face of the earth. God created everything from the origin of '**darkness**'. When a baby is born the fetus is formed in the '**darkness** of its mother's womb'. We have been taught that black is bad or of a lesser value. But in actuality, dirt devoid of color is considered granulated, sand or dessert. Real flour is called ' whole grain flour'. An healthier option is to eat whole grain flour. White flour is denatured brown flour.

We were taught that 'so called' Jesus was white, the angels in heaven were white. They told us that Tarzan was the 'King of the Jungle' in AFRICA, and he was white. I know that you remember the story Tarzan swinging from the trees in black Africa with a diaper on, beating his chest. Tarzan broke the lions jaw, and beat up all the Africans. Tarzan could even speak to the animals, but the Africans had been there for centuries. Yet they could NOT talk to the animals. Hilarious right! There's so many positive 'white' imaging infiltrated all around us. For years Miss America was always white. Every president of the United States always has **supposedly** been white white except for Barack Obama. Miss Universe used to always be white. You have 'white house cigars', 'white swan soap','white cloud tissue paper'.We were taught that 'black' was so negative, or undesirable. I mean just look at the language people use concerning 'black'. The words we use and how we use them really do have subconscious psychological effects on people. People say, "Don't get **black**-balled, or **black-** listed". They taught us that the '**white**' cake was angels cake and that the **chocolate** cake was the devils cake. We were taught to 'dream of a **white** christmas', and 'Mary had a little lamb with feet as **white** as snow. We were taught to love 'Snow **White**', and that Santa Claus, everyone's child hero, is **white.** We were also taught that Superman was **white,** Peter Pan was **white,** Popeye was **white,** batman was **white,** Paul was **white,** Jesus is **white,** Buddha was **Asian** with **white** skin, Beethoven was **white,** Mozart was **white** and even God is **white**. For years all our little girls had was Barbie and Ken and they were both **white**. The majority Policemen are **white**. Congress and the Senate are mostly **white**.

But everything bad was **black**. The little ugly duckling was the **black** duck. And the **black** cat was the bad luck. If someone threatens you they are **black**-mailing you! The Great **White** Shark is not **white**, they are **black** and grey mostly, but you still notice they are called 'Great **White**' but the **black** Whale is called the 'Killer Whale'. If you're buying something illegally its on what's called the **black** market! Children and stolen goods are sold on the **black** market. The streets we walk on is **black**, the exits signs are **black**. The book of whorish women and of ones's enemies is called the **black** book. The **white**-swan soap was the good soap, but 'Nigger Head' was the cheap **tar** soap was called ' I'm telling you this is psychological warfare at its best.

HIStory or OUR Story   **Chapter 1**

The Euro-Americans see the sun as a threat because **they are easily burned by the sun**. Nature's sun reveals the true identity of the Euro-Americans as the 'red man'. People of color **naturally** have no need to run or hide from the sun. Unconditioned pigmented skin is not in opposition with the sun, but in harmony with the sun because of its melanin. Euro-Americans' reduced melanin dictates a higher need for sun**block** to protect them from the sun's UV rays. Unconditioned pigmented skin, by nature, draws energy from the sun. Most of us with pigmented skin have had our skin denatured. It has been de-conditioned by the air conditioner. Through air-conditioning, our pores have been conditioned to breathe at an un-natural temperature. As a byproduct of being air-conditioned, we sweat easily when in the sun and we actually lose energy. Naturally our sweat glands were calibrated for nature's sun, but because of unnatural air-conditioning, our glands have been weakened and our pores constrict and clamp down.

Do you know where the 'Garden of Eden' was geographically speaking? Do you have any idea? Well, using the resources left to us we can get a pretty good idea of what Eden looked like. It may surprise you that the Garden of Eden according to the borders of the rivers, provided in the scriptures, was the third neighbor to Khemet/Egypt and Yahsrael/Israel.

In Genesis, it is revealed that there are four rivers outlining the Garden of Eden:
1. Pishon (**Nile**) of Egypt,
2. Gihon
3. Hiddekel (**Tigris**) of Egypt
4. The Euphrates.

The scriptures also refer to the land of Cush, which today is called Ethiopia. The Pishon river is the modern day **Nile river.** The scriptures denote that the Gihon River surrounded the land of Cush, while the Pishon River flowed around the land of Havilah (**the Arabian Peninsula**) Genesis 2:13. The land of Cush/**Ethiopia** is in Africa and **Cush means black.** (Genesis 10:8). We must also bear in mind the geographical jurisdiction of ancient Egypt and ancient Israel.

Bear in mind that Adam/Adamah was created from the **dust** (soil) of the ground.
Genesis 2:7 "And Yahuah formed man **from the dust (soil)** of the GROUND.." (See NET Bible)

The scriptures testify that in that region of the earth the **dust** (soil) was **black.**
Jeremiah 14:2 "Yahudah mourns, and the gates thereof languish; they are **black** like the GROUND."

Note that **Yahushua** (Christ) is also in Adamah's direct pedigree. **Luke 3: 23, 38.**

HIStory or OUR Story   Chapter 1

A common misconception that needs to be set right is about the ancient Eygptians/Kemetians. Egypt (Kemet) is in Africa and all of the ancient Egyptians were a black/colored people. The ancient people that built the wonder of the world--the pyramids, what Ptolemy called the cradle of civilization, of a truth was and is a 'colored' people, a.k.a. 'black' people. Here are some ancient temple drawings and ancient statues left to us by the ancient people to testify as to what they looked like. I'm sure nobody on earth today can know better then themselves.

So as you can see the ancient Egyptians was a black African people according to their own testimony. The ancient Egyptians created a calendar based on the farming season. There were three seasons - the flooding season, the planting season, and the harvest season. Each season was three months long that added up to 360 days. The ancient Egyptians noticed they needed a few more days to fit the seasons. So they added 5 days, holy days, to thank the gods. So thousands of years ago, the ancient Egyptians invented a calendar with 365 days!

An obelisk was a monument made of stone. Each obelisk was placed in a public place. In ancient Egypt, obelisks were often built in pairs. Some were not very high. But some were seventy feet (70 feet!) tall. A few were even taller! They were very heavy and very impressive.
An obelisk has four sides and tapers towards the top to a pyramid shaped point. In ancient Egypt, these huge structures were cut from one huge piece of incredibly heavy stone. The ancient Egyptians were clever. They found a way to stand these huge stones upright after they had been decorated and carved. Each obelisk had writing stating the wonderful life and great achievements of the person each obelisk honored. The pharaohs ordered these huge monuments built for them so that they would always be remembered. The writings on the obelisks tell us a great deal about the ancient Egyptian civilization. Most obelisks were commissioned by pharaohs, but anyone could build one if they had the money. The ancient Egyptians are not the only civilization to build obelisks. In relatively modern times, around the middle of the 1800's, about the same time in American history as the Gold Rush, the government of the United States began building an obelisk in Washington DC, to honor our first president, George Washington. We call this obelisk the Washington Monument. You can see the Washington Monument today. It's still standing. It was built using 36,000 huge heavy blocks of stone. The Washington Monument is 555 feet tall!

HIStory or OUR Story   Chapter 1

Egyptians Invented The Time Clock

The ancient Egyptians were either the first or one of the first ancient civilizations to divide a day into sections, so they could tell what time it was.

Around 3,500 BCE (Before Common Era), the Egyptians used the shadows the giant stone obelisks cast on the ground to tell the time of day. Each obelisk was built to tell a story. But they worked very well as shadow clocks.

Later on, the ancient Egyptians invented the first portable timepiece. It was also a shadow clock, but you could carry it around with you. It was lightweight, and about a foot long, maybe a little longer. It had a raised section in the middle. The rod was marked with 10 or 12 sections. To tell time, you pointed the end of the rod towards the east in the morning and towards the west in the afternoon. The raised center piece cast a shadow on the rod. Where the shadow fell on the markings would tell you what time it was. This creative invention is known as the ancient Egyptian shadow clock.

The Rosetta Stone

In the beginning, in ancient Egypt, over 5000 years ago, scribes wrote things down using pictures. That was a scribe's job, to write things down. Scribes used a system of pictures to do so. These pictures were called hieroglyphics. It was beautiful art. Each symbol had a meaning. But it took time to write things down using hieroglyphics. The scribes needed a faster way to write, because the ancient Egyptians loved to write things down. The scribes created a new written language called Demotic script.

Many years later, when archaeologists discovered hieroglyphic writing on the walls of tombs, they could not read it. They knew the pictures had meaning. But the best they could do was to guess what those pictures meant.

One day, about 200 years ago, someone found a stone in ancient Egypt, a very old stone. There was some writing on the stone. It was a very short story. The same story was written in Greek, in Demotic script, and again in hieroglyphics. Scientists could read Greek. They could even read Demotic script. And now they could read hieroglyphics!

This stone was named the Rosetta Stone. The Rosetta Stone is currently on display at the British Museum in London, England

HIStory or OUR Story Chapter 1

Courts and Justice System

In ancient Egypt, the head of government was Pharaoh.

The ancient Egyptians said "Pharaoh", not the pharaoh. That's because there was only one pharaoh at a time, and Pharaoh owned everything. You did not own your home or your jewelry or your food or anything else. Pharaoh owned everything.

Each pharaoh had an army, a police force, and a huge number of ministers and government officials to help him rule the country. The most important of these helpers was Pharaoh's right hand man, his Vizier.

The Vizier received reports from every top official every day. Every day, the Vizier gave Pharaoh a concise report on what was happening all over Egypt.

The ancient Egyptian legal system was based on common sense. The Egyptian goddess Ma'at was the goddess of justice. Basically, the law followed the teachings of Ma'at, according to the priests, about what was right and wrong. No remains of written laws have been found. However, since the ancient Egyptians loved lists and wrote everything down they could, it would not surprise historians to learn they did write down (codify) some laws at least.

The ancient Egyptians did have a court system. When a dispute was settled in court, both sides were heard, and a common sense decision was made by the lower court based on the facts presented. However, if you did not like the decision of the lower court, you could come before the Vizier on a first come, first served basis, and present your case again. It was not smart to come before the Vizier unless your case was serious, and you had evidence to show that the lower court's decision was in error, because the Vizier's decision was final. You could end up in more trouble than you were in already by demanding to have your case heard in the high court. But the Vizier did try to be fair.

HIStory or OUR Story Chapter 1

Papyrus

The Kemetians/Egyptians were the first people on earth to create paper. Papyrus is the first known form of paper used by humans. Papyrus was a weed that grew wildly along the banks of the Nile River. It grew about 10 feet high. It was used to make everything!

The ancient Egyptians used papyrus to make paper, baskets, sandals, mats, rope, blankets, tables, chairs, mattresses, medicine, perfume, food, and clothes. Truly, papyrus was an important "gift of the Nile".

They even tried to make boats out of papyrus, but that did not work very well. Papyrus absorbs water. Boats made of papyrus would become waterlogged and sink.

Using papyrus to make boats might not have worked, but making paper out of papyrus worked very well. The ancient Egyptians soaked papyrus to soften it, and then mashed it. They pushed the mashed papyrus together into sheets, and let the sheets dry. Then they cut the dried papyrus sheets into strips. They piled several strips on top of each other to make a thick paper. They beat the stack with a hammer to mash the strips together. Then, they placed a weight on top of each stack. That made the paper thin and sturdy. The final step was to dry to stack. That's how they made paper.

But it was still papyrus paper. That meant that even though it had been beaten to a pulp twice, and dried, it could still absorb water. To make sure what they wrote down was protected, the ancient Egyptians only wrote on one side of a sheet of paper. When the paper was full of writing, they rolled the paper into a cylinder with the writing inside, and left a hole down the middle. That way, if the paper picked up any moisture, it could more easily dry.

HIStory or OUR Story   **Chapter 1**

Pyramids

In ancient Egypt, pyramids were built during the time of the Old Kingdom. Pyramids were tombs, royal tombs, where the ancient Egyptians buried their kings. The first pyramid was the Step Pyramid. It was built about 5,000 years ago! You could see it for miles!

Beautifully Decorated: Most pyramids were huge. They had rooms inside like store rooms, bedrooms, and even inside courtyards. Pyramids took many years to build. The inside walls of the pyramids were beautifully decorated.

False Doors: As well as messages and prayers and stories painted on the inside walls in hieroglyphics, the walls were also painted with fake doors. These were not painted to trick anyone into walking into a solid wall. Painted false doors were considered the connectors between the living and the dead.

Pyramid Cities: Cities grew up around the base of a pyramid that was under construction. These cities were called pyramid cities. Pharaoh provided food, shelter, and clothing for the workers and their families. This is how the workers were paid.

After the Pyramids were built, the Pyramid city continued to flourish. The workers might be gone, but in their place were guards. A pyramid had to be guarded. Pharaohs, like all ancient Egyptians, were buried with grave goods so they could enjoy their afterlife. A Pharaoh's grave goods were made of gold and encrusted with jewels. Since pyramids were huge, there was no hiding them. Everybody knew that a pyramid held great wealth. This tempted many robbers. So the expense of a pyramid was not only in construction costs, it continued after the pyramid was built.

Tomb Robbing: To discourage theft, the punishment for robbing a tomb was severe. Traps and secret passages were built inside a pyramid to catch robbers. The pyramid was guarded. Just the same, robbers could not seem to resist the lure of the great wealth inside. Many tombs were successfully robbed.

After the time of the Old Kingdom, pyramids fell out of style. They cost a lot of time and money, and made it far too easy for robbers to know exactly where great wealth was buried.

HIStory or OUR Story   **Chapter 1**

With the overwhelming evidence that you have just seen I think it should be no doubt in your mind that the original Egyptians were what we call today so called 'black' people. And it should make sense being that **Egypt IS in Africa**. This should also give you the context clue that the Hebrew Yahsraelites were also a 'black' people. If we **just read our Bible** the scriptures even bear witness of this. Take note of the following scriptures.

Lamentations 5:10
10:"**Our skin was black** like an oven because of the terrible famine."

Job 30:30
30:"**My skin is black** upon me, and my bones are burned with heat".

Songs of Solomon 1:5-6
5: "**I am black** but **comely** (beautiful/attractive), O you daughters of Yahrushalom, as the tents of Ke'dar, as the curtains of Shelamoh.
6: Look not upon me, because **I am black,** because the sun has looked upon me..."

Description of the son of God
Daniel 10:5-6
5: **Then I lifted up my eyes, and looked and behold a certain** (specific) **man** clothed in **linen**, whose loins were **girded** with **fine gold** of U'phaz:
6: **His body** also was like the **beryl**, and **His face as the appearance of lightning**, and **His eyes as lamps of fire**, and **His arms** and feet LIKE IN COLOR to POLISHED BRASS, and the voice of His words like the voice of a multitude."

Revelation 1: 13-18
13 And in the midst of the seven candlesticks one like to **the Son of man** (son of a human/son of mankind), clothed with a garment down to the foot, and **girt about the paps** (covered his waist and chest) with a **golden girdle.**
14 His **head** (top of his head) and His **hairs** (beard) **were white** like **wool,** as **white as snow**; and **His eyes** were **as a flame of fire**;
15 And **His feet** were like to **fine brass**, as if they **burned in a furnace**; and His voice as the sound of many waters.
16 And He had in his right hand seven stars: and out of his mouth went a sharp two-edged sword: and **His countenance was as the sun shine in his strength.**
17 And when I saw Him, I fell at His feet as dead. And He laid his right hand upon me, saying to me, "Fear not; I am the first and the last:
18 I am He that lives, and was dead; and, behold, I am alive for evermore, Amen; and have the keys of hell and of death."

Daniel 7:9
9: I beheld till the thrones were cast down, and the **Ancient of days** (The Most High) did sit, whose **garment** was **white as snow**, and the **hair of His head were like the pure wool**: His throne was like the fiery flame, and His wheels as burning fire

HIStory or OUR Story — Chapter 1

Another thing to note is: when any of the Hebrews had leprosy if their hair was **black,** they were healed. If their hair was **yellow and thin**, then they were considered UNCLEAN. This goes to show that the Hebrews' hair was/is black. Yahushua a.k.a. 'Jesus' hair could not have been blonde. How could his hair be a color that for a Hebrew was only a condition of leprosy, making him UNCLEAN? Read **Leviticus 13:30-37** for reference.

Another supporting scripture is found in **Matthew 5:36**
36 "Neither shall you swear by your head, because you can not make one **hair WHITE** or **BLACK**"

When Hebrew men are young, **their hair is black in color.** When they grow old, their hair becomes **white in color**.
Now I know that this is a different image than you had in your mind of the Son of God. But, according to the BIBLE and HISTORY, **THIS IS IT!!**
As you can see, even the Son of the Most High **WAS NOT** *clean shaven*. These are some scripture references denoting what they did to Him. NOTE: I use more than one reference because you get more detail.

Isaiah 50:6
6 "I gave **my back** to the smiters, and my **cheeks** to them that **plucked off my beard**: I hid not my **face from shame and spitting**"

But in popular European culture, being *clean shaven* somehow denotes having more integrity or being more trustworthy!? Of course we all know this is not true, because nobody had more integrity than Christ, but He had a full beard. This is simply an observation in the culture we live in today.

HIStory or OUR Story Chapter 1

The Bible teaches that the Hebrew Yahsraelites (Israelites) had certain characteristics.
The Bible says that the Hebrew **men** and **women** wore **bonnets**. (**Isaiah 3:20, Leviticus 8:13, Exodus 32:2-3**)
The Bible teaches that both the biblical Hebrew **men** and **women** wore **earrings**. (**Genesis 35:1-4, Isaiah 3:20, Leviticus 8: 7-13,**)
The Bible teaches that the Hebrew **men** wore **girdles**. (**Exodus 29:9**, **2 Samuel 20:8, Ephesians 6: 14**)
The Bible teaches that the Hebrews wore **fringes**. (**Numbers 15:38-40, Deuteronomy 22:12,** even **Yahushua (Jesus)** wore them--(**Matthew 9:20**) "**hem**" means "fringe, tassel, or the border of a garment" (**Luke 8:44**)
The Bible also teaches that the Hebrew men wore **headbands**. (**Isaiah 3:20**)
Below are ancient depictions of Hebrew Yahsraelites. Notice the **bonnets, earrings, headbands, girdles** and **fringes**.

The above picture is a historically accurate picture of Hebrew Yahsraelites bringing their cakes to the Moon goddess called the 'Queen of heaven', which they worshiped in Babylon. **Jeremiah 44: 16-25**. Below are black Kemetians/Egyptians beating black Hebrews Yahsraelites which is historically accurate as well.

This is a historically accurate depiction of a Kemetian/Egyptian taskmaster whipping a Hebrew Yahsraelite man who was a slave. **Exodus 1:11, 13**

Back in ancient times it was **not about skin color**, it was about <u>tribe</u> and <u>nationality</u>. Black **was not**, **is not**, and **never will be** a nationality because BLACK IS NOT A NATION! There is no such thing as the 'Nation of Black' or the 'Black Nation'. There is no place called the 'Black Land'. Black Egyptians were the slave-owners of black Hebrews. This is and was a reality, and this is what it looked like.

So as you can see above Yosef/Joseph, according to ancient Egypt, is the really dark man with the golden <u>staff</u> (representing being in charge) and the **golden necklace** that pharaoh had given him. How would Yosef be able to blend in among black Egypt unless he, too, was black?? It's because he WAS BLACK!

This is how **Miriam** (Mary) and Yosef, Christ's parents, were able to flee into black Egypt and blend in with the people when King Herod ordered to kill all newborn Hebrew males, because they were ALL BLACK! This is why it was a **miracle** when Musa's (Moses') hand turned white because before it was black. If his hand was already white or tan and turned white, that's not a miracle! (**See Exodus 4: 6-7, Numbers 12:10**). This is how Jethro's daughters mistook **Musa** for a black Egyptian, because he was a black Hebrew!! (**Exodus 2: 11-19**)

On the same note, this is how black Hebrews from the tribe of Benyamin, **Sha'ul** (Paul) was mistaken as a black Egyptian. This occurrence is strongly suggestive of the Apostle Paul's physical appearance (**Acts 21:37-39, Romans 11: 1, Philippians 3: 4-5, 2 Corinthians 11:22, Romans 4:1**).

HIStory or OUR Story   **Chapter 1**

It also helps knowing what the Egyptians physically looked like back then. It's indicative of what the biblical, historical Hebrew Yahsraelites looked like as well. To start, if you look at a map of the land masses, you will see that they are very close, within walking distance--no different than the state line of Georgia is to Alabama. No boat was needed. You could walk to Egypt as did the children of Yahsrael when they were in a great famine.

So as you can see Yahsrael and Egypt are very close. Yahuah said Himself you could **walk** to Egypt read: **Isaiah 30:1-2**
1 "Woe to the **rebellious** children", says Yahuah," that take counsel, but not of me; and that cover with a covering, but not of My spirit, that they may add sin to sin:
2 That **WALK to go down into Egypt**, and have not asked at My mouth; to strengthen themselves in the strength of Pharaoh, and to trust in the shadow of Egypt!

Also it is interesting to note that if Yosef (Joseph) would have been white/or Jewish looking person today, his appearance would have startled his brothers for a Caucasian man to be in such a prestigious position, as governor of all black Egypt back then. Yosef blended in perfectly.

Genesis 42:8 "And Yosef recognized his brothers , but **they did not recognize him**"

Our Agreement/Covenant with the Most High

Long ago, The Most High made a **covenant** (relationship of responsibility) with our forefathers **Avram** (Abram), **Yizak** (Isaac) and **Yahkob/Yahsrael** (Jacob/Israel). He promised to give the land of **Yahsrael** (Israel) to them and to their descendants **FOR EVER**.

Agreement with Avram
Genesis 13: 14-17

14 And Yahuah said to A'vram after that Lot was separated from him, "Lift up now your eyes, and look from the place where you are **northward** and southward and **eastward** and **westward**
15 For **all the land** which you see, to you will I give it, and to your <u>seed</u> (descendants) **FOR EVER**
16 And I will make your <u>seed</u> (descendants) as the dust of the earth: so that if a man can number the dust of the earth, then shall your <u>seed</u> (descendants) also be numbered"

Agreement with Yizak
Genesis 26: 1-5

1 And there was a **<u>famine</u>** (lack of food) in the land, beside the first famine that was in the days of Avraham. And Yizak went to Abimelech king of the Philistines to Ge'rar
2 And Yahuah appeared to him, and said, "Go not down into E'gypt; dwell in the land which I shall tell you of
3 <u>Sojourn</u> (stay temporarily) in this land and I will be with you, and will bless you; for to you, and to your <u>seed</u> (descendants), I will give all these countries and I will perform **the oath** which **I swore** to Avraham (Abraham) your father:
4 <u>**And I will make your seed**</u> (descendants) to multiply as the stars of heaven, and will give to your <u>seed</u> (descendants) all these countries; and in your <u>seed</u> (descendants) shall all the nations of the earth be blessed
5 <u>Because that Avraham obeyed My voice, and kept My charge, My commandments, My statutes, and My laws."</u>

HIStory or OUR Story   **Chapter 2**

Agreement with Yahkob/Yahsrael
Deuteronomy 30:15-18
15 "See, I have set before you this day **life** and **good**, and **death** and **evil**;
16 In that I command you this day to love Yahuah your God, to walk in His ways, and to keep His commandments and His statutes and His judgments, that you may live and multiply: and Yahuah your God shall bless you in the land where you go to possess it.
17 But if your **heart** (mind) turn away, so that you will not hear, but shall be drawn away, and worship other gods, and serve them;
18 I **denounce** (publicly announce) to you this day, that you shall surely **perish** (be gone/not be seen/be out of sight), and that you shall not **prolong** (lengthen/extend) your days upon the land, where you go to pass over Jordan to go to possess it.
19 I call heaven and earth to record this day against you, that I have set before you life and death, **blessing** (good fortune/consequences) and **cursing** (bad fortune/consequences): therefore choose life, that both you and your **seed** (descendants) may live:
20 That you may love Yahuah your God, and that you may obey His voice, and that you may cleave to Him: for He is your life, and the length of your days: that you mayest dwell in the land, which Yahuah swore to your fathers, to Avraham (Abraham), to Yizak (Isaac), and to Yahkob (Jacob), to give them."
Genesis 28:10, 12-14

10 And Yahkob..
12 And he dreamed, and behold a ladder set up on the earth, and the top of it reached to heaven: and behold the **angels** (messengers) of God ascending and descending on it
13 And, bold, Yahuah stood above it, and said, "I am Yahuah God of Avraham your father, and the God of Yizak: the land whereon you lie, to you will I give it, and to your **seed** (descendants)
The Promise of the Land of Yahsrael was a conditional promise. Yahuah gave us positive consequences if we obeyed His voice and kept His commandments, but He also gave us negative consequences if we did not keep them.
As it is written:
14 And your **seed** (descendants) shall be as the dust of the earth, and **you shall spread abroad** to the **west**, and to the **east**, and to the **north**, and to the **south**: and in you and in your **seed** (descendants) shall all the families of the earth be blessed."

HIStory or OUR Story   Chapter 2

Exodus 19: 3-8

3. And Musa (Moses) went up to **God**, and Yahuah called to him out of the mountain, saying, "Thus shall you say to the house of Yah'kob and tell the children of Yahsrael:
4. You have seen what I did to the Egyptians, and how I <u>bore</u> (carried) you on <u>eagles' wings</u> (til the death), and brought you to Myself
5. Now therefore, <u>if</u> (in the condition) you will obey My voice indeed, and keep My <u>covenant</u> (agreement) then you shall be a <u>peculiar</u> (special) treasure to me <u>above</u> (more important than) all people: for all the earth is Mine
6. And you shall be to Me a kingdom of priests and a <u>holy</u> (set-apart) nation. These are the words which you shall speak to the children of Yahsrael"
7. And Musa came and called for the elders of the people, and laid before their faces all these words which Yahuah commanded him.
8. And all the people answered together, and said, "**All that Yahuah has spoken we will do**". And Musa returned the words of the people to Yahuah

The ten commandments are the **core values** of the entire law. The whole law is comprised of 613 laws. It is written: "<u>**IT IS GOOD**</u> to <u>keep the</u> <u>whole law</u> **for if you offend in one point, he is guilty of all. For He that said,** Do not commit adultery, **said also,** Do not kill. **Now if you commit no adultery, yet if you kill, you are become a transgressor of the law." James 2:10-11.**

Yahushua taught that the entire **law** (the Torah) and **the prophets** (books of the prophets) were centered around two basic **old testament** commands: "Love Yahuah with all your heart, and with all your soul, and with all your mind."(**Deuteronomy 6:5**), and "You shall love your neighbor as yourself." **Leviticus 19:18. Matthew 22: 36-40.**

Just like when a company or job has core values, in policy there are a lot more rules than just that of the core values. To say "we only have to keep the '10 commandments' " is equivalent to saying about your job, "I only have to keep the core values, I don't have to comply with all the other policies and procedures". Try that if you want to! You'll be at the Department of Labor before the week is out! Keep in mind folks, we are <u>laborers</u> (**Matthew 9:37**), and this is a <u>business</u>. (**Luke 2:49**) Let's work!

HIStory or OUR Story   **Chapter 2**

LET US REMEMBER THE TEN COMMANDMENTS, OUR CORE VALUES

DEUTERONOMY 6: 5-21

1 I am Yahuah your God, which brought you out of the land of Khemet (Egypt), from the house of bondage. You shall have none other gods before Me.

2 You shall not make you any graven image, or any likeness of any thing that is in heaven above, or that is in the earth beneath, or that is in the waters beneath the earth: You shall not bow down yourself to them, nor serve them: for I, Yahuah your God, am a jealous God visiting the iniquity of the fathers upon the children to the third and fourth generation of them that hate Me, And showing mercy to thousands of them that love me and keep My commandments

3 You shall not bring to nothing the Name of Yahuah your God: for Yahuah will not hold him guiltless that brings His Name to nothing

4 Keep the Sabbath day to sanctify it, as Yahuah your God have commanded you. Six days you shall labour, and do all your work: But the seventh day is the Sabbath of Yahuah your God: in it you shall not do any work, you, nor your son, nor your daughter, nor your manservant, nor your maidservant, nor your ox, nor your ass, nor any of your cattle, nor your stranger that is within your gates; that your manservant and your maidservant may rest as well as you. And remember that you was a servant in the land of Egypt, and that Yahuah your God brought you out from there through a mighty hand and by a stretched out arm: therefore Yahuah your God commanded you to keep the Sabbath day.

5 Honour your father and your mother, as Yahuah your God has commanded you; that your days may be <u>prolonged,</u> and that it may go well with you, <u>in the land</u> which Yahuah your God gives you

6 You shall not kill

7 Neither shall you commit adultery

8 Neither shall you steal

9 Neither shall you bear false witness against your neighbor.

10 Neither shall you desire your neighbor's wife, neither shall you covet your neighbor's house, his field, or his manservant, or his maidservant, his ox, or his ass, or any thing that is your neighbor's"

HIStory or OUR Story   Chapter 2

Yahuah confirmed in His word that He did not only make this agreement with our ancestors only, but also with us, who were in their loins. Read.

Deuteronomy 29:14-15

14 "NEITHER with you only do I make this **covenant** (agreement) and this **oath** (promise); 15 But with him that stands here with us this day before Yahuah your God and also with him that IS NOT here with us this day:"

This is why Yahuah brought us out of Egypt, because of His agreement with **our** forefather Avraham. Egypt descends from Ham **(Psalms 106:22)**, which the other African nations descend from Ham. We, Hebrews, do not come from Ham, but we descend from **Shem/Sem (Semites) (Luke 3:36) (Genesis 10:1)**. So the following passages of scriptures are in fact our history. We as a nation have already received the blessings of the covenant in **Deuteronomy 28:1-14**. They came to pass to their perfection through the life of Shelamoh (Solomon), which you will read about later, but following you will see our downfall in **Deuteronomy 28: 15-68**, which took place from 70.A.D.- up to this current day. If you know our history, even just a little bit, you will recognize these **curses** (consequences) that have already happened to us and are still clinging to our people.

Deuteronomy 28:1-68

1. And it shall come to pass, **if** you shall **hearken** (listen) diligently to the voice of Yahuah your God to observe and to do all His commandments which I command you this day, that Yahuah your God will set you **on high** (at the top) **above** (superior to) all nations of the earth
2. And all these **blessings** (good fortunes) shall come on you, and overtake you if you shall **hearken** listen to the voice of Yahuah your God
3. Blessed shall you be in the city, and blessed shall you be in the field
4. Blessed shall be the **fruit of your body** (children), and the fruit of your ground, and the **fruit of your cattle** (offspring), the increase of your cattle and flocks of your sheep
5. Blessed shall be your basket and your store
6. Blessed shall you be when you come in, and blessed shall you be when you go out
7. Yahuah shall cause **your enemies** that rise up against you to be **smitten** (defeated) before your face: they shall come out against you one way, and flee before you seven ways
8. Yahuah shall command the blessing upon you in your storehouses, and in all that you set your hand to do; and He shall bless you in the land which Yahuah your God gives you
9. Yahuah shall establish you a **holy** (set apart/special) people to Himself, as He has sworn to you, if you shall keep the commandments of Yahuah your God and walk in His ways
10. And all people of the earth shall see that you are called by the name of Yahuah; and they shall be **afraid** (intimidated by) of you

11. And Yahuah shall make you plenteous in goods, in the **fruit of your body** (offspring), and in the **fruit of your cattle** (offspring), and in the fruit of your ground, in the land which Yahuah swore to your fathers to give you
12. Yahuah shall open to you His good **treasure** (storehouse), the heaven to give the rain to your land in its season, and to bless all the work of your hand: and you shall lend to many nations, and you shall not borrow
13. And Yahuah shall make you **the head** (the master) and not **the tail** (servant); and you shall be **above** (on top) only, and you shall not be beneath; if that you **hearken** (listen) to the commandments of Yahuah your God which I command you this day to observe and to do them
14. And you shall not **go aside** (deviate) from any of the words which I command you this day, to the right hand, or to the left, to go after other gods to serve them
15. But it shall come to pass, if you will not **hearken** (listen) to the voice of Yahuah your Elohim to observe to do all His commandments and His statutes which I command you this day; that all these **curses** (supernatural punishments) shall come upon you, and overtake you
16. **Cursed** (under supernatural punishment) shall be you be in the city, and cursed shall you be in the field
17. **Cursed** shall be your basket and your store
18. **Cursed** shall be the fruit of your body, and the fruit of your land, the increase of your cattle and the flocks of your sheep
19. **Cursed** shall you be when you come in, and cursed shall you be when you go out
20. Yahuah shall send upon you **cursing** (hatred), **vexation** (confusion), and **rebuke** (rejection) in all that you set your hand to do, until you be **destroyed** (the process of causing so much damage to something that it no longer exists or cannot be repaired), and you perish quickly; because of the wickedness of your doings whereby you have forsaken Me
21. Yahuah shall make the **pestilence** (disease) cling to you, until He has **consumed** (destroyed reality of) you from off the land, where you go to possess it
22. Yahuah shall smite you with a **consumption** (illness/ruin/destruction/damage), and with a fever, and with an **inflammation** (irritation/pain/infection/soreness), and with **the sword** (war) and with **blasting** (bombed/demolished/killed/shattered/shot at) and with **mildew** (contamination/rotting); and they shall pursue you until you perish
23. And your **heaven** (sky) that is over your head shall be **brass** (as a solid surface/ not releasing rain) and the earth that is under you shall be **iron** (unproductive/famine) until you perish
24. Yahuah shall make the rain of your land powder and dust from **heaven** (sky): shall it come down upon you, until you be destroyed
25. Yahuah shall cause you to be **smitten** (defeated) before your **enemies**: you shall go out **one way** (one direction) against them: and flee **seven ways** (seven different directions to seven different continents) before them: and shall be removed into **all the kingdoms** (all nations) of the earth

HIStory or OUR Story   Chapter 2

26. And your **carcass** (body) shall be **meat** (food) to all of the **fowls** (birds) of the air, and to the beasts of the earth, and no man shall **fray** (frighten) them away
27. Yahuah will smite you with the **botch** (boils) of Egypt, and with the **emerods** (tumors) and with the scab, and with the itch, whereof you cannot be healed
28. Yahuah shall smite you with **madness** (insanity), and **blindness** (lack of vision), and **astonishment of heart** (confusion/daze/surprise)
29. And you shall **grope** (search blindly) at noonday, **as** (similar to) the **blind** (unable to see/lacking perception) **gropes** (searches blindly) in darkness,: and you shall not prosper in your ways: and you shall be only **oppressed** (subject to harsh and authoritarian treatment) and **spoiled** (diminished or destroy the value or quality of/robbed) evermore, and **no man** (human) shall **save you** (redeem)
30. You shall **betroth** (marry) a wife, and **another man shall lie with her** (rape/have sex with): you shall build a house, and you shall not **dwell therein** (live in it): you shall plant a vineyard, and shall not gather the grapes thereof
31. Your ox shall be slain before your eyes, and you shall not eat thereof: your **ass** (mule) shall be violently taken away from before your face, and shall **not be restored**: your sheep shall be given to your **enemies** (people who dislike you, hold you back, do not have your best interest in mind, people who **hate** you (**Leviticus 26:17**) and you shall have none to rescue them.
32. Your sons and your daughters shall be given to **another people** (different race/foreigners), and your eyes shall look, and fail with longing for them all the day long: and there shall be **no might** (power) in your hand
33. The fruit of your land, and all your **labors** (efforts), shall a nation **which you know not of** (unaware) eat up; and you shall be only **oppressed** (subject to harsh and authoritarian treatment/ keep someone in subservience and hardship, especially by the unjust exercise of authority) and **crushed** (deformed, pulverized) always
34. So that you shall **be mad** (upset/made crazy) for the sight of your eyes which you shall see
35. Yahuah shall smite you in the knees, and in the legs, with a sore **botch** (boil) that **cannot be healed**, from the sole of your foot to the top of your head
36. Yahuah shall bring you, and your king which you shall set over you, to a nation which **neither you nor your fathers have known** (not aware of); and there shall you serve other gods, **wood** (Christianity's Cross) and **stone** (Islam's Kaaba Stone)
37. And you shall become an **astonishment** (amazement/a wonder), a **proverb** (example of), and a **byword** (nickname/word used to get by without knowing identity) among all nations where Yahuah shall lead you

38 You shall carry much seed out into the field, and shall gather but little in; for the locust shall consume it.
39 You shall plant vineyards, and dress them, but shall neither drink of the wine, nor gather the grapes; for the worms shall eat them
40 You shall have olive trees throughout all your **coasts** (territory) but you shall not anoint yourself with the oil; for your olive shall **cast** (lose) its fruit
41 You shall father sons and daughters, but you shall not enjoy them; for they shall **go into captivity** (be taken as slaves)
42 All your trees and fruit of your land shall the locust consume
43 **The stranger** (foreigner) that is **inside you** (in your communities) shall **get up above you very high** (be more prosperous than); and you shall **come down very low** (be demoted/decrease)
44 He shall lend to you, you shall not lend to him: he shall be the **head** and you shall be the **tail**
45 Moreover all these **curses** shall come upon you, and shall **pursue** (follow/stalk/chase) you, and **overtake** (conquer) you, till you be destroyed; because you **hearkened** (listened) not to the voice of Yahuah your God to keep His commandments and His statutes which He commanded you:
46. And they shall be upon you for a **sign** (representation/marker) and for a **wonder** (miracle/spectacle) and upon your **seed** (descendants) **forever** (in Hebrew, the word for forever is "olam" meaning "long duration")
47. Because you served not Yahuah your God with joyfulness, and with gladness of heart, for the **abundance of all things** (great wealth)
48. **Therefore** (this is why) shall you **serve** (work for) your **enemies** (people who dislike you), people who **hate** you (**Leviticus 26:17**),
49. which Yahuah shall send against you, in **hunger** (to eat), and in **thirst** (to drink) and **in nakedness** (to clothe yourself), and **in want of all things** (whatever one desires/severe desperation): and he shall put a **yoke of iron upon your neck**, until He have **destroyed** (ruined/broken) you
Yahuah shall bring a nation against you from far, **from the end of the earth** (other side of the planet/NEW WORLD) as **swift** (quick/very intelligent) as the **eagle (emblem of the United States)** flies; a nation whose **tongue** (language) you shall not understand
50. A nation of **fierce** (hostile/intense aggressiveness/very violent/brave/proud/eager to fight or kill/strong emotion) **countenance** (behavior/attitude), which shall not **regard** (respect/care for) the **person of the old** (elder/old person) nor show **favor** (approval/liking/preference/act of kindness/mercy) to the young

51. And he shall eat the fruit of your cattle, and the fruit of your land, until you be **destroyed** (ruined/broken): which also shall not leave you either corn, wine, or oil, or the increase of your cattle, or flocks of your sheep, until he have **destroyed** (ruined/broken) you
52. And he (shall **besiege** (surround) you in all **your gates** (entrances/exits), until your high and **fenced** (guarded) walls come down, wherein you trusted, throughout all **your land**: and he shall: and he shall **besiege** (surround) you in all your gates throughout all your land, which Yahuah your God has given you
53. And you shall eat the **fruit of your own body** (your own children), the flesh of your sons and of your daughters, which Yahuah your God has given you, in the **siege** (serious attack/ a military operation in which enemy forces surround a town) and in the **straitness** (very tight/suffocating) wherewith your **enemies** (people who dislike you), people who **hate** you (**Leviticus 26:17**) shall **distress** (cause worry/cause extreme anxiety/make afraid/stress out) you
54. So that the man that is **tender** (gentle/harmless/nice) among you, and very **delicate** (charming/soft/fragile/charming), his eye shall be evil toward his **brother,** and toward the **wife** of **his bosom** (intense love/intimacy), and toward the **remnant** (remaining) of his children which he shall leave:
55. So that he will not give to any of them of **the flesh** (skin) of his children whom he shall eat: because **he has nothing left** (foodless) in the **siege** (serious attack/a military operation in which enemy forces surround a town), and in the **straitness** (very tight/suffocating) wherewith your enemies shall **distress** you in all your gates
56. The **tender** (gentle/harmless/nice) and **delicate** (precious/soft/fragile/charming) woman among you, which would not **adventure** (dare) to set the sole of her foot upon the ground for **delicateness** (classiness) and **tenderness** (very high regard), her eye shall be evil toward the **husband** of her **bosom** (intense love/intimacy), and toward her **son**, and toward her **daughter**
57. And toward her **young one** (newborn baby) that comes out from between her feet, and toward her **children** which she shall bear: for she shall eat them for **want of all things** (severe desperation) **secretly** (privately/not in the open) in the **siege** (very tight/suffocating) and **straitness** (very tight/suffocating) wherewith your **enemies**, people who **hate** you (**Leviticus 26:17**) shall **distress** you in your gates
58. If you will not **observe to do** (practice) all the words of this law that are written in **this book** (In Hebrew, "Torah" means "Book of the Law"/the first five books of the Old Testament), that you may **fear** (greatly respect/honor/revere) this **glorious** (beautiful/awesome) and **fearful** (awe-inspiring/breath-taking/too great to be described) Name, **YAHUAH YOUR GOD**

HIStory or OUR Story Chapter 2

59. Then Yahuah will make your **plagues** (supernatural consequences/afflictions) **wonderful** (unbelievable/outstanding/phenomenal/startling), and the **plagues** (supernatural consequences/afflictions) of your **seed** (descendants) even great **plagues** (supernatural consequences/afflictions) and of **long continuance** (very long time), and sore **sicknesses** (diseases), and of **long continuance** (extremely long time)
60. Moreover He will bring upon you all the diseases of Egypt, which you were afraid of; and they shall **cling** (stay very close) to you
61. Also every **sickness** (disease) and every **plague** (supernatural consequences/afflictions) **which is not written** (have not come into existence yet) in this **book of this law**, them will Yahuah bring upon you, until you be **destroyed** (ruined/broken) you
62 And you shall be left few in number, whereas you were as the stars of heaven for multiple; because you would not obey the voice of Yahuah your God
63 And it shall come to pass, that as Yahuah rejoiced over you to do you good, and to multiply you; so Yahuah will rejoice over you to **destroy** (ruin/break) you, and to **bring you to nothing** (tear down); and you shall be **plucked** (removed) from off the land where you go to possess it
64 And Yahuah shall scatter you among **all people from the one end of the earth** even to the other; and there you shall serve other gods, **which neither you nor your fathers have known** even **wood** (Christianity's Cross) and **stone** (Islam's Kaaba Stone)
65 And among these nations shall you find no **ease** (freedom from work/relief), neither shall the sole of your foot **have rest** (peace); but Yahuah shall give you there a **trembling heart** (fearful/great anxiety/overly worried) and **failing of eyes** (lacking perception), and **sorrow of mind** (depression)
66 And your life shall hang in doubt before; and you shall fear day and night, and you shall have **no assurance of life** (guarantee of survival)
67 In the morning you shall say, "**Would God it were evening**" (Only if I can survive til night) and at **evening** you shall say, "**Would God it were morning**" (only if I can survive til morning) for the **fear** (dread) of your heart wherewith you shall **fear** (dread) and for the sight of your eyes which you shall see
68 And Yahuah shall bring you into **Egypt** (BONDAGE, See Scriptures Exodus 20:1-2/Deuteronomy 5:6/Exodus 13:3,14/Deuteronomy 13:5/Deuteronomy 6:12/Deuteronomy 8:14) again with **SHIPS,** by the way whereof I spoke to you, "You shall see **it** (the land) no more again: and there you shall be sold to your **enemies**, people who **hate** you (**Leviticus 26:17**) for **bondmen** (male slaves) and **bondwomen** (female slaves) and no **man** (human) shall **buy you** (redeem you).

Back in those days there was a law that a man could save enough money to buy/redeem their own freedom, or a the next closest of kin could buy/redeem you. But what Yahuah is saying here is that NOBODY will be able to buy you your freedom in this slavery. See **Leviticus 25: 47-55**.

HIStory or OUR Story Chapter 2

Deuteronomy 30: 15-18

15 "See, I have set before you this day **life** and **good**, and **death** and **evil**;
16 In that I command you this day to love Yahuah your God, to walk in His ways, and to keep His commandments and His statutes and His judgments, that you may live and multiply: and Yahuah your God shall bless you in the land where you go to possess it.
17 But if your **heart** (mind) turn away, so that you will not hear, but shall be drawn away, and worship other gods, and serve them;
18 I **denounce** (publicly announce) to you this day, that you shall surely **perish** (to die or be destroyed), and that you shall not **prolong** (lengthen/extend) your days upon the land, where you go to pass over Jordan to go to possess it.
19 I call heaven and earth to record this day against you, that I have set before you life and death, **blessing** (good fortune/good consequences) and **cursing** (bad fortune/ bad consequences): therefore choose life, that both you and your seed (descendants) may live:
20 That you may love Yahuah your God, and that you may obey His voice, and that you may cleave to Him: for He is your life, and the length of your days: that you mayest dwell in the land which Yahuah **swore to your fathers**, to Avraham, to Yizak, and to Yahkob, to give them."

Exodus 24:3-8
3. And Musa (Moses) came and told the people all the words of Yahuah, and all the **judgments** (rules): and all the people answered with **one voice** (in unity), and said, "**All the words which Yahuah has said, we will do.**"
4. And Musa wrote all the words of Yahuah, and rose up early in the morning, and built an altar under the hill, and twelve pillars, according to the twelve tribes of Yahsrael
5. And he sent young men of the children of Yahsrael, which offered burned offerings, and sacrificed peace offerings of oxen to Yahuah
6. And Musa took half of the blood, and put it in **basins** (big bowls): and half of the blood he sprinkled on the altar
7. And he took the **book of the covenant** (terms and conditions) and read in the **audience** (hearing) of the people: and they said, "**All that Yahuah has said will we do, and be obedient**"
8. And Musa took the blood, and sprinkled it on the people, and said, "Behold the **blood of the covenant**, (terms and conditions), which Yahuah has made with you concerning all these words"

HIStory or OUR Story   **Chapter 2**

In **the Hebrew culture,** they lived by the Commandments and Laws that Yahuah gave them which are the first five books of the 'Torah': (Genesis-Joshua). This included keeping the **7th day weekly Sabbath,** and the annual **Passover, seven-day Feast of Unleavened bread** where the 1st and 7th day are Sabbaths, the **Feast of First Fruits**, the **Feast of Pentecost**, the **Feast of Trumpets**, and the 8-day **Feast of Tabernacles**. God's laws are meant to set apart Yahsrael from all the other nations, through their practices.

1. The Hebrews were commanded **NOT** to get any tattoos on their bodies.
Leviticus 19:28, Leviticus 18:22, Leviticus 20:13, Romans 1:18-32

2. The Hebrews were commanded **NOT to eat swine's flesh aka 'pork'/'pig' Deuteronomy 14:8, Leviticus 11:7**

3. **Food Laws- Leviticus 11 (the entire chapter)** outlines the entire food law.

4. The Hebrews were commanded **NOT to seek mediums and psychics- Leviticus 19:31, Leviticus 20:16**

5. The Hebrews were commanded **NOT** to be rumor-spreaders/tale-bearers. **Leviticus 19:16**

6. Hebrew men **were commanded NOT to cut their beards. Leviticus 19:27**

7. The Hebrews were told and taught strictly: <u>**DO NOT**</u> inter marry with other nations.
Genesis 28:1-9, Deuteronomy 7:1-4, Ezra 9:1-2, Nehemiah 13: 23-28, I Kings 11:1-3, Exodus 23:32-33, Exodus 33:16, Deuteronomy 23: 2-3, Numbers 36: 3, 6-13

8. The Hebrews wore fringes and they were commanded to do so. **Numbers 15: 38-40**

9. The Hebrews were to pray towards the east, towards the land of Yahsrael, towards the city of Yahrushalom while in captivity as commanded, in order to get released
Daniel 6:10, 1 Kings 8:26-59, I Kings 11:36

HIStory or OUR Story   **Chapter 2**

Yahuah delivered us out of Egypt to keep His promise to our forefathers. It had nothing to do with anything our people were doing right or wrong.
The Hebrew Yahsraelites were the people that Yahuah was dealing with at this time.

Exodus 4:22
22. "And you shall say to Pharaoh, Thus says Yahuah, **Yahsrael is My son**, even **My firstborn**:
23. And I say to you, **Let MY SON** go, that he may serve Me: and if you refuse to let him go, behold, I will <u>slay</u> (murder/kill) your son, even your firstborn."

Exodus 8: 23
23. "And I will put a <u>division</u> (distinction/difference) between **My people** and your people: tomorrow shall this sign be"

Exodus 11:7
7. "..Yahuah does put a <u>difference</u> between the Egyptians and Yahsrael."

Amos 3: 1-2
1 "Hear this word that Yahuah has spoken against you, O children of Yahsrael, against the whole family which I brought up from the land of Egypt saying,
2 <u>YOU ONLY</u> have I <u>known</u> (developed a relationship with) <u>of all the families of the earth</u>: therefore I will punish you for all your iniquities"

Yahuah told Yahsrael that they would lose their heritage and that they would lose the memory of who they were as a people because He knew they would refuse His laws and commandments. Yahuah even said we would forget His name through the process of time.

Jeremiah 17: 4
4: And you even yourself shall **LOSE** from your <u>heritage</u> (history, birthright, land) that I gave you; and I will cause you to serve your enemies in the land which you <u>know not</u> (have no knowledge of): for you have kindled a fire in My anger, which shall burn <u>forever.</u>

Deuteronomy 32: 26
26. I said, I would scatter them into <u>corners</u> (four corners of the earth), I would make the <u>remembrance of them</u> (self identity/memory of self) to <u>cease</u> (stop/disappear) from among men."

Jeremiah 44: 26 "Nevertheless hear the word of Yahuah, all Yahudah who are living in the land of Egypt, 'Behold, I have sworn by **My Great Name**,' says Yahuah, 'that **My Name shall NO MORE be INVOKED by the mouth** of ANY MAN of Yahudah in all the land of Egypt, saying, "Yahuah GOD lives."

                                     Amos 8: 11-13

11 Behold, the days come**, says Yahuah,** that I will send **a famine** in the land, not a famine of bread, nor a thirst for water, but **of hearing the words of Yahuah:**
12 And **they shall wander from sea to sea**, and from the north even to the east, **they shall run to and fro to seek the word of Yahuah, and shall not find it.**
13 In that day shall the young women and young men **faint for thirst.**

HIStory or OUR Story   Chapter 2

A nationality is supposed to reveal your homeland of nativity as a people.
Below are some examples. If you are a Vietnamese man/woman, then it is understood your land of nativity is Vietnam. If you are a Liberian, then your land of nativity is Liberia.

Chinese = China	Irish= Ireland	Mexican= Mexico
Japanese- Japan	British= Britain	Italian= Italy
Korean= Korea	Polish= Poland	Hawaiian= Hawaii
Pakistani = Pakistan	German= Germany	Kenyan= Kenya
Brazilian= Brazil	Englishman= England	Ethiopian= Ethiopia
Norwegian= Norway	Indian= India	Egyptian= Egypt
Sudanese = Sudan	Russian= Russia	Nigerian= Nigeria
Grecian= Greece	Puerto Rican= Puerto Rico	Somalian= Somalia
Australian= Australia	Spaniard= Spain	Haitian= Haiti
Trinidadian= Trinidad	Jamaican= Jamaica	Arabian= Arabia
Scottish= Scotland	Swedish= Switzerland	French= France

Khazarians are from Khazaria. Khazarians are called Jews today, but there is no homeland named Jews or Jewish. The Jews are merely 'called' Jewish, but Jewish is a religion, not a land. There is no Jewish land. The truth is: "Jews" is a made up word. Now, there is the tribe of Yahudah which a man of Yahudah would be called Yahudim or Yahudite. But truthfully, the people they call the "Jews" today are nothing more than Khazarians from the land of Khazaria who migrated to Israel in 1948. They are not the Biblical Israelites. Notice we call them Israelis not Israelites. Israelis means 'sort of' Israel or 'like' Israel. Israelis are citizens or nationals of the <u>modern state of Israel</u>. The true Israelites would be called Israelites (Yahsraelites) and their land is Israel (Yahsrael).

Now on to us

Black=???? Black is a color, not a land of origin. I am brown in color, not even truly black! There is no such thing as a 'black' homeland'!

Negro= ???? Negro is a word that means black. It is not a land of origin either. There is no such thing as a 'negro land' or even 'negroid land'!

Colored= ???? Colored is a word that means "having pigmentation", but is not a land of origin. There is no such thing as a 'colored land'!

Nigger= ??? Nigger is a derogatory term adopted by our oppressors, not a land of origin. There is no so such thing as a 'nigger land'.

African American - Africa is a Continent so I cannot get my nationality from being called an African anything. Likewise, America is a country named after a man named Amerigo Vespucci, which was an Italian man. Black people are not Italian so we cannot be American by bloodline or be related to Amerigo Vespucci. Black people cannot claim "American" as a nationality of ORIGIN but of citizenship only.

HIStory or OUR Story   **Chapter 2**

Now in dealing with citizenship, America is a nation. Anybody can get American citizenship and become an American citizen. A Japanese, Chinese and even a Nigerian man or woman can become an American citizen. Our president, Barack Obama, is an American citizen by birth, but his heritage is Kenyan on his father's side and English on his mother's side.

But back to us, we don't know what our True nationality is!! I am here to show you what the Bible says it is. If Yahsraelite (Israelite) is your true nationality, then according to our maps today, Yahsrael (Israel) is not a part of Africa so it would be wrong to call you an African. Let's review the evidence.

HIStory or OUR Story   **Chapter 2**

Yahuah even foretold Avraham of our enslavement before it took place.

Read Genesis 15:12-16

12. And when the sun was going down, a deep sleep fell upon A'vram; and, lo, **a Horror** of **Great Darkness** fell upon him.
13. And He said to A'vram, "<u>Know of a surety</u> that your <u>seed</u> (descendants) shall be a <u>stranger</u> (temporary resident) in a land that is not theirs, and shall serve them; and they shall afflict them <u>Four Hundred years</u>;
14. And also that nation whom they shall serve, will I judge: and afterward shall they come out with great substance (possessions).
15. And you shall <u>go to your fathers</u> (die) in peace; you shall be buried in a good old age.
16. But in the fourth generation they shall come <u>here</u> (to this place) again: for the <u>iniquity</u> (sins) of the Am'orites is not yet full."

So as you can see this agreement/covenant was between Yahuah and the children of Yahsrael only. Not with the world. That is why the curses as a collective were only poured out upon the children of Yahsrael as a collective. There is no other entire nation of people on the face of the earth who was brought across the world on boats, but the Hebrew Yahsraelites. There is no other entire nation of people on the face of the earth who had their identities, names, language, culture, and way of telling time and history wiped out except for the Hebrew Yahsraelites.

The reason it is **IMPERATIVE** that our enemies keep us devoid of our truth, calling on the wrong names and divided is because they know that Yahuah has already said that He would put the curses we endured on our enemies. Our enemies will go into a 1,000 year servitude, during Christ's 100 year reign with His people Yahsrael gathered back to the land. They know this and they will do everything in their power to discourage this. See scriptures

Deuteronomy 30:1-7
1 "Now it shall come to pass, when all these things come upon you, the blessing and the curse which I have set before you, and you **call them to mind** among all the nations where Yahuah your God drives you
2 And you return to Yahuah your God and obey His voice, according to all that I command you today, you and your children, with all your heart and with all your soul,
3 That **Yahuah your God will bring you back from captivity**, and have compassion on you, and **gather you again from all the nations** where **Yahuah your God has scattered you**.
4 If any of you are driven out to the farthest parts under heaven, from there Yahuah your God will gather you, and from there He will bring you.
5 Then Yahuah your God will bring you to the land which your fathers possessed, and you shall possess it. He will prosper you and multiply you more than your fathers.
6 And Yahuah your God will circumcise your heart and the heart of your descendants, to love Yahuah your God with all your heart and with all your soul, that you may live.
7 "Also Yahuah your God WILL PUT THESE **CURSES ON YOUR ENEMIES** and on those **WHO WHO HATE YOU,** who persecuted you.
For more Scriptures about this go to: **Obadiah 1:15, Jeremiah 14:7, Isaiah 45:11-14, Isiah 14:1-3, Jeremiah 16:16, Genesis 15:14, Isaiah 61:1-9, Revelation 18:5-6**

HIStory or OUR Story   Chapter 3

Our Nations Pinnacle

Key: Daud= David
      Shelamoh= Solomon

Yahuah made good on His promise to our people that if we kept His commandments and were obedient to His laws then he would set us on high, above all of the people of the earth. (**Deuteronomy 28:1**). As a result of Daud's obedience, Daud's son, Shelamoh, was blessed beyond measure. Daud ruled the kingdom of Yahsrael in righteousness (**I Kings 9:2-4**).

See the following passage of scriptures
I Kings 10:1-29

1 And when the Queen of She'ba heard the **fame** (reputation) of Shelamoh concerning **the name of Yahuah** , she came to **prove** (try/test) him with **hard** (difficult) questions
2 And she came to Yahrushalom with a very great **train** (assistants accompanying an important person) with camels that **bore** (carry) spices and very much **gold** and **precious** (expensive/valuable) stones: and when she was come to Shelamoh she **communed** (enter deep discussion/intimate conversation) with him of all that was **in her heart** (on her mind)
3 And Shelamoh **told her** (answered) all her questions: there was not **any thing hidden from the King** (no question) which he told her not
4 And when the Queen of She'ba had seen all Shelamoh's **wisdom** (quality of having experience/good judgment), and the house that he had built
5 And the **meat** (food) of his table, and the **sitting** (posture) of his servants, and the **attendance** (appearance) of his ministers, and their **apparel** (clothes) and his **cupbearers** (waiters responsible to refill wine) and his ascent by which he went up to the house of Yahuah there was **no more spirit in her** (overwhelmed/took her breath away)
6 And she said to the King, "It was a true **report** (story) that I heard in my own land of your **acts** (actions) and of your **wisdom** (quality of having experience/good judgment)
7 However I believed not the words, until I came, and my eyes had seen it: and **behold the half was not told me:** your **wisdom** (quality of having experience/good judgment) and **prosperity** (wealth/affluence/plenty/well-being/security) **exceeds** (surpasses/goes beyond) the **fame** (reputation) which I heard
8 Happy are your men, happy are these your servants, which stand continually before you, and that hear your **wisdom**
9 Blessed be Yahuah your God which delighted in you, to set you on the throne of Yahsrael: because Yahuah loved Yahsrael for ever, therefore made He you king to do **judgment** (make decisions) and **justice** (make even/be fair)

HIStory or OUR Story   **Chapter 3**

10 And she gave the king a hundred and twenty **talents** (1 talent =100lbs) of **gold** and of spices very great **store** (quantity/abundance) and **precious** (expensive/valuable) stones: there came no more such **abundance** (large amount) of spices as these which the Queen of She'ba gave to King Shelamoh
11 And the **navy** (fleet of ships) also of Hi'ram, that brought **gold** from O'phir, brought in from O'phir **great plenty** (very many) of almug trees, and **precious** (expensive/valuable) stones
12 And the King made of the almug trees pillars for the house of Yahuah, and for the King's house, **harps** also and **psalteries** (lyres/medieval musical instrument) for singers: there came no such almug trees, nor were seen to this day
13 And King Shelamoh gave to the Queen of She'ba **all her desire** (whatever she wanted), whatsoever she ask, beside that which Shelamoh gave her of his **royal bounty** (his very best), So she turned and went to her own country, she and her servants
14 Now the weight of **gold** that came to Shelamoh in one year was **six hundred threescore and six** (666) talents of **gold**
15 Beside that he had the **merchantmen** (trading ships), and of the **traffic** (trade) of the spice **merchants** (businessmen/traders), and of all the kings of Arabia, and of the governors of the country
16 And King Shelamoh made two hundred **targets** (large shields) of beaten **gold**: six hundred **shekels** (coin unit of weight/money) of **gold** went to one went to one target
17 And he made three hundred shields of beaten **gold**; three pounds of **gold** went to one shield: and the King put them in the house of the forest of Lebanon
18 Moreover the King made a **great** (above normal) throne of **ivory** and overlaid it with **the best gold**
19 The throne had six steps, and the top of the throne had six steps, and the top of the throne was round behind: and there were **stays** (seat arms) on either side on the place of the seat, and **two lions** stood beside the **stays** (seat arms)
20 And **twelve lions** stood there on the one side and on the other upon the six steps: there was not the **like** (equal) made in any kingdom
21 And **all King Shelamoh's drinking vessels** (cups) were of **gold, all the vessels** of the house of the forest of Leb'anon were of **pure gold; none were of silver**: it was **nothing accounted of** (not valued high) in the days of Shelamoh
22 For the King had at sea a **navy** (fleet of ships) of Thar'shish with the **navy** (fleet of ships) of Hi'ram: once in three years came the **navy** (fleet of ships) of Thar'rish, bringing **gold** and **silver, ivory**, and apes, and peacocks
23 So King Shelahmoh exceeded all the kings of the earth for **riches**(wealth) and **wisdom** (quality of having experience/good judgment)
24 And **all the earth** (every nation) **sought to** (seeks/desires/wants) Shelahmoh, to hear his **wisdom** (quality of having experience/good judgment), which God had put in his **heart** (mind)

HIStory or OUR Story   **Chapter 3**

25 And they brought every man his **present** (gift) **vessels** (cups) of **silver** and **vessels** (cups) of **gold** and **garments** (clothes) and **armor** and **spices**, **horses** and **mules**; a rate year by year

26 And Shelamoh gathered together **chariots** and **horsemen** (skilled riders): and he had a **thousand and four hundred chariots** and **twelve thousand horsemen** (skilled riders), whom he **bestowed** (stationed) in the cities for **chariots**, and with the King of Yahrushalom

27 And the King made **silver** to be in Yahrushalom **as stones** (common/having little value) and **cedars** (wood with lovely fragrance) made he to be as the sycamore trees that are in the **valley** (lowland) for **abundance**

28 And Shelahmoh had **horses** brought out of Egypt/Kemet and linen yarn: the King's **merchants** (traders/businessmen) receive the linen yarn at a price

29 And a chariot came up and when out of Egypt/Kemet for **six hundred shekels of silver,** and a horse for a hundred and fifty: and so for all the kings of the Hittites, and for the kings of Syria, did they bring them out by their **means** (expense).

So as you can see Yahuah already delivered His promise of obedience for keeping His commandments to the nation of Yahsrael.

Shelamoh (Solomon) and his golden kingdom, as it was describing **everything in his kingdom was made of pure gold**. Silver was common and unimportant as stones or rocks are to us today. The word "gold" is mentioned 13 times alone in describing everything in Shelamoh's kingdom. **I Kings 10: 21**

The Hellenization of the Hebrews

The experiment with the opulence and power of the great eastern kingdoms had ended on disaster for Yahsrael. King Shelamoh created the wealthiest and most powerful central government the Hebrews would ever see, but he did so at an impossibly high cost. Land was given away to pay for his extravagances and people were sent into forced labor into Tyre in the north. When Shelamoh died between 926 and 922 BCE (Before Current/Christian Era; an alternative to Before Christ--abbreviated B.C.), the ten northern tribes refused to submit to his son, Rehaboam, and revolted. Read all of **1Kings Chapter 12**.

From this point on, there would be two kingdoms of Hebrews: in the north-the house of Yahsrael and in the south the house of Yahudah. The house of Yahsrael split into two houses. This was the beginning of their downfall as it is written **Mark 3:25** "And if a house be divided against itself, that house will not be able to stand". The northern kingdom Yahsrael formed their capital in the city of Samaria, and the Yahudites kept their capital in Yahrushalom. These kingdoms remained separate states for over two hundred years. They both endured many ineffective, disobedient, and corrupt kings.

From the beginning when the Hebrews first asked for a earthly king, in the book of Judges, they were told that only God was their King. When they approached Shemuel the prophet, he told them the desire for a king was an act of disobedience and that they would pay dearly if they established a monarchy. The Hebrew empire eventually collapsed, Moab successfully revolts against Yahudah, and Ammon successfully secedes from Yahsrael. Within a century of Shelamoh's death, the kings of Yahsrael and Yahudah were left as tiny little states- no bigger than Connecticut- on the larger map of the Middle East. Because of their small size, Rome would eventually conquer them. As history proved time and time again in the region, tiny states never survived long. In 722 BC, the Assyrians conquered Yahsrael. The Assyrians were aggressive and effective; the history of their dominance over the Middle East is a history of constant warfare. In order to assure that conquered territories would remain pacified, the Assyrians would force many of the native inhabitants to relocate to other parts of their empire. When they conquered Yahsrael, they forced the ten tribes to scatter throughout their empire. From this point on Yahsrael went on to be called 'the ten lost tribes of Yahsrael'. Sometime after this, Babylon would conquer Yahudah and hold them captive for 70 years, but they came out of captivity and migrated back to their land. **See Daniel Chapter 1-5 for detailed account.**

HIStory or OUR Story — Chapter 4

When Greece rule was spread through Alexander the Great, Egypt was conquered in 332 B.C. A young Greek prince arrived in Egypt after it had already been weakened by defeat by the Assyrians, the Babylonians and the Persians. Alexander the Great's army was the head of one of the most brutal armies the Egyptians had ever seen. When he came to Egypt, the Egyptians did not want to war with him so instead welcomed him as a liberator of Persian rule.

Alexander spends the winters in Egypt. His actions there are the first indication of how he will set about keeping control of distant conquests, places with their own cultural traditions. One method was to establish outposts of Greek culture. In Egypt, he founded the greatest of the cities known by his name, Alexandria. Alexander the Great played the role of a local ruler to the point of carrying out a sacrifice to Apis, a sacred bull at Memphis, where the priests of Egypt crown him Pharaoh. He made long pilgrimages to the famous oracle of the sun god Amon-Ra, at Siwa, where the priest duly recognizes Alexander as the son of god.

This period is known as the Hellenization period. "Hellenize" means to make Greek in character such as Greek ideas and customs. The Greeks made it law that only Greek gods were to be worshipped; only the Greek language was permitted to be spoken; and all forms of writing had to be translated into Greek including the Old and New Testament scriptures. Under Hellen rule, the writings in any language but Greek was burned. They destroyed the images of the black gods of Egypt and set up the pantheon of Greek gods with their main god being Zeus. Religious Greek festivals were forced on Egypt along with all nations under Greek rule. The Greeks charged Egypt along with all nations under Greek rule an annual tax. The Greeks instituted their sports and used the scattered indentured servant Hebrews primarily as their primary participants in their Greek games. The Greeks established their culture in Egypt. Any resistance at this time was punishable by death. Hence, we still have the saying to this day "**Go Greek**"!!

Napoleon arrived in Egypt and he saw an amass of statues and monuments with black African physical features. He subsequently had his soldiers shoot the nose off the sphinx in order to hide the true ethnic origin of it and to hide the true identity of the builders.

Also, Hellen felt that it would be bad for Greek youth to worship Egyptian gods that looked like Egyptians so they changed the images of the gods to look like Greek men and women.

When Rome overthrew Greece they continued in the Hellenization process.

HIStory or OUR Story   Chapter 4

This is a passage of scripture from the 2nd book of Maccabees which was apart of the original Hebrew holy scriptures. The book of Maccabees was even in the original King James Bible printed in 1611. FYI: the original King James Bible had 80 books in it. The Apocrypha, or so called "Lost books of the Old Testament, goes back to 200 B.C. and was in the canonized King James Bible until the year 1885.

2Maccabees Chapter 6

1 Not long after this the king sent an old man of Athens to compel the Yahudites to **depart from the laws of their fathers, and not to live after the laws of God:**
2 And to pollute also the temple in Yahrushalom, and to call it the temple of Jupiter Olympius; and that in Garizim, of Jupiter the Defender of strangers, as they did desire that dwelt in the place.
3 The coming in of this mischief was sore and grievous to the people:
4 For the temple was filled with riot and revelling by the Gentiles, who had sex with harlots, and had women within the circuit of the holy places, and besides that brought in things that were not lawful.
5 The altar also was filled with profane things, which the law forbiddes.
6 **Neither was it lawful for a man to keep sabbath days or ancient fasts, or to profess himself at all to be a Yahudite**.
7 And in the day of the king's birth every month they were brought by bitter constraint to eat of the sacrifices; and when the fast of Bacchus was kept, the Yahudites were compelled to go in procession to Bacchus, carrying ivy.
8 Moreover there went out a decree to the neighbor cities of the nations, by the suggestion of Ptolemy, against the Yahudites, that they should **observe the same fashions, and be partakers of their sacrifices:**
9 And w**hoso would not conform themselves to the <u>manners</u>** (ways/traditions) of the **<u>Gentiles</u>** (nations) should be put to death. Then might a man have seen the present misery.
10 For there were two women brought, who had circumcised their children; whom when they had openly led round about the city, the babes handing at their breasts, they cast them down headlong from the wall.
11 And others, that had run together into caves nearby, to **keep the sabbath day secretly**, being discovered by Philip, were all burnt together, because they made a conscience to help themselves for the honor of the most sacred day.
12 Now I beg those that read this book, that they be not discouraged for these calamities, but that they judge those punishments not to be for destruction, but for a chastening of our nation.
13 For it is a token of His great goodness, when wicked doers are not suffered any long time, but forthwith punished.
14 For not as with other nations, whom Yahuah patiently waits to punish, till they come to the fullness of their sins, so deals He with us,

15 Unless that, being come to the height of sin, afterwards He should take vengeance of us.
16 And therefore he never withdraws His mercy from us: and though he punish with adversity, yet **He never totally forsakes His people**.
17 But let this that we at spoken be for a warning to us. And now will we come to the declaring of the matter in a few words.
18 Eleazar, one of the principal scribes, an old man, and of a well favored countenance, was **constrained to open his mouth, and to eat swine's flesh**.
19 But he, **choosing rather to die gloriously, than to live stained with such an abomination**, <u>spit it forth</u>, and came of his own accord to the torment,
20 As it behoved them to come, that are resolute to stand out against such things, as are not lawful for love of life to be tasted.
21 But they that had the charge of that **wicked feast**, for the old acquaintance they had with the man, taking him aside, besought him to bring flesh of his own provision, such as was lawful for him to use, and make as if he did eat of the flesh taken from the sacrifice commanded by the king;
22 That in so doing he might be delivered from death, and for the old friendship with them find favor.
23 But he began to consider discreetly, and as became his age, and the excellency of his ancient years, and the honor of his gray head, whereon was come, and his most honest education from a child, or rather the **holy law** made and given by God: therefore he answered accordingly, and willed them straightway's to send him to the grave.
24 "For it becomes not our age", said he, in any wise to dissemble, "whereby many young persons might think that Eleazar, being fourscore years old and ten, were now gone to a strange religion;
25 And so they through my hypocrisy, and desire to live a little time and a moment longer, should be deceived by me, and I get a stain to my old age, and make it abominable.
26 For though for the present time I should be delivered from the punishment of men: yet should I not escape the hand of the Almighty, neither alive, nor dead.
27 Wherefore now, manfully changing this life, I will show myself such an one as my age requires,
28 And leave a notable example to such as be young to die willingly and courageously for the **honorable and holy laws**. And when he had said these words, immediately he went to the torment:
29 They that led him changing the good will they bare him a little before into hatred, because the foresaid speeches proceeded, as they thought, from a desperate mind.
30 But when he was ready to die with stripes, he groaned, and said," It is manifest to Yahuah, that has the **holy knowledge**, that whereas I might have been delivered from death, I now endure sore pains in body by being beaten: but <u>in soul am well content to suffer these things</u>, **because I fear Him**."
31 And so this man died, leaving his death for an example of a noble courage, and a memorial of virtue, not only to young men, but to all his nation.

HIStory or OUR Story   Chapter 4

The Beginning of The End

The 12 tribes of Yahsrael separated themselves into two separate kingdoms. The northern kingdom and the southern kingdom. The northern kingdom was referred to as the house of Yahsrael (10 tribes), and the southern kingdom was referred to as the house of Yahudah (2 tribes). King Shelamoh (Solomon) was given to pagan gods and the idols of the surrounding nations. Only the house of Yahudah remained true to Yahuah. **Read below 1Kings Chapter 12**.

1 And Rehoboam went to Shechem: for all Yahsrael were come to Shechem to make him king.
2 And it came to pass, when Jeroboam the son of Nebat, who was yet in Egypt, heard of it, (for he was fled from the presence of king Shelamoh, and Jeroboam dwelled in Egypt;)
3 That they sent and called him. And Jeroboam and all the congregation of Yahsrael came, and spoke to Rehoboam, saying,
4 "Your father made our yoke grievous: now therefore make you **the grievous service** of your father, and his heavy yoke which he put upon us, lighter, and we will serve you."
5 And he said to them, "Depart yet for three days, then come again to me." And the people departed."
6 And king Rehoboam consulted with the old men, that stood before Shelamoh his father while he yet lived, and said, How do you advise that I may answer this people?
7 And they spoke to him, saying, "If you wilt be a servant to this people this day, and will serve them, and answer them, and speak good words to them, then they will be your servants forever".
8 But he forsook the counsel of the old men, which they had given him, and consulted with the young men that were grown up with him, and which stood before him:
9 And he said to them, "What counsel give you that we may answer this people, who have spoken to me, saying, "Make the yoke which your father did put upon us lighter?"
10 And the young men that were grown up with him spoke to him, saying, "Thus shall you speak to this people that spoke to you, saying, Your father made our yoke heavy, but make you it lighter to us; thus shall you say to them, "My little finger shall be thicker than my father's loins
11 And now whereas my father did lade you with a heavy yoke, I will add to your yoke: my father has chastised you with whips, but I will chastise you with scorpions."
12 So Jeroboam and all the people came to Rehoboam the third day, as the king had appointed, saying, "Come to me again the third day."
13 And the king answered the people roughly, and forsook the old men's counsel that they gave him;
14 And spoke to them after the counsel of the young men, saying," My father made your yoke heavy, and I will add to your yoke: my father also chastised you with whips, but I will chastise you with scorpions."

15 Wherefore the king listened not to the people; for the cause was from Yahuah, that he might perform his saying, which Yahuah spoke by Ahijah the Shilonite to Jeroboam the son of Nebat.
16 So when all Yahsrael saw that the king listened not to them, the people answered the king, saying, What portion have we in Daud? neither have we inheritance in the son of Yishai: to your tents, O Yahsrael: now see to your own house, Daud. So Yahsrael departed to their tents.
17 But as for the children of Yahsrael which dwelt in the cities of Yahudah, Rehoboam reigned over them.
18 Then king Rehoboam sent Adoram, who was over the tribute; and all Yahsrael stoned him with stones, that he died. Therefore king Rehoboam made speed to get him up to his chariot, to flee to Yahrushalom.
19 So Yahsrael rebelled against the house of Daud to this day.
20 And it came to pass, when all Yahsrael heard that Jeroboam was come again, that they sent and called him to the congregation, and made him king over all Yahsrael: there was none that followed the house of Daud, but the tribe of Yahudah only.
21 And when Rehoboam was come to Yahrushalom, he assembled all the house of Yahudah, with the tribe of Benyamin, an hundred and fourscore thousand chosen men, which were warriors, to fight against the house of Yahsrael, to bring the kingdom again to Rehoboam the son of Shelamoh.
22 But the word of God came to Shemaiah the man of God, saying,
23 Speak to Rehoboam, the son of Shelamoh, king of Yahudah, and to all the house of Yahudah and Benyamin, and to the remnant of the people, saying,
24 Thus saith Yahuah, "You shall not go up, nor fight against your brothers the children of Yahsrael: return every man to his house; for this thing is from Me". They listened therefore to the word of Yahuah, and returned to depart, according to the word of Yahuah.
25 Then Jeroboam built Shechem in mount Ephraim, and dwelled therein; and went out from there, and built Penuel.
26 And Jeroboam said in his heart, "Now shall the kingdom return to the house of Daud:
27 If this people go up to do sacrifice in the house of Yahuah at Yahrushalom, then shall the heart of this people turn again to their lord, even to Rehoboam king of Yahudah, and they shall kill me, and go again to Rehoboam king of Yahudah.
28 Whereupon the king took counsel, and made **two calves of gold**, and said to them," It is too much for you to go up to Yahrushalom: **behold your gods**, O Yahsrael, **which brought you up out of the land of Egypt**."
29 And he set the one in Bethel, and the other put he in Dan.
30 And this thing became a sin: for the people went to worship before the one, even to Dan.
31 And he made an house of high places, and made priests of the lowest of the people, which were **not of the sons of Levi**.
32 And **Jeroboam ordained a feast in the eighth month**, on the fifteenth day of the month, **like to the feast that is in Yahuah**, and he offered upon the altar. So did he in Bethel, sacrificing to the calves that he had made: and he placed in Bethel the priests of the high places which he had made.

HIStory or OUR Story   **Chapter 4**

33 So he offered upon the altar which he had made in Bethel **the fifteenth day of the eighth month**, even in **the month** which **he had devised of his own heart**; and ordained **a feast** to the children of Yahsrael: and he offered upon the altar, and burned incense.

Furthermore, Yahsrael was taken captive to Assyria. Read below **2Kings 17:6-23**

6 In the ninth year of Hosheyah the king of Assyria took Samaria, and carried Yahsrael away into Assyria, and placed them in Halah and in Habor by the river of Gozan, and in the cities of the Medes.
7 For so it was, that the children of Yahsrael had sinned against Yahuah their God, which had brought them up out of the land of Egypt, from under the hand of Pharaoh king of Egypt, and had feared other gods,
8 And walked in the statutes of <u>**the heathen**</u> (the nations), whom Yahuah cast out from before the children of Yahsrael, and of the kings of Yahsrael, which they had made.
9 And the children of Yahsrael did secretly those things that were not right against Yahuah their God, and they built them high places in all their cities, from the tower of the watchmen to the fenced city.
10 And they set them up images and groves in every high hill, and under every green tree:
11 And there they burned incense in all the high places, as did the **heathen** (nations) whom Yahuah carried away before them; and wrought wicked things to provoke Yahuah to anger:
12 For they served idols, whereof Yahuah had said to them, "You shall not do this thing."
13 Yet Yahuah testified against Yahsrael, and against Yahudah, by all the prophets, and by all the seers, saying,"Turn you from your evil ways, and keep My commandments and My statutes, according to all the law which I commanded your fathers, and which I sent to you by My servants the prophets."
14 Notwithstanding they would not hear, but hardened their necks, like to the neck of their fathers, that did not believe in Yahuah their God.
15 And they rejected His statutes, and His covenant that He made with their fathers, and His testimonies which He testified against them; and **they followed vanity**, and **became vain**, and went after the **heathen** (nations/ non-Hebrews) that were round about them, concerning whom Yahuah had charged them, that they should not do like them.
16 And they left all the commandments of Yahuah their God, and made them molten images, even two calves, and made a grove, and worshipped all the host of heaven, and served <u>**the Lord**</u> (Baal).
17 And they caused their sons and their daughters to pass through the fire, and used divination and enchantments, and sold themselves to do evil in the sight of Yahuah, to provoke Him to anger.
18 Therefore **Yahuah was very angry with Yahsrael**, and removed them out of His sight: there was none left but the tribe of Yahudah only.
19 Also Yahudah kept not the commandments of Yahuah their God, but walked in the statutes of Yahsrael which they made.

HIStory or OUR Story   **Chapter 4**

20 And Yahuah rejected all the seed of Yahsrael, and afflicted them, and delivered them into the hand of spoilers, until he had cast them out of his sight.

21 For He rent Yahsrael from the house of Daud; and they made Jeroboam the son of Nebat king: and Jeroboam drove Yahsrael from following Yahuah, and made them sin a great sin.

22 For the children of Yahsrael walked in all the sins of Jeroboam which he did; they departed not from them;

23 Until Yahuah removed Yahsrael out of his sight, as He had said by all His servants the prophets. So was Yahsrael carried away out of their own land to Assyria to this day.

Then they were REPLACED by foreigners from other lands and they came in and inhabited the land of Yahsrael and Samaria while the children of Yahsrael was in captivity. These people also had a Hebrew priest come back from captivity to teach them the laws and commandments of Yahuah. Read below **2Kings 17: 24-39**

24 And the king of Assyria **brought men from Babylon, and from Cuthah, and from Ava, and from Hamath, and from Sepharvaim**, and **placed them in the cities of Samaria instead of the children of Yahsrael**: and they possessed Samaria, and dwelled in the cities thereof.

25 And so it was at the beginning of their dwelling there, that they feared not Yahuah: therefore Yahuah sent lions among them, which killed some of them.

26 Wherefore they spoke to the king of Assyria, saying," The nations which you have removed, and **placed in the cities of Samaria, know not the manner of the <u>God</u>** (power) **of the land**: therefore he has sent lions among them, and, behold, they slay them, because they know not the manner of the God of the land."

27 Then the king of Assyria commanded, saying," Carry there one of the priests whom you brought from there; and let them go and dwell there, and let him teach them the manner of the God of the land."

28 Then one of the priests whom they had carried away from Samaria came and dwelled in Bethel, and taught them how they should fear Yahuah.

29 Howbeit **every nation made gods of their own**, and put them in the houses of the high places which the Samaritans had made, every nation in their cities wherein they dwelt.

30 And the men of Babylon made Succothbenoth, and the men of Cuth made Nergal, and the men of Hamath made Ashima,

31 And the Avites made Nibhaz and Tartak, and the Sepharvites burned their children in fire to Adrammelech and Anammelech, the gods of Sepharvaim.

32 So they feared Yahuah, and made to themselves of the lowest of them priests of the high places, which sacrificed for them in the houses of the high places.

33 They feared Yahuah, and served their own gods, after the manner of the nations whom they carried away from there.

34 To this day they do after the former manners: they fear not Yahuah, neither do they after their statutes, or after their ordinances, or after the law and commandment which Yahuah commanded the children of Yahkob, whom he named Yahsrael;

HIStory or OUR Story   **Chapter 4**

35 With whom Yahuah had made a covenant, and charged them, saying, "You shall not fear other gods, nor bow yourselves to them, nor serve them, nor sacrifice to them:"
36 But Yahuah, who brought you up out of the land of Egypt with great power and a stretched out arm, Him shall you fear, and Him shall you worship, and to Him shall you do sacrifice.
37 And the statutes, and the ordinances, and the law, and the commandment, which He wrote for you, you shall observe to do forevermore; and you shall not fear other gods.
38 And the covenant that I have made with you, you shall not forget; neither shall you fear other gods.
39 But Yahuah your God you shall fear; and He shall deliver you out of the hand of all your enemies.

Read 2Kings 18:11-13. In verse 13 it references when the house of Yahudah was also taken captive Read **2Kings 18:13**. It was prophesied ahead of time in the year 626 B.C. that Yahudah would be taken captive by the Babylonians. Read **Jeremiah 25: 1-14**. It historically happened in the year 605 B.C. that the house of Yahudah was defeated and taken to Babylon by king Nebuchadnezzar. **Read Daniel 1:1-7**. The house of Yahudah remained in captivity there for 70 years as prophesied, but then came out by the hand of Cyrus as prophesied read the following scriptures for full understanding: **Isaiah 44:28, Isaiah 45:1-13**, and **Ezra Chapter 1**.
As Yahushua prophesied in **Mark 3:24-25** "And if a kingdom be divided against itself, that kingdom cannot stand. And if a house be divided against itself, that house cannot stand."

With No UNITY, there is NO COMMUNITY.

The Warning From On High

Yahushua (Christ, the Messiah) was born to save **His people** the Hebrew Yahsraelites from their sins as it is written in Matthew 1:21 "And she (Mary/Miriam) shall bring forth a son, and you shall call His name <u>**YAHUSHUA**</u> ("Yah who saves") for He shall **save His people** from t**heir sins**."

Luke 1:68 "Blessed be Yahuah God of Yahsrael: for He has visited and redeemed **His people**"
Psalms 28:9"Save **Your people**; and bless Your inheritance: feed them also, and lift them up forever"

Matthew 10:5-6
5. "These twelve Yahushua sent forth, and commanded them, saying "Go not into <u>the way</u> (area) of the <u>Gentiles</u> (nations), and into any city of the Samaritans enter you not;
6. But go rather to the <u>lost</u> (misplaced) sheep of the house of Yahsrael"
Matthew 15:24
24. "But He answered and said, "I am not sent <u>but</u> (except) to the lost sheep of the house of Yahsrael"

So the warning Yahushua issued out was **specifically to His people**, to whom the covenant or agreement was made, Yahsrael. It would not make sense that Yahuah be angry with the world at this point, when He had not dealt with the other nations nor entrusted them with any laws or commandments at this time. **Yahuah had no covenant with the other nations at this time, only Yahsrael.**

Amos 3: 1-2
1 "Hear this word that Yahuah has spoken against you, O children of Yahsrael, against the whole family which I brought up from the land of Egypt saying,
2 <u>YOU ONLY</u> (just you) have I <u>known</u> (developed a relationship with) of all the families of the earth: therefore I will punish you for all your iniquities"
Psalms 147:19-20
19 "He shows His word **to Yahkob**, His statutes and His judgments **to Yahsrael**
20 **He has not dealt so with any nation**: and as for His judgments, **they have not known them**. Praise you Yahuah"

Isaiah 63:18-19
18 "**Your holy people** have possessed the land but a little while: our enemies have trodden down your sanctuary.
19 **We are yours: you never bore rule over them; they were never called by your Name**"

HIStory or OUR Story — Chapter 5

Psalms 28:9 "Save your people! Bless Yahsrael, your special possession. Lead them like a shepherd, and carry them in your arms forever"

Yahuah sent Yahushua to redeem us, Yahsrael, for we were the only ones under the law. Nobody else was under the law but Yahsrael, only we had made a covenant with the Most High.

Galatians 4:4-5
4 "But when the fullness of the time was come, God sent forward his Son, made of a woman, made under the law,
5 To **REDEEM THEM** THAT WERE UNDER THE LAW, that we might receive the adoption of sons."

Psalms: 105:43
43 "And He brought forth His people with joy, His chosen ones with a joyful shout."

Acts 13:23-24
23 "From the descendants of this man, according to promise, **God has brought to Yahsrael a Savior**, Yahushua,
24 After John had proclaimed before His coming a baptism of **repentance to all the people of Yahsrael**"

Acts 5:31
31" Him has God exalted with his right hand to be a Prince and a Saviour, for to give **repentance TO YAHSRAEL**, and forgiveness of sins."

As you can see, **ONLY** the nation of Yahsrael had a covenant with God, which they violated so they were the ones in need of forgiveness.

HIStory or OUR Story — Chapter 5

EXPLAINING THE TRUE MEANING OF **JOHN 3:16**

John 3:16 "For God so loved the world, that He gave His only begotten Son, that whosoever believes in Him should not perish, but have everlasting life".

When people see the word **'world'** they automatically insert their own meaning to what the word world means. They have been taught that, the word means the entire planet. They fail to comprehend that there are over 17 different definitions of the word 'world' in the Bible.

In the Bible, it clearly tells you there's **more than one meaning** of the word 'world'.

Hebrews 1:1-2
1 "In the past God spoke to our ancestors through the prophets at many times and in various ways
2 Has in these last days spoken to us by His Son, whom He has appointed heir of all things, by whom also He made **THE WORLDS**"

Worlds, plural!! Worlds with an "s" at the end. And so now, the next question you have to ask yourself is: What 'world' is John Chapter 3 verse 16 referring to? Since we know now, there are multiple "worlds" according to the Bible.

HIStory or OUR Story **Chapter 5**

So from here, let's examine the scriptures to figure this out.
From the scriptures **Malachi 1:2,** we have the reference taken of
Romans 9:13.
As it is written, "Yahkob have I loved, but Esau have I hated"

Esau became a nation called the Edomites (see **Genesis Chapter 36**). Because of God hating Esau, and his descendants (**Ezekiel Chapter 35** and book of **Obadiah**) God could not have meant 'world' as in 'everybody' because he hates the nation of Esau period. That would be a biblical contradiction, which we know that the scriptures cannot be broken (**John 10:34**) . So, let's examine this further.

Isaiah 45:17
"But **YAHSRAEL SHALL BE SAVED** in Yahuah with an everlasting salvation: you shall not be ashamed nor confounded **WORLD** without end"

The **'world'** in **Isaiah 45:17** is talking about the same **'world'** it was talking about in **John 3:16**, it was the **'world' of Yahsrael**.

Now, let's examine the word 'whosoever' in **John 3:16**. The 'whosoever' of **John 3:16** does not apply to everybody. It's all about application. If you stay in correct context, you'll understand. Prior to **John 3:16**, you must read:

John 3:14
14 "And as Musa lifted up the serpent in the wilderness, **EVEN SO** must the Son of man be lifted up:"
Even so, meaning **the same way** the serpent was lifted up, so the Son of man will be lifted in the same way.

Let's review **Numbers 21: 5-9**.
5 And the people spoke against God, and against Musa (Moses), "Why have you brought us up out of Egypt to die in the wilderness? For there is no bread, neither is there any water; and our soul loathes this light bread."
6 And Yahuah sent fiery serpents among the people, and they bit the people; and **MUCH** people **of Yahsrael died.**
7 Therefore the people came to Musa, and said, "We have sinned, for we have spoken against Yahuah, and against you; pray to Yahuah, that He take away the serpents from us." And Musa prayed for the people.
8 And Yahuah said to Musa, "Make you a fiery serpent, and set it upon a pole: and it shall come to pass, that **EVERY ONE** that is **bitten**, when **he looks** upon it, shall live."
9 And Musa made a serpent of brass, and put it upon a pole, and it came to pass, that if a serpent had bitten **ANY MAN**, when he beheld the serpent of brass, he lived.

Notice that the words 'any man' and 'every one' is used, but it is understood that 'every one' or 'any man' from Yahsrael would live. Because it says Yahuah sent serpents among the people of Yahsrael. It was the people of Yahsrael who died and were bitten. The dead did not get a chance to live again once they died, but it was those who were bitten who, once they lifted up their heads (which one had to be alive to do), would live.

The people who were in the wilderness were called 'the church' and they were exclusively the children of Yahsrael. See **Acts 7:38**. Only Yahsrael made the covenant with Yahuah and broke it, so only on Yahsrael (Israel) were the curses of the law poured out.

Here's an example. Imagine you are a classroom teacher with 40 students and you give out a test and say, "Whosoever (or Who ever because its the modern term for the word 'whosoever') finishes the test first can leave early." Does that mean you're talking to somebody in the classroom next door?? Or someone in a classroom in China? Or someone in a classroom in Russia? No! It's pertaining to the 'whosoever' in your specific classroom; in that environment. That's who the statement is directed to, and that's the same thing with the Bible. In truth, the Bible is directed to the Hebrew Yahsraelites so the 'whosoever' of **John 3:16** w**as of Yahsrael (Israel)**. When Yahushua was making this speech, He was speaking to **YAHSRAEL**!

Notice even our every day usage of the word **'WORLD'** in the phrases **'Sea WORLD'** or **'Disney WORLD'**. Within context, the word **'WORLD'** is not talking about the entire planet, but rather the **WORLD** of Disney or the **WORLD** of the Sea. When Columbus arrived in America, he called it the **NEW WORLD**. He did not mean new planet, but rather a new geographical territory.

Here is another reference note in...

Exodus 12:15 "Seven days you shall eat unleavened bread, but on the first day you shall remove leaven from your houses; for **WHOSOEVER** eateth leavened bread from the first day until the seventh day, that soul shall be cut off **FROM YAHSRAEL**."

The same way that **WHOSEVER** in Exodus was from the people of Yahsrael, so is the **WHOSOEVER** in **John 3:16**.

Yahsrael is its own nation. 'Whosever' is not all inclusive. Yahsrael is the world God was talking about. This is very simple. Remember, it's all about context. Without the proper context, you will have an improper conclusion.

HIStory or OUR Story   **Chapter 5**

Keep in mind that Yahushua Himself was a Hebrew Yahsraelite from the tribe of Yahudah. **(Hebrews 7:14)**

The purpose for Yahushua's birth is given right here:

Luke 2:34 "And Sim'eon blessed them, and to Miriam (Mary), His mother, Behold, this Child is set for **the FALL and RISING AGAIN** of many in **Yahsrael**; and for **a sign** which shall be spoken against;"

Yahushua represented Yahsrael's fall and rising again as a nation. Yahushua is the son of God and Yahsrael is the son of God . Yahushua is the chosen one. Yahsrael is the chosen nation. There were many similarities to the Messiyah and Yahsrael. Yahushua was kidnapped, mocked, spit on, ill treated and killed and beaten beyond recognition because He was destined to be the ruler. The nation of Yahsrael was kidnapped, mocked, spit on, ill treated and killed and beaten beyond recognition because we were chosen to be the ruler.

Isaiah 50:6
6 "I gave **my back** to the smiters, and my **cheeks** to them that **plucked off my beard**: I hid not my **face from shame and spitting**"

Everything that Yahushua did was a rehearsal of what was going to happen to our ancestors. Yahuah killed Pharaoh's first-born son and all of Egypt's first born's for the disobedience of the fathers. It was Pharaoh's disobedience and that of all the fathers in Egypt, who did not follow Yahuah's law and cover their door posts with the blood of a first born lamb, unblemished, that caused their innocent sons to be slaughtered.

It was the disobedience of Yahsrael's (our) forefathers that caused our ancestors to go through all the tribulation that they did and continue to endure.

Lamentation 5:7 "<u>**Our fathers**</u> (our ancestors) have sinned, **and are not;** (are dead); and we have <u>**borne**</u> (paid for/carried) their <u>**iniquities**</u> (sins)"

We know that Yahuah will punish up to four generations (400 years) for the sins of the ancestors.

Exodus 20:5 "..I, Yahuah your God, am a jealous God, <u>**visiting**</u> (bringing) <u>the iniquity of the fathers</u> **upon the children** to the third and fourth generation of them that hate Me

HIStory or OUR Story Chapter 5

Yahushua came to warn Yahsrael of the soon coming judgement from Yahuah. That everything written in the covenant, all the curses of disobedience will be poured on them and that they should flee into Africa. Do not go into the cities. Yahushua was the last prophet given to Yahsrael before the destruction that would scatter them and leave their land in ashes.

Luke 19: 41-44
41: And when **He** (Yahushua) was come near, **He** (Yahushua) **beheld** (looked down on) the **city** (Yahrushalom) and wept over it,
42: Saying, "If you had known, even you, at least in this your day, the things which **belong to** (are needed for) your peace! But now they are hidden from your eyes.
43: For the days shall come upon you that your **enemies** (Roman Army) shall cast a trench **about you** (around you), and **compass you round** (surround you), and **keep** (hem) you in on ever side
44: And shall **lay you** (level you) (bring you down) even with the ground, and your children within you; and they shall not leave in you one stone upon another; because you knew not the time of **your visitation** (judgment)."

Knowing that all **of the prophets die in Yahrushalom (Jerusalem)**, because every prophet of Yahsrael was killed in Yahrushalom, Yahushua made his way back to Yahrushalom.

Luke 13:33-35
33 "Nevertheless I must walk today, and tomorrow, and the day following: for **it cannot be that a prophet perish out of Yahrushalom**
34 O Yahrushalom, **Yahrushalom which kills the prophets**, and stones them that are sent to you; how often would I have **gathered your children together**, as a hen does gather her **brood** (family) under her wings, and **you would not** (would not obey)!
35 Behold, your house is left to you **desolate** (destruction); and verily I say to you, You shall not see Me, till you shall say, Blessed is He that comes **in the name of** Yahuah"

HIStory or OUR Story   **Chapter 5**

Yahsrael's people had become proud and boastful and Yahushua came to prophesy to them of their pending doom unless they repent just like Yahonon (John) the Baptist did. After many years of living a luxurious lifestyle, Yahsrael had gotten proud and worshipped other gods as it was prophesied of them by Musa (Moses).

Deuteronomy 32:15-26

15. But Jeshu-run (Yahsrael) grew **fat** (rich), and kicked: you are grown **fat** (rich), you are grown **thick** (wealthy), you are covered with **fatness** (much wealth); then he forsook God which made him, and **lightly esteemed** (took for granted) the Rock of his salvation.
16. They provoked Him to jealousy with strange gods, with **abominations** (detestable idols) provoked they Him to anger.
17. They sacrificed to devils, not to God, to gods whom they knew not, to new gods that came newly up, who your fathers feared not.
18. Of the Rock that fathered you, you are unmindful, and have forgotten God that formed you.
19. And when Yahuah saw it, He **abhorred** (detested) them, because of the provoking of His sons, and of His daughters.
20. And He said, "**I will hide My face from them**, I will see what their end shall be: for they are a very **froward** (perverted) generation, children in whom is no **faith** (faithfulness).
21. They have moved Me to jealousy with that which is not God; they have provoked Me to anger with their **vanities** (idols) and I will move them to jealousy with those which are **not a people**; I will provoke them to anger with a **foolish nation** (imposters).
22. For a fire is kindled in My anger, and shall burn to the lowest **hell** (grave), and shall consume the earth with her increase, and set on fire the foundations of the mountains.
23. I will heap mischiefs upon them; I will spend My arrows upon them.
24. They shall be burned with hunger, and devoured with burning heat (famine), and with bitter destruction: I will also send the teeth of beasts (fierce nations) upon them, with the poison (lies) of serpents (liars) of the dust.
25. The sword outside, and terror inside, shall destroy both the young man and **the virgin** (young woman) the **suckling** (babies) also with the **man of gray hairs** (old man).
26. I said, I would scatter them into **corners** (four corners of the earth), I would make the **remembrance** (memory of self identity) of them to **cease** (disappear) from among men."

HIStory or OUR Story   **Chapter 5**

Luke 21: 5-6, 20-25

5. And as some spoke of the temple how it was **adorned** (decorated) with **goodly** (beautiful) stones and gifts, He said,
6. "As for these things which you **behold** (see) the days will come, in which there shall not be left one stone upon another, that shall not be thrown down."..
…
20. "And when you shall see Yahrushalom **compassed** (surrounded) **with armies** (Roman Army in 70 A.D.), then **know** (recognize) that the desolation **(destruction)** thereof is near.
21. Then let them which are in **Yahudah** (the city) flee to the mountains: and let them which are in the midst of it depart out; and let not them that are in the **countries** (fields) enter thereto.
22. For these be the days of **vengeanance** (punishment) that all things which are written may be **fulfilled** (carried out).
23. But woe to them that are **with child** (pregnant), and to them that **give suck** (breast-feed/nursing) in those days! For there shall be great **distress** (pain/anxiety/sorrow) in **the land** (Yahsrael) and **wrath** (extreme anger) upon this people.
24. And **they** (Yahsrael) shall **fall** (be defeated) by the **edge of the sword** (war), and shall be **led away** (taken)(escorted)(brought) **captive** (slave)(war prisoner)(confined)(enslaved)(held in bondage) into **all nations** (all over the world): and Yahrushalom shall be **trodden down** (inhabited by) of **Gentiles** (foreign nations)(Arabs), until the times of the **Gentiles** (foreign nations) be fulfilled.
25. And there shall be **signs** (darkness) in the **sun**, and (blood) in the **moon**, and in the **stars** (multiple fallen stars); and upon the earth **distress** (sorrow/pain and torment) of nations, with **perplexity** (confusion); the **sea and the waves roaring** (hurricanes).

Our Fall

In the year 66 A.D., the Yahudites of Yahudah rebelled against their Roman masters. In response, the Emperor Nero dispatched an army under the generalship of Vespasian to restore order. By the year 68 A.D., resistance in the northern part of the province had been eradicated and the Romans turned their full attention to the subjugation of Yahrushalom. That same year, the Emperor Nero died by his own hand, creating a power vacuum in Rome. In the resultant chaos, Vespasian was declared Emperor and returned to the Imperial City. It fell to his son, Titus, to lead the remaining army in the assault on Yahrushalom.

The Roman legions surrounded the city and began to slowly squeeze the life out of the Yahsraelite stronghold. On top of this, the land of Yahsrael was suffering from a famine as well, so food was scare. The Hebrew children, being the weaker vessels with less body fat to survive on would die first. Upon dying, the parents would eat the flesh of their children and they even fought over it. This is in accordance with the scriptures:

Deuteronomy 28: 52-57
52. And he shall **besiege** (surround) you in all **your gates** (entrances/exits), until your high and **fenced** (guarded) walls come down, wherein you trusted, throughout all **your land**: and he shall: and he shall **besiege** (surround) you in all your gates throughout all your land, which Yahuah your God has given you
53. And you shall eat the **fruit of your own body** (your own children), the flesh of your sons and of your daughters, which Yahuah your God has given you, in the **siege** (serious attack/ a military operation in which enemy forces surround a town) and in the **straitness** (very tight/suffocating) wherewith your **enemies**, people who **hate** you (**Leviticus 26:17**) shall **distress** (cause worry/extreme anxiety/fear) you
54. So that the man that is **tender** (gentle/harmless/nice) among you, and very **delicate** (charming/soft/fragile/charming), his eye shall be evil toward his **brother,** and toward the **wife** of **his bosom** (intense love/intimacy), and toward the **remnant** (remaining) of his children which he shall leave:
55. So that he will not give to any of them of **the flesh** (skin) of his children whom he shall eat: because **he has nothing left** (foodless/resourceless) in the **siege**, and in the **straitness** wherewith your enemies shall **distress** you in all your gates

HIStory or OUR Story   Chapter 6

56. The **tender** (gentle/harmless/nice) and **delicate** (precious/soft/fragile/charming) woman among you, which would not **adventure** (dare) to set the sole of her foot upon the ground for **delicateness** (classiness) and **tenderness** (very high regard), her eye shall be evil toward the **husband** of her **bosom** (intense love intimacy), and toward her **son**, and toward her **daughter**

57. And toward her **young one** (newborn baby) that comes out from between her feet, and toward her **children** which she shall bear: for she shall eat them for **want of all things** (severe desperation) **secretly** (privately/not in the open) in the **siege**(very tight/suffocating) and **straitness** (very tight/suffocating) wherewith your **enemies** (Leviticus 26:17) shall **distress** you in your gates

By the year 70 A.D., the attackers had breached Yahrushalom's outer walls and began a systematic ransacking of the city. The assault culminated in the burning and destruction of the Temple that served as the center of the Hebrews.

The rebellion sputtered on for another three years and was finally extinguished in 73 A.D. with the fall of the various pockets of resistance including the stronghold at Masada. In victory, the Romans slaughtered thousands. Of those spared from death, thousands more were enslaved and sent to toil in the mines of Egypt/Kemet. Others were dispersed to arenas throughout the Empire to be butchered for the amusement of the public. The Temple's sacred relics were taken to Rome where they were displayed in celebration of the victory. Pregnant women were ripped open, babies' heads were stomped against the rocks. The religious scriptures were burned, and the temple was burned down. One stone was not left upon another just as prophesied. The Hebrew refugees were caught and taken as slave to Rome, but the ones who escaped, fled into Egpyet and then into deeper parts of Africa to avoid death and slavery. Then after this, Roman Emperor, Vesapian, put a hefty bounty on any Hebrew Yahsraelites returned to the Roman province. Because of this, the Hebrew Yahsraelites hid themselves by integrating and infiltrating with various African tribes and different countries. The Africans were considered Gentiles to the Hebrew Yahsraelites, but they were the same color so they took the opportunity to blend in. The Hebrews learned the different African languages, religions, philosophies, customs and even married into their culture. Most of them forsook the laws and ways of Yahuah. They blamed Yahuah for allowing their land to be taken by strangers and their families split up. They were taken into slavery, raped, and murdered. A lot of the Yahsraelites settled into Ethiopia and others settled in various minute countries in West Africa. The Torah (books of the Law) was an oral history for the Hebrews so they still passed it down from generation to generation. Because 10 of the 12 tribes had already migrated into Africa, a few of the Yahudites from the tribe of Yahudah and Benyamin were able to settle in areas were their brothers and sisters were already assembled and continue to keep the laws and pass down their heritage to their children.

HIStory or OUR Story   Chapter 6

The nations had long awaited this day that Yahsrael fell. As a matter of fact, they knew it was coming because of the constant fighting within ourselves. Even the nations all praised Yahsrael and Yahrushalom outwardly for it's beauty and riches, but they secretly were jealous of Yahsrael. Observe the following scriptures:

Lamentations 2:16
16: **All your enemies mock you**: they hiss and gnash their teeth: the say, "We have **swallowed her up** (destroyed her/devoured her): certainly **THIS IS THE DAY THAT WE LOOKED FOR**; we have lived to see it"!!

They especially didn't like the idea that Yahsrael considered themselves the '**chosen people**'. This is evident by what was said to them when they were carried away into captivity. And in the aftermath of when Yahsrael fell, scripture suggests that the nations even knew why they fell.

Psalms 137:3-4
3: For there they that carried us away captive **required of us** (requested) a song; and they that **wasted** (mocked) us **required of us mirth** (demanded that we be happy) saying, "Sing us one of the songs of Zion"
4: **How** shall we sing Yahuah's song in **a strange land**?

The nations not only anticipated Yahsrael's fall, but plotted against them and conspired to make sure that they never rose to power again. **Read** the following passages of scriptures:
Psalms 83: 1-8, 12

1 Keep not Your silence, O God: hold not Your peace, and be not still, O God
2 For, lo, Your enemies make a **tumult** (uproar/loud noise by multiple of people) and they that hate You have **lifted up the head** (exalted themselves)
3 **They** (your enemies) have taken **crafty** (clever/devious/scheming/tricky) **counsel** (interchange of opinions as to future procedure/plan) **against** (in opposition to) Your **hidden ones** (diamonds in the rough/people whom Yah has concealed)
4 **They** (Yahuah's enemies/Yahsrael's enemies) have said, "Come let us **cut them off** (block/isolate/separate/bring to an end/segregate/intercept/sever/obstruct/intrude) from **being a nation** (being united); that the **name** (identity/reputation/title/character) of Yahsrael may be **no more in remembrance** (no longer relevant/forgotten/abandoned)
5 For they have **consulted** (agreed/plotted) together with **one consent** (mind): they are **confederate** (united) against You
6 The tabernacles of **E'dom** (Europeans) and the **Ish'malites** (Arabs); of **Moab** (Asians) and the **Hagarenes** (Egyptians)

HIStory or OUR Story   **Chapter 6**

7 **Geba**l (people of India) and **Ammon** (central Africans), and **Amalek** (Russians); the **Philistines** (Hamas) with the inhabitants of **Tyre** (Hezbollah)

8 **As'sur** (west Africans) also is joined with them: they have helped the **children of Lot** (Hispanics) **Selah** (meditate on that)
…
12 Who said, "**Let us** (Yahuah's enemies/Yahsrael's enemies) **take to ourselves** (steal for ourselves) **the houses of God in possession**"

Jeremiah 11:16-19

16 "Yahuah called your (Yahsrael's) name, a green olive tree (prosperous)(**psalms 52:8**, **Hosea 14:5-6, Isaiah 61:3**) fair (just/upright) and of goodly fruit (full of good deeds **Matthew 7:17-20**): with the noise of a great tumult (uproar, loud noise caused by people) He has kindled fire upon it, and the branches of it are broken

17 For Yahuah of hosts that planted (established/placed) you, has pronounced (declared) evil against you, for the evil of the house of Yahsrael and of the house of Yahudah which they done against themselves to provoke Me to anger in offering incense to the Lord"

18 And Yahuah has given **me** (Yirimiyahu) knowledge of it, and I know it, then you showed me **their** (house of Yahsrael and house of Yahudah) doings

19 But **I**(house of Yahsrael and house of Yahudah) was **like a lamb** (innocent/silent) or an **ox** (dumb) that is brought to the slaughter; and I knew not (didn't understand) that they had **devised** (planned/plotted/carefully thought out) **devices** (schemes/tricks/designs) against me, saying, "**Let us** (the nations/Gentiles/Yahsrael's enemies) **destroy the tree** (genealogical tree/family tree/heritage/lineage/origin) with **the fruit** (language/religion/customs) thereof, and let us **cut him off** (block/isolate/discontinue/disconnect/separate/bring to an end/segregate/intercept/catch/obstruct/intrude) from the land of **the living** (to be awake/to be alive/to be aware/to be conscious), that **his name** (identity/reputation/title/character) **may be no more remembered.**

Yahuah also said that he would cause us to Forget His Name once we left the land of Yahsrael.

Jeremiah 44: 26-29

26 Therefore hear you the word of Yahuah, all Yahudah that dwell in the land of Egypt; "Behold, I have sworn by **My Great name**", says Yahuah, that My name shall **NO MORE be named in the mouth of any man of Yahudah** in all the land of Egypt, saying, Yahuah God lives.

27 Behold, I will watch over them for evil, and not for good: and all the men of Yahudah that are in the land of Egypt shall be consumed by the sword and by the famine, until there be an end of them.
28 Yet a small number that escape the sword shall return out of the land of Egypt into the land of Yahudah, and all the remnant of Yahudah, that are gone into the land of Egypt to sojourn there, shall know whose words shall stand, Mine, or their's.

HIStory or OUR Story   **Chapter 6**

See **Psalms 74:1-11**

1 O God, why have You cast us off **forever** (unspecified amount of time)? Why does Your anger smoke against the sheep of Your pasture?
2 Remember Your **congregation** (group of people), which You have **purchased** (obtained/gotten) of **old** (in the past); the **rod** (tribe) of Your inheritance, which You have **redeemed**;(saved), this mount Zi'on, wherein You have **dwelled** (spent time)
3 Lift up Your feet to the **perpetual** (ongoing) **desolations** (empty/barren/solitary); even all that the **enemy** (people who dislike you, hold you back).
4 Your enemies **roar** (threaten/intimidate) **in the midst** (in the communities) of your **congregations**; they set up their **ensigns** (flags/symbols/territory markers) for **signs** (territory markers)
5 A **man** (Yahuah/Exodus 15:3/Exodus 9:14-16) was famous according as **he had lifted up axes upon the thick trees** (Daniel 4:10-15 22-23)
6 But now they break down **the carved work** (Exodus 31:18) thereof at once with axes and hammers
7 They have cast fire into Your sanctuary, they have **defiled** (profaned/violated) by casting down the dwelling place of Your name to the ground
8 **They** (Yahsrael's enemies) said in their **hearts** (minds), "Let us **destroy** (ruin/break) **them** (Yahsrael) **together** (as a unit): **they** (Yahsrael's enemies) have burned up **all** the **synagogues** (temples/churches) of God in the land
9 **We** (Yahsrael) see not our signs: there is **no more any prophet** (we have no leader): neither is there any that knows how long
10 **O God, how long shall the adversary** (enemy) **reproach** (disrespect)? Shall the **enemy** blaspheme Your name for ever?

Not only did the heads of the nations plot to destroy us as a nation, but they also knew who we were. Notice the **following scriptures:**

1 By the rivers of **Babylon** (confusion), there we sat down, yea, we wept, when we remembered Zion.
2 We hanged our harps upon the willows in the midst thereof.
3 For there they that carried us away **captive** required of us a song; and they that **wasted** (destroyed) us required of us **mirth**, (be happy) saying, Sing us one of the **songs of Zion**.
4 How shall we sing Yahuah's song in a strange land?
5 If I forget you, O Yahrushalom, let my right hand forget her **cunning** (skills)
6 If I do not remember you, let my tongue cling to the roof of my mouth; **if I prefer not Yahrushalom** above my chief joy

7 Remember, O Yahuah, the children of Edom in the day of Yahrushalom; who said, **<u>Raze it</u>** (destroy it), **<u>raze it</u>**, even to the foundation thereof.

You know they knew who we were if they were asking us to sing them a 'song of Zion'. You also know that our ancestors knew who they were because they remembered Yahrushalom. As a matter of fact, our ancestors prefered to be in their homeland more than anything else (their chief joy). Our ancestors would rather their tongues stick to the top of their mouths and they be mute if they ever did not prefer to live in Yahrushalom, their homeland, over any other land.

Here is another scripture showing that they knew who they were, at that time.

Deuteronomy 29:22-28

22 So that the generation to come of your children that shall rise up after you, and the stranger that shall come from a far land, shall say, when they see the plagues of that land, and the sicknesses which Yahuah hath laid upon it;
23 And that the whole land thereof is brimstone, and salt, and burning, that it is not sown, nor beareth, nor any grass groweth therein, like the overthrow of Sodom, and Gomorrah, Admah, and Zeboim, which Yahuah overthrew in his anger, and in his wrath:
24 Even **all nations** shall say, "**<u>Wherefore</u>** (why) has Yahuah done this to this land? What means the heat of this great anger?"
25 Then **men shall say**, "Because **they** have forsaken the covenant of Yahuah God **OF THEIR FATHERS**, which he made with them when he brought them forth out of the land of Egypt:
26 For they went and served other gods, and worshipped them; gods whom they knew not, and whom He had not given to them:
27 And the anger of Yahuah was kindled against this land, to bring upon it **all the curses** that are written in this book:
28 And Yahuah rooted them out of their land in anger, and in wrath, and in great indignation, and cast them into **another land**, as it is this day"

Lamentations 1:10 "The adversary has spread out his hand upon all her **pleasant things**: for she has seen that the **<u>heathen</u>** (nations/**non-Hebrews**) entered into her sanctuary, whom You did commmand that they should not enter into Your congregation."

HIStory or OUR Story Chapter 6

The **Romans** carried away the Hebrew **Menorah** of Yahuah off like a 'trophy', which was called the "candle of God", which had seven golden candlesticks. (**Exodus 25:33-36, Exodus 27:20-21, Numbers 8:4, Revelations 1:12**)

Yahuah set four fates over Yahsrael because of their transgressions. This is what He said in His word.

Jeremiah 15: 1-4
1 Then Yahuah said to me, "Even though Musa and Shemuel were to stand before Me, My heart would not be with this people; send them away from My presence and let them go!
2 And it shall be that when they say to you, 'Where should we go?' then you are to tell them, 'Thus says Yahuah:
"Those destined for **death**, to **death**;
And those destined for the **sword**, to the **sword**;
And those destined for **famine**, to **famine**;
And those destined for **slavery**, to **slavery**."
3 I will appoint over them **four kinds of doom**," declares Yahuah: "**the sword to slay**, the **dogs to drag off**, and the **birds** of the sky and the **beasts** of the earth **to devour and destroy**.
4 I will make them an object of horror among all the kingdoms of the earth because of Manasseh, the son of Hezekiah, the king of Yahudah, for what he did in Yahrushalom.

Deuteronomy 28:48 "Therefore you shall **serve your enemies** whom Yahuah will send against you, in hunger, in thirst, in nakedness, and in the lack of all things; and **He will put an YOKE OF IRON UPON YOUR NECK** until He has destroyed you."

HIStory or OUR Story   Chapter 6

The Prophecy of Daniel and Revelation Explained

These books are able to be understood now. It was already written that the books would be sealed for a certain period of time, but afterwards 'knowledge would increase' (**Daniel 12:4**). Knowledge of what? Essentially, the Hebrews would **REMEMBER** themselves, their God, their ancestors, the truth of the Covenant and the Law, and would realize where they are and why. The truth of the Bible would be revealed to them for the first time. Heretofore, the book had been sealed and anybody trying to understand the book would not be able to until the end time, which is now (**Daniel 12:9,**

Revelation 22:10)

1. In the first year of Belshazzar king of Babylon, Daniel had a dream and visions of his head upon his bed: then he wrote the dream, and told the sum of the matters.
2. Daniel spoke and said, I saw in my vision by night, and, behold, the four winds of the heaven strove upon the great sea.
3 And four great beasts came up from the sea, **diverse one from another**.

Summary Daniel 7:1-3
In Daniel 7:23, the angel says: "The **fourth beast shall be the fourth kingdom upon the earth**." Even today, we portray nations with animal symbols (US: Eagle, Russia: Bear, England: Lion, etc**.**)**. In prophecy,** Babylon = Lion, Medo-Persia = Bear, Greece = Leopard, Rome/America = Eagle (**2 Esdras Chapter 11**)
Winds in Bible prophecy depict war, strife and bloodshed. See **Jeremiah 25:31-33. The** "Four winds" indicate that the strife is coming from all directions of the compass. See **Matthew 24:31**. The "sea" and waters symbolize many people. See **Revelation 17:15. So, beasts arising from the turbulent waters symbolize nations arising from wars among many people.**
4 The first was like a lion, and had eagle's wings: I beheld till the wings thereof were plucked, and it was lifted up from the earth, and made **stand upon the feet as a man**, and **a man's heart** was given to it
5. And behold another beast, a second, like to a bear, and it raised up itself on one side, and it had **three ribs in the mouth** of it between the teeth of it: and they said thus to it, Arise, devour much flesh.

Summary Daniel 7:4-5
7:4 Babylon is fitly represented by a "lion." See **Jeremiah 4:7; 50:17, 43-44. Just as gold is supreme among the metals, so the** "lion" is king among beasts and the "eagle" is king of the birds. Babylon's rise from a basal state of Assyria to ruler of the known world was breathtakingly swift. In the 21 years after Babylon gained its independence from Assyria, it had conquered the surrounding nations, and become the most powerful empire in the region; thus the "eagle's wings" portray speed. See **Habakkuk 1:6-8.**
Later, this nation ceased to expand and conquer, represented by the wings being "plucked" off. After the death of Nebuchadnezzar, **the succeeding kings of Babylon chose to ignore God's law and mock him**. See note on **Daniel 5:22**. Then **Babylon lost its lion-like nobility. It was given a "man's heart"** and made **to stand upon its "feet as a man."**

HIStory or OUR Story   **Chapter 6**

7:5 The next kingdom, corresponding to the chest and arms of silver from the image of **Daniel 2**, is Medo-Persia. Persia was dominant over Media, which is represented by the "bear raised up on one side". The **"three" ribs** in the bear's mouth likely represent the major kingdoms which Medo-Persia conquered—**Babylon, Lydia and Egypt**. At the height of its power, this empire conquered more than six times as much land as had its predecessor, Babylon. It did "devour much flesh."

6 After this I beheld, and lo another, **like a leopard**, which had upon the back of it four **wings** of a fowl; the beast had also four heads; and dominion was given to it.

7 After this I saw in the night visions, and behold a fourth beast, dreadful and terrible, and strong exceedingly; and it had great iron teeth: it devoured and broke in pieces, and stamped the residue with the feet of it: and it was diverse from all the beasts that were before it; and it had ten horns.

Summary Daniel 7:6-7
7:6 Medo-Persia was defeated by Macedonian Greece, represented as a "leopard" with "four heads" and "four wings." The "four wings" represented unprecedented swiftness. See **Habakkuk 1:6**. The conquests of Macedonian Greece under Alexander the Great were more rapid than even those of Babylon. In just three short years, from 334-331 BC, he conquered the entire Persian Empire. The leopard is more agile and swift than a lion or bear, yet more frail. Alexander died in 323 BC at the age of thirty-two. **His four strongest generals (Cassander, Lysimachus, Ptolemy, and Seleucas)** divided the kingdom among themselves, symbolized by the leopard's "four heads."

7:7 The previous empires were represented by some of the most ferocious animals of prey; but this fourth "beast" is represented by a frightful monster. This is a fitting description of the Roman Empire, which dominated the world with its iron legions. The "iron teeth" of this monster give it a direct parallel to the iron in the image in **Daniel 2:40**

It was Rome that ruled the Mediterranean world when Yahushua lived on earth, and it was the Roman governor, Pilate, who sent Him to the cross, where he died for the sins of all mankind. The "ten horns," like the leopard's "four heads," show a splintering of the kingdom into multiple parts. See notes on verse 24-25.

Daniel 7:8-10
8 I considered the horns, and, behold, there came up among them another little horn, before whom there were three of the first horns plucked up by the roots: and, behold, in this horn were eyes like **the eyes of man**, and **a mouth speaking great things**.

9 I beheld till the thrones were cast down, and the **Ancient of days** did sit, whose garment was white as snow, and **the hair of His head like the pure wool**: His throne was like the fiery flame and His wheels as burning fire.

10 A fiery stream issued and came forth from before Him: thousand thousands ministered to Him, and ten thousand times ten thousand stood before Him: the judgment was set, and the books were opened.

HIStory or OUR Story   **Chapter 6**

Summary of versus Daniel 7:8-10
7:8 Verse 24 tells us, "The ten horns out of this kingdom are ten kings." So this horn is a little kingdom. See notes on verses 24-25. Also another title for the office of the Pope is 'Holy See' in reference to the 'eyes of a man'.
7:9-10 In Daniel 2, we saw a stone crush the statue to powder then fill the whole earth, vividly portraying the time when these nations will be judged and destroyed. At that time, God will set up His Kingdom and reign forever. This chapter addresses the fact that God will "sit" for a solemn day of judgment before He sets up His "everlasting dominion." See verses 9-12, 22 and 26. His verdict will be both just and merciful, because He commits the judgment to His Son, who gave His life for us.
John 5:22, 27

11 I beheld then because of **the voice of the great words** which the horn spoke: I beheld even till the beast was slain, and his body destroyed, and given to the burning flame.
12 As concerning the rest of the beasts, they had their dominion taken away: yet their lives were prolonged for a season and time.

Summary Daniel 7:11-12
The territory and subjects of the three previous kingdoms were not destroyed even though they ceased to exist as separate empires. In contrast, the fourth kingdom ends in the lake of fire and has no existence beyond. See **Revelation 19:20**.

20 And of the ten horns that were in his head, and of the other which came up, and before whom three fell; even of that horn that had eyes, and a mouth that spoke very **great things**, whose look was more stout than his fellows.
21 I beheld, and **the same horn made war with the chosen people,** and prevailed against them;
22 Until the **Ancient of days** came and judgment was given to the chosen people of the Most High; and the time came that the saints possessed the kingdom.
23 Thus he said, **The fourth beast shall be the fourth kingdom upon earth,** which shall be **diverse from all kingdoms**, and shall devour the whole earth, and shall tread it down, and break it in pieces.
24 And the ten horns out of this kingdom are ten kings that shall arise: and another shall rise after them; and he shall be diverse from the first, and **he shall subdue three kings**.
25 And **he shall SPEAK GREAT WORDS against the Most High**, and shall persecute **the chosen people of the Most High**, and **think to change TIMES and LAWS**: and **THEY shall be given into his hand** until a time and times and the dividing of time.

> One way that the fourth Beast a.k.a. the Mother Church a.k.a. the Roman **Catholic Church changed the times** was by giving us the Gregorian Calender. The **Gregorian calendar** is today's internationally accepted civil **calendar** and is also known as the "Western **calendar**" or "Christian **calendar**". It was named after the man who first introduced it in February 1582: **Pope Gregory XIII. Therefore, it is called the Gregorian Calender**.

Louis Gaston Segur, *Plain Talk about the Protestantism of Today*
(London: Thomas Richardson and Son, 1874): 213:

"Thus the observance of Sunday by the Protestants is a homage they pay to the authority of the Catholic Church."

Stephen Keenan, *Catholic—Doctrinal Catechism 3rd Edition, Page* 174

Question: Have you any other way of proving the Church has power to institute festivals of precept?

Answer: "**Had she not such power,** she could not have done that in which all modern religionists agree with her, **she could not have substituted the observance of Sunday the 1st day of the week,** for the observance of Saturday the 7th day, **a change for which there is no Scriptural authority."**

Our Sunday Visitor (February 5, 1950):

"**Practically everything Protestants regard as essential or important, they have received from the Catholic Church**... The Protestant mind does not seem to realize that in **accepting the Bible and observing Sunday, in keeping Christmas and Easter, they are accepting the authority of the spokesman for the church, the Pope."**

Chancellor Albert Smith for Cardinal of Baltimore Archdiocese, letter dated February 10, 1920:

"**If Protestants would follow the Bible**, they should worship God on the Sabbath day by God which is Saturday. In **keeping the Sunday, they are following a law of the Catholic Church**."

The Catholic Mirror (September 23, 1893):

"The Catholic Church, for over one thousand years before the existence of a Protestant, by virtue of her divine mission, **changed the day from Saturday to Sunday**"

"Pope," *Ferraris' Ecclesiastic Dictionary*:

"The **Pope is of SO GREAT** dignity and so exalted that **he is not a mere man, but as it were God,** and the vicar of God"

HIStory or OUR Story   **Chapter 6**

Some keys of knowledge for you. (**Luke 11:52**). The official title for the Pope is Vicarius Filii Dei (Latin: Vicar or Representative of the Son of God). If you add up the Latin values for V.F.D. you get 666. Man was made on the 6th day thus 6 is the number of man. The hands represents works (**Ecclesiastes 9:10**), the mind represents ones beliefs (**Jeremiah 31:33/Hebrews 8:10**)
The vision in the book of Revelation is the Revelation of the vision in the book of Daniel. Both books are mates meant to be studied together. In Daniel he is told to "**shut up the vision**", meaning to hide or conceal it (**Daniel 12:9**). But in the book of Revelation, John is told to "**SEAL NOT the book**" for the time is at hand". (**Revelation 22:10**)

So in the book of Revelation, John is looking back at the Babylonian kingdom, the Medo-Persian Kingdom, the Grecian kingdom, up to the Roman kingdom which was the fourth kingdom upon the earth ruling at that current time. For reference, when the scriptures in this prophecy use the terminology (beast), it is not a literal beast, but a **king** and a **kingdom.** See the below scriptures.

Daniel 7:17 "These great **beasts**, which are **four**, **are four kings**, which shall arise out of the earth."
Daniel 7:23 "Thus he said, "**The fourth beast** shall be **the fourth kingdom** upon the earth, which shall be **different** from all kingdoms, and shall devour the whole earth and shall tread it down and break in pieces."

The reason this fourth kingdom is different is because the Babylonian, Medo-Persian, and Grecian kingdoms were all clearly pagan in their religion. Rome re-packaged itself from appearing clearly pagan to being Catholic. Rome went from being known as Pagan Rome to Papal Rome. Rome is the only entity that took the Holy Scriptures and made it their primary religion. The exception is that they held on to their own ancestral traditions. They have hidden a lot of truth, and decided which books they wanted to follow and not. It was in 321 A.D. that Constantine of the Roman Empire held an assembly to decide which scrolls of scripture were authoritative and which were not. Later in history, you will find that the Catholic Church had the Apocrypha removed in 1885. The Original King James Bible assembled in 1611 contained 80 books. We were only limited to 66 books within the last 130 years.

In **Daniel 7:4-7** Daniel orders the beasts as follows: lion, bear, leopard, and a most dreadful and terrible beast. You'll notice the fourth beast is not described as a particular animal at this time, and that is because the full meaning of the book at this time was sealed or hidden. In the book of **Revelation 13: 1-3,** John starts off with the **third beast** (Greece) depicted as a leopard beast,working his way back down to the **first beast** (Babylon) depicted as a lion. He did not make an anamalistic representation of the fourth beast which was described as **dreadful, terrifying, strong exceedingly**, with great **iron** teeth. We know that **iron** was representing Rome in Daniel's interpretation of Nebuchadnezzar's statue. Historically after Greece lost rulership, Rome was the successor. Pagan Rome and Papal Rome are described as the beast. It is also important to note that ancient Rome and America's **imperial national symbols** are **the bald eagle**. The same pilgrims who came here on the Mayflower were nothing more than re-packaged Romans. You'll notice the eagle appears to come in peace leading with a symbol of peace, the **olive branch,** but in it's back paw it has 13 arrows representing war. The eagle also represents great foresight and strength. The lion used by the Babylonians represented the king of the beasts of the earth, as he is often called the 'king of the jungle'. The eagle is used by Rome and America and it is called the 'king of the sky'.

HIStory or OUR Story   Chapter 6

In Ezra's vision (described in the Apocryphal book, 2 Ezra), the eagle is depicted as having three heads. The following excerpt is from the 2nd book of Ezra from the Apocrypha. The vision given in **2 Ezra Chapter 11** as follows:

1: Then saw I a dream, and, behold, there came up from the sea **an eagle**, which had twelve feathered wings, and **three heads**.
2: And I saw, and, behold, she spread her wings over all the earth, and all the winds of the air blew on her, and were gathered together.
3: And I beheld, and out of her feathers there grew other contrary feathers; and they became little feathers and small.
4: But her heads were at rest: the head in the midst was greater than the other, yet rested it with the residue.
5: Moreover I beheld, and, lo, **the eagle flew with her feathers**, and reigned upon earth, and over them that dwelled therein.
6: And I saw that all things under heaven were subject to her, and **no man spoke against her**, no, not one creature upon earth.
7: And I beheld, and, lo, **the eagle** rose upon her talons, and spoke to her feathers, saying,
8: Watch not all at once: sleep every one in his own place, and watch by course:
9: But let the heads be preserved for the last.
10: And I beheld, and, lo, the voice went not out of her heads, but from the midst of her body.
11: And I numbered her contrary feathers, and, behold, there were eight of them.
12: And I looked, and, behold, on the right side there arose one feather, and reigned over all the earth;
13: And so it was, that when it reigned, the end of it came, and the place thereof appeared no more: so the next following stood up. and reigned, and had a great time;
14: And it happened, that when it reigned, the end of it came also, like as the first, so that it appeared no more.
15: Then came there a voice to it, and said,
16: Hear **you that have bore rule over the earth so long**: this I say to you, before **you begin to appear no more**,
17: There shall none after you attain to your time, neither to the half thereof.
18: Then arose the third, and reigned as the other before, and appeared no more also.
19: So went it with all the residue one after another, as that every one reigned, and then appeared no more.
20: Then I beheld, and, lo, in process of time the feathers that followed stood up upon the right side, that they might rule also; and some of them ruled, but within a while they appeared no more:
21: For some of them were set up, but ruled not.
22: After this I looked, and, behold, the twelve feathers appeared no more, nor the two little feathers:
23: And there was no more upon **the eagle's** body, but three heads that rested, and six little wings.
24: Then saw I also that two little feathers divided themselves from the six, and remained under the head that was upon the right side: for the four continued in their place.

HIStory or OUR Story   Chapter 6

25: And I beheld, and, lo, these little wings thought to set up themselves and to have the rule.
26: And I beheld, and, lo, there was one set up, but shortly it appeared no more.
27: And the second was sooner away than the first.
28: And I beheld, and, lo, the two that remained thought also in themselves to reign:
29: And when they so thought, behold, **there awakened one of the heads that were at rest, namely, it that was in the midst; for that was greater than the two other heads**.
30: And then I saw that the two other heads were joined with it.
31: and behold, the head turned with those that were with it, and it devoured the two little wings which were planning to reign.
32: But t**his head put the whole earth in fear**, and bore rule in it over all those that dwelled upon the earth with **much oppression**; and it had the governance of the **world more than all the wings that had been**.
33: And after this I beheld, and, lo, the head that was in the midst suddenly appeared no more, like as the wings.
34: But there remained the two heads, which also in like sort ruled upon the earth, and over those that dwelled therein.
35: And I beheld, and, lo, the head upon the right side devoured it that was upon the left side.
36: Then I heard a voice, which said to me, Look before you, and consider the thing that you see.
37: And I beheld, and lo, as it were **a roaring lion** chased out of the wood: and I saw that he sent out **a man's voice** to **the eagle,** and said,
38: Hear you, I will talk with you, and Yahuah shall say to you,
39: "**Are not you it that remains of the four beasts**, whom I made to reign in My world, that the end of their times might come through them?
40: **You, the fourth that has come**, have conquered all the beasts that have gone before; and **you have held sway over the world with much terror,** and over all the earth with grievous oppression; and for so long **you have dwelled on the earth with DECEIT.**
41: **For the earth YOU HAVE NOT judged with truth.**
42: For you have afflicted the meek, you have hurt the peaceable, **you have loved liars**, and destroyed the dwellings of them that brought forth fruit, and have cast down the walls of such as did you no harm.
43: Therefore is your wrongful dealing come up to Yahuah, and your pride to the Mighty.
44: Yahuah also has looked upon the proud times, and, behold, they are ended, and his abominations are fulfilled.
45: And therefore **APPEAR NO MORE, you eagle,** nor your horrible wings, nor your wicked feathers, nor your malicious heads, nor your hurtful claws, nor all your vain body:
46: That all the earth may be refreshed, and may return, being delivered from your violence, and that she may hope for the judgment and mercy of Him that made her.

HIStory or OUR Story   **Chapter 6**

2 Ezras Chapter 12

1: And it came to pass, while **THE LION** spoke these words to **THE EAGLE**, I saw,
2: And, behold, the head that remained and the four wings appeared no more, and the two went to it and set themselves up to reign, and their kingdom was small, and full of uproar.
3: And I saw, and, behold, they appeared no more, and **the whole body of the eagle was burned so that the earth was in great fear**: then awaked I out of the trouble and trance of my mind, and from great fear, and said to my spirit,
4: Lo, this have you done to me, in that you search out the ways of Yahuah.
5: Lo, yet am I weary in my mind, and very weak in my spirit; and little strength is there in me, for the great fear wherewith I was afflicted this night.
6: Therefore will I now beg Yahuah, that He will comfort me to the end.
7: And I said, Yahuah that bears rule, if I have found grace before your sight, and if I am justified with you before many others, and if my prayer indeed be come up before your face;
8: Comfort me then, and show me your servant the interpretation and plain difference of this fearful vision, that you may perfectly comfort my soul.
9: For you have judged me worthy to show me the last times.

Now the interpretation is given:

10: And he said to me, This is the interpretation of the vision:
11: **The eagle**, whom you saw come up from the sea, **is the kingdom which was seen in the vision of your brother Daniel.**
12: But it was not explained to him, therefore now I declare it to you.
13: Behold, the days will come, that **there shall rise up a kingdom upon earth, and it shall be feared above all the kingdoms that were before it**.
14: In the same, shall twelve kings reign, one after another:
15: Whereof the second shall begin to reign, and shall have more time than any of the twelve.
16: And this do the twelve wings signify, which you saw.
17: As for the voice which you heard speak, and that you saw not to go out from the heads but from the midst of the body thereof, this is the interpretation:
18: And in the midst of the time of that kingdom, there shall arise great strivings, and it shall stand in peril of failing: nevertheless **it shall not then fall, but shall be restored again to his beginning**.
19: And whereas you saw the eight small wings sticking to her wings, this is the interpretation:
20: That in him there shall arise **eight kings**, whose times shall be but small, and their years **swift**.
21: And two of them shall perish, the middle time approaching: four shall be kept until their end begins to approach: but two shall be kept to the end.

22: And whereas you saw three heads resting, this is the interpretation:
23: In his last days shall Yahuah raise up three kings, and renew many things therein, and they shall have the dominion of the earth,
24: And of those that dwell therein, with **much oppression**, **ABOVE ALL THOSE WHO WERE BEFORE THEM**: therefore, are they called the heads of the eagle.
25: For these are they that shall accomplish his wickedness, and that shall finish his last end.
26: And whereas you saw that the great head appeared no more, it signifies that one of them shall die upon his bed, and yet with pain.
27: For the two that remain shall be slain with the sword.
28: For the sword of the one shall devour the other: but at the last shall he fall through the sword himself.

Now if we look at the various coat of arms, banners of the Holy Roman Empire, we see how it fits with this vision. The banners feature a one or two headed eagle with wings outstretched, and six "wing feathers" hanging down on each side, making twelve wing feathers:

HIStory or OUR Story   Chapter 6

Now let's look at the last twelve kings of the Holy Roman Empire:

Rulers	Begin Reign	Reign years
1 Francis	1637	21
2 Leopold I	1658	47
3 Joseph I	1705	6
4 Charles VI	1711	29
5 Charles VII	1742	3
6 Francis I	1745	20
7 Joseph II	1765	25
8 Leopold II	1790	2
9 Francis II	1792	14
10 William I	1871	17
11 Frederick III	1888	3 months
12 William II	1888-1918	30

These are the twelve feather wings which are twelve kings which each reigned in turn. Note the second king ruled longer than the others, more than twice as long as any of the first nine. While it was not more than twice as long as the 12th king, **remember the last three were not crowned by the Pope**. This fulfilled the prophecy "Then I beheld, and, lo, in the process of time the feathers that followed stood up upon the right side, that they might rule also; and some of them ruled, but within a while they appeared no more: For some of them were set up, but ruled not." (**2Ezras 11:20-21**)

Ezra had it right. The last three kings were set up, but the Pope did not crown them as Roman Emperors, so they did not officially rule. **Amazing how Ezra knew this 2,500 years before hand!**

In the wake of WW I, three major powers rose up from the "Barbarians of Europe" in the vacuum of the fall of the Holy Roman Empire: **The United States (whose symbol is the eagle):**

HIStory or OUR Story   **Chapter 6**

Britain died "upon his bed" in that Britain passed from being a major power as if from old age. Britain slept while Nazi Germany grew in power.

The United States slew Nazi Germany "with the sword" (by war).

This leaves the United States as the last remaining head, which will be slain "with the sword" by MessiYAH upon his return.

29: And whereas you saw two feathers under the wings passing over to the head that is on the right side;
30: It signifies that these are they, whom Yahuah has kept to their end: this is the small kingdom and full of trouble, as you saw.
31: And **THE LION**, whom you saw **rising up out of the wood, and roaring**, and speaking to **the eagle**, and **rebuking her for her unrighteousness** with all the words which you have heard;
32: **This is the MessiYah**, which **Yahuah has kept for them and for their wickedness** to the end of days, **who will arise from the seed of Daud**, and **will come and speak to them: He shall reprove them**, and **shall upbraid them with their cruelty**.
33: For **He shall set them before Him alive in judgment**, and **shall rebuke them**, and **correct them**.
34: For **the rest of my people, shall he deliver with mercy**, those that have been pressed upon my borders, and **He shall make them joyful until the coming of the day of judgment**, whereof I have spoken to you from the beginning.
35: This is the dream that you saw, and these are the interpretations.
36: And you alone were worthy to learn this secret of Yahuah.
37: Therefore write all these things that you have seen in a book, and hide them:
38: And **teach them to the wise of the people**, whose hearts you know may comprehend and keep these secrets.

This last heir to the Roman Empire (the USA) will not heed to the words of Yahuah and will be judged and Yahuah's people will be delivered out of her.

HIStory or OUR Story   **Chapter 6**

The ten kings of (**Revelation 13:1**) are ten kingdoms (**Revelation 17:9,10**) that made up the pagan Roman Empire and are as follows:

1. **Vandals** (East Germanic tribe, from which we have the word **'vandalism'** due to their violent exploits)
2. **Visigoths** (German nomadic tribe)
3. **Suevi** (German tribe)
4. **Alans** (Iranian nomadic tribe)
5. **Burgundians** (East Germanic tribe)
6. **Franks** (a mixed group of Germanic tribes)
7. **Britons** (modern day Celtics)
8. **Huns** (Eastern European tribe from Caucasia from which the term 'Caucasian' derives.)
9. **Lombards** (Germanic tribe)
10. **Ravenna** (was the capital of the Western Roman Empire)

After Pagan Rome fell, then one of its heads was resurrected again as Papal Rome (**Revelation 13:3**). All of these seven kingdoms ruled with unity. (**Revelation 17:13**). The seven kingdoms of Papal Rome is as follows:

1. **Babylon**
2. **Medo**
3. **Persia**
4. **Greece**
5. **Assyria**
6. **Egypt**
7. **Rome, Italy**

The third head of the of the eagle rose and is called **'the eighth'** of the seven. That means the people of this new kingdom is a mixture of people from the previous seven. The scriptures states that the seven kingdoms support this eighth kingdom (see **Revelation 17:10-13**) Papal Rome was made up of seven kingdoms from which came forth the Anglo-Saxon Americans.

See **Revelation 13:11-17** and **Revelation 17:9-14**.

HIStory or OUR Story   **Chapter 6**

Summary Daniel 7:20-25
The ten horns of the beasts, like the feet of iron mixed with clay in **Daniel 2**, predicted that the Roman Empire would fragment into ten parts. Barbarian tribes invaded the empire's territory from the north and east and eventually became the nations of modern Europe.

26 But the judgment shall sit, and **they shall take away his dominion**, to consume and to destroy it until the end.

27 And the kingdom and dominion, and the greatness of the kingdom under the whole heaven, shall be given to **the people of the saints** of the most High, whose kingdom is an everlasting kingdom, and all dominions shall serve and obey him.

28 Hitherto is the end of the matter. As for me Daniel, my cogitations much troubled me, and my countenance changed in me: but I kept the matter in my heart.

Summary Daniel 7:26-28
The climax of this prophecy is God's final judgment. The beast and the little horn power are judged and their kingdom is taken away; at the same time, the verdict is made in favor of the saints and dominion is given to them.

These same events were portrayed in Daniel 2 when the stone crushed the statue of power and filled the whole earth.

God will set up His everlasting kingdom full of love, joy and peace; there will be no sickness or death. **Revelation 21:3-4**

Daniel Chapter 8

1 In the third year of the reign of king Belshazzar a vision appeared to me, even to me Daniel, after that which appeared to me at the first.

2 And I saw in a vision; and it came to pass, when I saw, that I was at Shushan in the palace, which is in the province of Elam; and I saw in a vision, and I was by the river of Ulai.

Summary Daniel 8:1-2
8:1-2 Daniel received this vision twelve years before the fall of Babylon. Since Babylon was about to be overthrown, the vision of this chapter begins with Medo-Persia. This chapter is also a repeat of chapter 7, with more emphasis on the judgment scene.

3 Then I lifted up my eyes, and saw, and, behold, there stood before the river a ram which had two horns: and the two horns were high; but **one was higher than the other**, and **the higher came up last.**

4 I saw the ram pushing westward, and northward, and southward; so that no beasts might stand before him, neither was there any that could deliver out of his hand; but he did according to his will, and **became great**.

Summary Daniel 8:3-4
8:3-4 Verse 20 identifies this "ram" as Medo-Persia. The "two horns" represent the two parts of the empire with the Persians, the younger of the two nations, becoming dominant over the Medes. See also notes on **Daniel 7:5**

5 And as I was considering, behold, an he goat came from the west on the face of the whole earth, and **touched not the ground**: and the goat had a notable horn between his eyes.
6 And he came to the ram that had two horns, which I had seen standing before the river, and ran to him in the fury of his power.
7 And I saw him come close to the ram, and he was moved with choler against him, and smote the ram, and broke his two horns: and there was no power in the ram to stand before him, but **he cast him down to the ground, and stamped upon him**: and there was none that could deliver the ram out of his hand.
8 Therefore the he goat waxed **very great**: and when he was strong, the great horn was broken; and for it came up four notable ones toward the four winds of heaven.

Summary Daniel 8: 5-8
8:5-8 Verses 21 and 22 identify the "goat" as Greece the "notable horn between his eyes" was **Alexander the Great**, who came from the west and defeated the armies of Persia. Alexander died without an heir at the height of his power. His generals fought each other until there were only **four left**, represented by the "**four horns**." See also notes on **Daniel 7:6**.
The two animals used to represent **Medo-Persia** and **Greece** are not wild animals of prey, but clean animals used in the sanctuary service. The next power to come into view is represented by a horn. The focus of this vision is how this power affects **God's Sanctuary**, **His people** and His work of saving souls from sin.

Daniel 8:9-12
9 And out of one of them came forth a little horn, which waxed **exceeding great**, toward the south, and toward the east, and toward the pleasant land.
10 And it waxed great, even to the host of heaven; and it **cast down some of the host and of the stars to the ground, and stamped upon them**.
11 Yea, he magnified himself even to the prince of the host, and by him the daily sacrifice was taken away, and the place of the sanctuary was cast down.
12 And a host was given him against the daily sacrifice by reason of transgression, **and it cast down the truth to the ground**; and it practiced, and prospered.

Summary Daniel 8:9-12
8:9-12 We know from **Daniel 2 and 7** and from history that the power which followed Greece was Rome. In chapters 2 and 7 it was shown in two phases: Pagan Rome and Divided Rome. We saw in Chapter 7 that the religious power of Papal Rome rose to dominate the divided empire.
This vision represents power. The physical actions of Pagan Rome against God's people are symbolic of Papal persecution of God's people and their true worship.

HIStory or OUR Story — Chapter 6

13 Then I heard one saint speaking, and another saint said to that certain saint which spoke, How long shall be the vision concerning the daily sacrifice, and **the transgression of desolation**, to **give both the sanctuary and the host to be trodden under foot**?
14 And he said to me, until two thousand and three hundred days; then shall the sanctuary be cleansed.

Summary Daniel 8:13-14
8:13-14 A day in Bible prophecy equals one literal year, so the 2300 days allotted for the events in this vision are 2300 years. See **Ezekiel 4:6; Numbers 14:34. This time period cannot be 2300 literal days**—a little over 6 years—because this vision encompasses the Persian, Grecian, Roman, and Papal powers, and because verses 17 and 19 state that the vision extends to the end of time. The angel does not give the starting date in this chapter, but we know that is sometime during the reign of Medo-Persia **(539-331 BC)**, which was the first kingdom in this prophecy. The exact starting date will be given in chapter 9

15 And it came to pass, when I, even I Daniel, had seen the vision, and sought for the meaning, then, behold, there stood before me as the **appearance of a man**.
16 And I heard **a man's voice** between the banks of Ulai, which called, and said, Gabriel, **make this man to understand** the vision.
17 So he came near where I stood: and when he came, I was afraid, and fell upon my face: but he said to me, Understand, O son of man: for at the time of the end shall be the vision.
18 Now as he was speaking with me, I was in a **deep sleep** on my face toward the ground: but he touched me, and set me upright.
19 And he said, Behold, I will make you know what shall be in the last **end of the indignation**: **for at the time appointed the end shall be.**
20 The ram which you saw having two horns are the kings of Media and Persia.
21 And the rough goat is the king of Grecia: and the great horn that is between his eyes is the first king.
22 Now that being broken, whereas four stood up for it, four kingdoms shall stand up out of the nation, but **not in his power**.

Summary Daniel 8:15-22
The angel Gabriel is given a divine command to instruct Daniel so he will "understand the vision." However, Daniel faints before Gabriel can give him the starting date of the 2300 days/years. Daniel later states that no one understood the vision in verse 27.

HIStory or OUR Story   Chapter 6

23 And in the latter time of their kingdom, when the **transgressors are come to the full**, a king of fierce countenance, and **understanding dark sentences**, shall stand up.

24 And his power shall be mighty, but **not by his own power**: and he shall destroy wonderfully, and shall prosper, and practice, and shall destroy **the mighty** and **the holy people**.

25 And **through his policy also he shall cause craft to prosper in his hand**; and **he shall magnify himself in his heart,** and **by peace shall destroy many**: <u>he shall also stand up against the Prince of princes</u>; but he shall be broken without hand.

Summary Daniel 8: 23-25
This power is broken "without hand" (vs. 25), an expression alluding to the rock cut out without hand that destroys **the image of Daniel.**
By a quick comparison of the "fourth Beast" and its "little horn" from chapter seven with the "little horn" of chapter eight, we see that **they both represent the same power:**
By a quick comparison of the "fourth Beast" and its "little horn" from chapter seven with the "little horn" of chapter eight, we see that they both represent the same power.

Take a look at the following verses in Daniel, Chapter 7.
Verse 21: "make war with the saints"
Verse 8: "mouth speaking great things"
Verse 19: "exceeding dreadful"
Verse 11: "beast was slain… given to the burning"

Take a look at the following verses in Daniel, Chapter 8.
Verse 24: "destroy **the mighty** and **the holy people**"
Verse 11: "magnified himself"
Verse 23: "king of fierce countenance"
Verse 25: "broken without hand"

The angel explained all parts of the vision except the 2300 days (evenings and mornings) and the cleansing of the sanctuary. Where the interpretation for these parts of the vision would be expected, Daniel instead is told to close up the vision.

26 And the vision of the evening and the morning which was told is true: wherefore shut you up the vision; for **it shall be for many days.**

27 And I Daniel fainted, and was sick certain days; afterward I rose up, and did the king's business; and I was astonished at the vision, but none understood it.

HIStory or OUR Story Chapter 6

Daniel 2 Explained

God gave King Nebuchadnezzar of Babylon a very important prophetic dream. Part of that dream is about our modern times.

This story is similar to the story of Yosef (Joseph), who stood before Pharaoh in Egypt. The great Egyptian ruler had dreamed a dream that disturbed him greatly. Because of a gift from God, Yosef had a reputation for being able to interpret dreams, so he was brought before Pharaoh to interpret his dream.

Like the Egyptian Pharaoh, King Nebuchadnezzar of Babylon also dreamed a dream that he could not remember. The Hebrew Prophet Daniel was called upon to reveal and interpret the dream, because Daniel also possessed a divine gift, like Yosef. In both stories, God was working profoundly to place a Hebrew into a strategic position of power within a pagan government. There he would play a divine role that would serve the purpose of God for Yahsrael and other nations in his day. In the long term, Daniel's roles in Babylon and Persia left an eternal testimony for all the nations of the world, and for all of time to come. God used both Yosef and Daniel to speak to the most powerful heathen powers of their day, to give a witness that Yahuah is in control over ALL the affairs of men, and that He sets kings and kingdoms in order. Both kings eventually recognized the miraculous power of Yahuah and worshipped Him from their thrones.

In the end, we can see that God sent the dreams to Pharaoh and Nebuchadnezzar. God also sent the interpreters, Yosef and Daniel. It was all divinely orchestrated for the glory of God.
"In the second year of the reign of Nebuchadnezzar he dreamed dreams, wherewith his spirit was troubled, and his sleep brake from him," **Daniel 2:1**.

Nebuchadnezzar could not remember the dreams that troubled him, so he demanded his magicians, astrologers and sorcerers to reveal and interpret them. Naturally, they could not, so Nebuchadnezzar ordered them all to be put to death.

But Daniel intervened. He begged for time to show the answer. "Then Daniel went to his house, and made the thing known to Hananiyah, Mishael, and Azariyah that they would desire mercies of the God of heaven concerning this secret."

They Desired Mercies Of The God Of Heaven

Daniel 2:19 - "Then was the secret revealed to Daniel in a night vision what we desired of you."

Daniel 2:20-21 - "Blessed be the name of God for ever and ever: ...He changes the times and the seasons: He removes kings, and sets up kings."
None of King Nebuchadnezzar's counselors could reveal his troubling dreams to him, so he ordered them all to be killed. But by intercessory prayer, Daniel obtained a revelation from God which answered the King's wishes, and saved the lives of Daniel and his companions. Daniel immediately gave thanks and praise to God.

HIStory or OUR Story   Chapter 6

Daniel 2:23 - "I thank you, and praise you, O you God of my fathers, who hast given me wisdom and might, and hast made known to me now what we desired of you: for you hast now made known to us the king's matter."

God Reveals Secrets Of The Latter Days

The wisest men in Babylon had no clues about the future. Nebuchadnezzar would have killed them for their ignorance. But all wisdom and knowledge comes from Yahuah, and wise men of God, like Daniel, save many lives. God knows EVERYTHING. Daniel saw things 2500 years in the future.

Daniel 2:27-28 - "Daniel answered... The secret which the king hath demanded cannot the wise men, the astrologers, the magicians, the soothsayers, show to the king; but there is a God in heaven that reveals secrets, and makes known to the king Nebuchadnezzar what shall be in the latter days."

God Tutored Nebuchadnezzar, A Pagan King
When all else had failed, the man of God, Daniel, had the answers that Nebuchadnezzar could find nowhere else. Nebuchadnezzar was the most powerful man on earth in his day, ruling over the sprawling Babylonian Empire. But he did not have a clue about the future. God decided to teach him a few things.

Daniel 2:29 - "As for you, O king, your thoughts came into your mind upon your bed, what should come to pass hereafter: and he that reveals secrets makes known to you what shall come to pass.... You, O king, saw, and behold a great image."

Nebuchadnezzar's Statue

God gave the dream to Nebuchadnezzar. He saw a great statue of a man. It was bright, excellent and terrible, and foretold the sequence of coming world empires. Its golden head represented the current Babylonian Empire; its silver breast and arms represented the successor, the Medo-Persian Empire. The brass thighs prophesied of Greece. Iron legs foresaw the Roman Empire; iron and clay feet, the now Papal Church mixed with the Hebrews.

Yahushua Will Come And Crush the mixture of the Iron And Clay Feet
Nebuchadnezzar's Statue **Daniel 2:45** - "...the stone was cut out of the mountain without hands, and... broke in pieces the iron, the brass, the clay, the silver, and the gold"
Nebuchadnezzar fell on his face and worshipped Daniel for his ability to describe and interpret the dream he had forgotten. He ordered his officers to offer an oblation and sweet odors to Daniel. He made him a great man, gave him many great gifts, made him ruler over the whole province of Babylon, and chief of the governors. People can recognize that our God is the greatest.

Daniel 2:47 - "Of a truth it is, that your God is a God of gods, and a Master of masters, and a revealer of secrets, seeing you could reveal this secret."
Summary: The great statue depicted successive world kingdoms.

HIStory or OUR Story   **Chapter 6**

These are the empires that have successively dominated the Euro-Asian-Mideast region for 2500 years. As such, these empires have had profound, even dramatic effects on the "diaspora" - the dispersed Hebrews that descended from ancient Yahsrael. Bible prophecies rarely have any comment on world events that do not have some association with the nation and people of Israel. These are the empires that most affected the people and/or land of Israel since ancient times.

The Roman Empire collapsed around 300 A.D. and the next and last world empire before Yahushua returns was illustrated by iron and clay feet, **which are the Hebrews (clay) scattered** and **mixed with Romans (iron). Daniel's 2:43**

"And whereas you saw the feet and toes, part of potter's clay, and part of iron, the kingdom shall be divided; but there shall be in it of the strength of the iron, forasmuch as you saw the iron mixed with **muddy clay**. And as the toes of the feet were part of iron, and part of clay, so the kingdom shall be partly strong, and partly broken." (**Daniel 2:41,42**)

The stone struck and destroyed the iron and clay feet.

What do the iron and clay feet represent? **An empire with a dual nature: Religion & Politics, Church & State.**

Columbus Discovered America- OR DID HE?

Many of the Hebrews were indentured servants in the foreign African countries for years before they were given any relief. Many of the Yahsraelites were sold by the Africans to the Arabs for thousands of years. Then in turn the Arabs sold the Hebrews to other nations around the world.

During this time period, our people were forced into different religions. Some Hebrews went into some of the different religions in Africa. The vast majority of the Hebrews became Muslims and adopted the religion of the Arabs. Back in those days, they either worshiped Allah or it was 'off with their heads'.

Some groups of Hebrew Yahsraelites of the tribe of Gad, Nephtali and Mannaseh primarily migrated even further than Africa because they were tired of being oppressed and being pilgrims. They wanted to go to a place where they could have their own territory to establish their own culture and live in peace. They already had knowledge of today's America which in that time was called "**Arsareth**". The **Olmec**'s a.k.a. the Xi people from West Africa of the Mende stock were here. The Australoids and the African pygmies were also in the **Americas** (Arsareth) to live and be left alone. They left because they were often oppressed by surrounding nations in Africa so they came to **America** (Arsareth) for a safe haven.

Walter Neves, an anthropologist, went to Sao Paulo -South Polo University Brazil and says he found evidence that the first people in **America** (Arsareth) were black. Mongoloid was an ancestor of the American Indian which predates the American Indian. The oldest skulls in America were here 10,000 years before American Indians ever showed up. The fact is, the so called 'colored people' circumnavigated the earth many times before the European knew the earth was round.
http://raceandhistory.com/historicalviews/ancientamerica.htm)

Shelamoh (Solomon) and the Hebrews knew that the earth was round. Even Yeshayahu (Isaiah) knew this, take note of this scripture.

Isaiah 40: 22 "It is He that sits upon **the circle** of the earth..."
Caucasians just recently only 500 years ago thought the world was flat, but the black Africans knew well over 4,000 years ago in Egypt that the world was round.

The land mass of America was known in Shelamoh's/Solomon's time. His navy made regular excavations to the **Americas** (Arsareths) for resources and trade. On a side note, Mansa Musa an African, who was the richest person who ever lived to this date, also came to the **Americas** (Arsareths) for trade. It was known that the civilizations that settled in the **Americas** (Arsareths) were peaceful civilizations so the scattered Hebrews went there. Notice the following scriptures describing this voyage.

HIStory or OUR Story   Chapter 7

2 Esdras 13: 22-48

22 Whereas you have spoken of them that are left behind, this is the interpretation:
23 He that shall endure the peril in that time have kept himself: they that be fallen into danger are such as have works, and faith toward the Almighty.
24 Know this therefore, that they which be left behind are more blessed than they that be dead.
25 This is the meaning of the vision: Whereas you sawest a man coming up from the midst of the sea:
26 The same is He whom God the Highest has kept a great season, which by His own self shall deliver His creature: and He shall order them that are left behind.
27 And whereas you saw, that out of His mouth there came as a blast of wind, and fire, and storm;
28 And that He held neither sword, nor any instrument of war, but that the rushing in of Him destroyed the whole multitude that came to subdue him; this is the interpretation:
29 Behold, the days come, when the most High will begin to deliver them that are upon the earth.
30 And He shall come to the **astonishment** (surprise) of them that dwell on the earth.
31 And one shall undertake to fight against another, one city against another, one place against another, one people against another, and one realm against another.
32 And the time shall be when these things shall come to pass, and the signs shall happen which I showed you before, and then shall my Son be declared, whom you saw as a man ascending.
33 And when all the people hear His voice, every man shall in their own land leave the battle they have one against another.
34 And an innumerable multitude shall be gathered together, as you saw them, willing to come, and to overcome him by fighting.
35 But He shall stand upon the top of the Mount Zion.
36 And Zion shall come, and shall be showed to all men, being prepared and built, like as you sawest the hill graven without hands.
37 And this My Son shall rebuke the wicked **inventions of those nations**, which for their wicked life are fallen into the tempest;
38 And shall lay before them their evil thoughts, and the torments wherewith they shall begin to be tormented, which are like to a flame: and He shall destroy them without labor by the law which is like to Me.
39 And whereas you saw that He gathered another peaceful multitude to Him;
40 Those are the **ten tribes**, which were **carried away prisoners out of their own land** in the time of Osea the king, whom Salmanasar the king of Assyria led away captive, and he carried them over the waters, and **so came they into another land.**

41 But they took this counsel among themselves, that they would leave the multitude of the **heathen** (nations/non-Hebrews), and go forth into a further country, where never mankind dwelled,
42 That they might there keep their statutes, which they never kept in their own land.
43 And they entered into Euphrates by the narrow places of the river.
44 For the most High then shows signs for them, and held still the flood, till they were passed over.
45 For through that country, there was a great way to go, namely, of a year and a half: and the same region is called **Arsareth** (modern day America).
46 Then dwelled they there until the latter time; and now when they shall begin to come,
47 The Highest shall **stay** (separate) the **springs** of the stream again, that they may go through: therefore saw you the multitude with peace.
48 But those that be left behind of your people are they that are found within my borders."

So as you can see the truth is that we, Hebrews, were already in the Americas before Christopher Columbus ever came.

In 1993, the United Nations Center for Human Rights, recognized the Washitaw de DugdahmoundYAH Muur Empire as the Oldest Indigenous group of people on Earth. The United Nations recognizes the Washitaw Muurs Nation within the United States along with the other Indigenous people of America. The Declaration 'On Rights Of' Indigenous People includes the Washitaw Nation, a nation that is made up of Black People who have the archaeological and historical evidence to prove that the original inhabitants of North and South America (so called "Indians") were Black People who came here from Africa. Black Indians are not solely a result of African slaves mixing with so-called Red Indians who were fleeing from slavery as many documented sources would have you to believe. Black Indians are indigenous to America—North, South, and Central before the so-called Red Man, before the Europeans, before the so-called Bering Strait crossings. The Olmecs, Washitaw, Moors, Yamasee, Mound Builders planted the seed of civilization in the Americas—Black Indians!"

The Washitaw were direct descendants of the Olmecs who mixed in the Malian Moors. The name "Washitaw" comes from the Washita River which flows along Northwest Texas and Oklahoma to the Red River where the Cheyenne Native Americans lived with the Chawasha, meaning "Raccoon People." The Washo were a Negroid tribe living above the New Orleans Bayou and were of Tunican linguistic stock. The name "Washitaw" is a derivative of the term "Ouachita" or what is now "Wichita." The term is a Choctaw term which means "Big Arbor". The Washitaw were originally from lower Mississippi, Louisiana, and Alabama (named after Nubian-Sudanese Ali Baba). The tribe was officially named "Wichita" by the US Government in the Camp Holmes Treaty of 1835. The Wichita were also known as "Paniwassaha" or by the French Panioussa which means "Black Pawnee."

HIStory or OUR Story   **Chapter 7**

French traders from Illinois called them "Pani Pique" which means Tattooed Pawnee. The Washitaw or Raccoon People were called Raccoons because of their black faces. When describing the Washitaw, the French describes the blacks who lived in the large grass houses. The tribe is the descendants of the Olmecs and Toltecs of Mexico.

During Pangaea, the Afrikan and American continents were joined. The Black Mound Builders were the Washitaw-Muurs (Ouachita-Moors), **the ORIGINAL** inhabitants of North and South America. Columbus **was not** entirely wrong in calling these people "**Indians**"! The true meaning of word "Indian" is ("INDI" meaning black, as in <u>INDI</u>a ink, h<u>IND</u>u and <u>INDI</u>go the darkest color of the color spectrum). The massive remains of this ancient BLACK civilization empire still stand in both North and South America.

The earliest people in the Americas were people of the **Negroid African** race, who entered the Americas by way of the Bering Straight. About 30,000 years ago a worldwide maritime undertaking included journeys from the Sahara, towards the Indian Ocean, and the Pacific Ocean. From West Africa across the Atlantic Ocean to the Americas men migrated.
Ancient NATIVE Black Nations of America before and after Columbus include:
The Washitaw of the Louisiana/Midwest, the Yamasee of the Southeast,
The Iroquois, The Cherokee Indians, The Blackfoot Indians, The Pequot and Mohegans of Connecticut, The Black Californians (Calafians) (CAL in CALifornia literally means BLACK, after the name of the Great Mamma KALi / Queen KALifa), and the Olmecs of Mexico.

The statistics state only .05% or 1/2 of 1% of all Indigenous people of North and South America are in existence as a result of Christopher Columbus and his European travelers' conquests. Ninety-five (95%) percent were massacred by Columbus and his European crews shortly after 1492. Around 1900, it was thought Native Americans were on the brink of extinction with only 250,000 left. Below are the **earliest pictures of <u>true native Americans</u>, before a lot of race mixing began creating the so called 'red man'**, and you will see that they were what the world called at that time **NEGROES!!**

The Hebrews also wore **fringes. Numbers 15:38-40, Deuteronomy 22:12.**

And they are wearing **headbands (Isaiah 3:20),** and just as the scriptures said they did.

These people are the true Native Americans, the so called "American Indians". But they are in truth, the Hebrew Yahsraelites. From the overwhelming evidence of these pictures you should clearly know the truth by now.

The Greatest Cover Up of All Time

Now that the Hebrew Yahsraelites and the Egyptians have been conquered and scattered throughout the world, the greatest hoax in history was able to take place. Today in America, identity theft is a Federal crime. Well the United Nations, the Khazarians, and the United States of America have committed this very heinous crime. Concerning the Egyptians, they stole their land, and their gold treasures, mummy caskets, ideas, culture, nationality, symbols, and their identity as far as birthright is concerned. They sold the gold as if it was theirs, and took Egyptian remains and set them up in museums. They profited from taking tourists on vacations inside of the Pyramids, but they do not give any of the true living descendants of the Egyptians a dime. All the money is going to the Turks, Europeans, Khazarian Jews, and the Arabs.

When it comes to the so called 'blacks' of America they have taken everything. They have taken our **wealth, gold, ideas, religion, culture, symbols, names, history, identity, nationality, language** and mainly they have TAKEN US!!! Our ancestors were KIDNAPPED!! That also is a Federal Crime that the United States Government is guilty of and is punishable by law. It is written: **Exodus 21: 16** "And he that steals (kidnaps) a man, and sells him, or if he be found in his hand, he shall SURELY BE PUT TO DEATH"

So there is a pending judgment on this nation (America), and all the nations who participated in our kidnapping. Not only did they kidnap us, but we are still here, meaning "we are found in their hand". They also broke many other laws, too many to name. What they also have done, even worse, is they have lied to us about who we are and it is no surprise for it is also written:

Deuteronomy 33:29 "Happy are you, O Yahsrael: who is like you, O people saved by Yahuah, the shield of your help, and who is the sword of your excellency! And **YOUR ENEMIES** shall be found **LIARS to YOU**; and you shall tread upon (trample down) their high places."

So it was prophesied that they would lie to us. Who are the "they"? Our enemies! Who are our enemies? Chapter 12 will prove in great detail that these people are your enemies beyond a doubt. The Bible speaks of our historical enemies here. Keep in mind when our ancestors came to this continent on the ships they were not "friends" with the people who brought them here.

HIStory or OUR Story   Chapter 8

They were considered enemies. They still are our enemies. Not only had the Europeans took them from the land of their antiquity, but they brought them here without consent and did unspeakable crimes along the way. Recently, I encountered a quote from the **National Wiki:**

"American Indian Holocaust" is a term used by American Indian activists to bring attention to what they contend is the deliberate mass destruction of American Indian populations following the Europeans' arrival in the Americas. It's a subject which the activists allege has hitherto received very limited mention in history, partially because most of the deaths happened before European chroniclers arrived to record them.

Estimates of the pre-Columbian population vary widely, though the figures for North, Central and South America have been estimated at a combined 80 million, with scholars' estimates approaching 18 million for North America alone. An estimated **90% of this population died after the arrival of Europeans**. Europeans, especially the Spanish conquistadors, also **killed thousands deliberately**".

For Europeans and the Spaniards to kill almost 70 million people, that was no accident. They did this on purpose, but why? The Europeans and Spaniards wanted to profit off the land, slavery, and the natural resources. In order to do that, they had to greatly decrease the population of the people who were already here. The Europeans knew their plans to bring slaves over to this land in order to cultivate and colonize it for their own benefit. They were afraid. Had the Europeans brought the rest of the black Hebrews here, when some (Hebrews) were already here in America, the Hebrews could possibly have joined together and fought against the Europeans. So, the Europeans had to kill most of the ones here off.

Mark 3:27 "No man can enter into a strong man's house, and spoil his goods, except he will first bind the strong man; and then he will spoil his house"

The Europeans covered up the truth that so called 'black Africans' were already here hundreds of thousands of years before the white Europeans ever showed up on the American scene. The black Africans knew about the Americas in ancient times because their sailors had circumnavigated the earth hundreds of times before. This fact is in recorded African history and is emphasized in Egyptian hieroglyphics. Through racial intermixing between the Spaniards and the Hebrews the 'red man' was created in Spain. The descendants of this union over time migrated to the Americas, but it was after the Hebrew and African nations were already in the Americas. European historians have deceitfully lied to us in making us believe that the so called 'red-man' was more Native to the Americas than the so called 'black man', which as you can see from chapter 5 is a complete lie.

HIStory or OUR Story   Chapter 8

Khazar history

The Jewish Encyclopedia:
"The Khazars, a **non-Semitic**, Asiatic, Mongolian tribal nation who emigrated into Eastern Europe about the first century, were converted as an entire nation to Judaism in the seventh century by the expanding Russian nation. Russia absorbed the entire Khazar population, which accounts for their presence in Eastern Europe and the great numbers of Yiddish speaking Jews in Russia, Poland, Lithuania, Galatia, Besserabia and Rumania."
Khazar: Ashkenazi Modern Jew

"Khazars was a national group of general Turkic type, independent and sovereign in Eastern Europe between the seventh and tenth centuries C.E. (Common Era). During part of this time, the leading Khazars professed Judaism…In spite of the negligible information of an archaeological nature, the presence of Jewish groups and the impact of Jewish ideas in Eastern Europe were considerable during the Middle Ages. Groups that have been mentioned as migrating to Central Europe from the East often have been referred to as Khazars, thus making it impossible to overlook the possibility that they originated from within the former Khazar Empire."

"The primary meaning of Ashkenaz and Ashkenazim in Hebrew is Germany and Germans. This may be due to the fact that the home of the ancient ancestors of the Germans is Media, which is the Biblical Ashkenaz…Krauss is of the opinion that in the early medieval ages, the Khazars were sometimes referred to as Ashkenazim…About 92 percent of all Jews or approximately 14,500,000 are Ashkenazim."
The Bible: Relates that the Khazar (Ashkenaz) Jews were/are the sons of Japheth not Shem:

HIStory or OUR Story — Chapter 8

Psalms 83:4

They have said,

>"Come let us <u>cut them off</u>

>>from <u>being a nation</u>;

>>>that the <u>name</u> of <u>Yahsrael</u>

>>>>may be

>><u>no more in</u> REMEMBRANCE"

It was already prophesied by Yahushua that there would be imposters or a people on the earth claiming to be 'Jews' that are not.

Revelation 2:9 "I know your works, and tribulation, and poverty, but you are rich and I know the blasphemy of them which **say they are Jews, and are not**, but are of the synagogue of Satan."

Revelation 3:9 "Behold, I will make them of the synagogue of Satan, which **say they are Jews and are not, but do lie**, behold **I will make them to come and worship before your feet**, and <u>to know that I have loved you</u>."

So the question is what will you choose to believe? HISTORY which is OUR STORY, the truth, or will you continue to believe the "white fairy-tale lie"?

HIStory or OUR Story   Chapter 8

There is an image of what people believe Yahushua looked like and that has been ingrained in the minds of most individuals for all of their lives. However that image is believed to be false. Yet it is the vision of Yahushua (Christ) that Christians, and even people of other/no faiths, have grown accustomed to. The image of Yahushua (Christ) that has been adopted began many years ago, back after Leonardo da Vinci started a very close relationship with Cesare Borgia.

Leonardo and the child of Rodrigo Borgia, who would later became Pope Alexander VI, were so close it was believed they were lovers. Under the power of the Catholic Church, Pope Alexander VI decided that he would have his son, **Cesare Borgia used as the model for Jesus in paintings that da Vinci was commissioned to do.**

Wisdom of Solomon Chapter 14 (1611 Bible)

8 But **that which is made with hands, is cursed**, as well as he that made it: because he made it, and it, because being corruptible **it was called god**.
9 For the ungodly and his ungodliness are both alike hateful to God.
10 For **that which is made, shall be punished together with him that made it.**
11 Therefore even upon the idols of the <u>Gentiles</u> (nations/non-Hebrews) shall there be a visitation: because in the creature of god they are become an abomination and stumbling blocks to the souls of men, and a snare to the feet of the unwise.
12 For the **devising of idols was the beginning of spiritual fornication**, and the invention of them the corruption of life.
13 For neither were they from the beginning, neither shall they be for ever.
14 For by the vain glory of men they entered into the world, and therefore shall they come shortly to an end.
15 For a father afflicted with untimely mourning, when **he has made an image of his child** soon taken away, now **honored him as a god**, which was then **a dead man**, and delivered to those that were under him, ceremonies and sacrifices.
16 Thus in process of time an ungodly custom growing strong, was kept as a law, and **graven images were worshipped by the commandments of kings**,
17 Whom men could not honor in presence, because they lived far off, they took **the counterfeit of his visage from far**, and **made an expressed image of a king whom they honored**, to the end that by this their forwardness, they might flatter him that was absent, as if he were present.
18 Also the singular diligence of the artificer did help to set forward the ignorant to more superstition.
19 For he peradventure willing to please one in authority, forced all his skill to make the resemblance of the best fashion.
20 And so the multitude allured by the grace of the work, **took him now for a god**, which a little before **was but honored as a man**.
21 And **this was an occasion to deceive the world**: for men **serving either calamity or tyranny**, did ascribe to stones, and stocks, **the incommunicable Name (not spoken/un-communicated).**
22 Moreover this was not enough for them, that **they erred in the knowledge of God**, but whereas they lived in the great **war of ignorance**, those so **great plagues** called they **peace**.

HIStory or OUR Story   Chapter 8

That fact of the matter is, images are very important. The Greeks and Romans knew this, which is why they altered the images. You will run into people that will say that the color of historical man does not matter. Well if that were really true, why is it that when creating images of Christ, Zeus, and many other great historical figures they always appear white?? Why don't they use multiple races and colors when depicting them. Why not sometime Asian, Japanese, Mexican, African, Hispanic, or Irish with red hair?? They all appear white even if it contradicts historical evidence. The fact of the matter is **image must have mattered to somebody** because otherwise since **the original images were black** then why didn't they leave them 'black'?? It seems that people only say that skin color does not matter when you try to suggest or proclaim that **Christ was Black**. The biggest Deception of ALL is when WE WENT FROM '**HEEBOES**' (which is Hebrews) to NEGROES!!

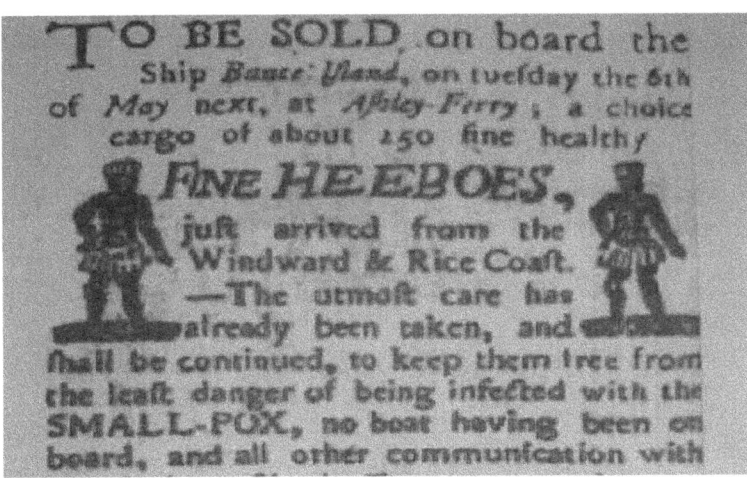

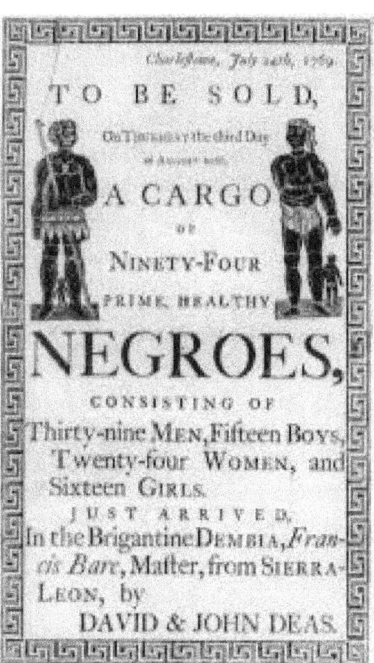

HIStory or OUR Story   Chapter 8

"The Renaissance" marks the time period of **European** history at the close of the Middle Ages and the rise of the Modern world. It represents t**heir cultural rebirth** from the 14th through the middle of the 17th centuries.

The period is characterized by a relative **scarcity of historical and other written records** for most of Europe, rendering it obscure to historians. The term "**Dark Ages**" originally was intended to denote the entire period between **the fall of Pagan Rome** and **the Renaissance** (rebirth). After **Pagan Rome** fell (**Revelation 13:3), it** was reborn as Papal Rome. It was after this 'rebirth' that everything changed. When Rome prevailed, so did their religion of Catholicism. Slowly but surely, all of the black images of Christ, the biblical Hebrew Israelites, and the Egyptians were altered and changed.

The Dark ages, plainly put, was the time period in which the so called "*dark races*" ruled the earth. While the "*dark races*" ruled, the lighter races were still in ignorance in the Caucasus mountains from which we have the word 'Caucasians'. At this time, the Europeans still thought the world was flat, but once they rose to power they began taking the knowledge, wealth, religion, history, and culture of the so called "*dark races*" as their own.

Origins of our so called 'American Traditions'

During the Nicean council of 325 A.D. Constantine, a group of priests, monks, and Roman government officials came together in a meeting in which Constantine's goal was to make a religion out of the faith, history and holy scriptures of the Hebrews. There were no Hebrew Yahsraelite men or women present or considered at this meeting. At this time, the nations worshiped a pantheon of different gods ranging from the sun, the planets, and animals. At this point in history, Rome had taken over the Greek empire and had established a one world government politically. Every nation under the sun hailed to Caesar. Constantine's goal was to also unite the world in religion as well. Constantine took the major common denominators between the major religions of the world at that time and in order to reach a common consensus to create unity he combined those practices and traditions. The universal day of worship for the rest of the world at this time was **SUN**day, the 1st day of the week. This is because the religions of the world worshiped the Sun as the supreme god.

Constantine was a Roman emperor who reigned from A.D. 306 to 337. According to his own account on his way to an important battle in 312 A.D., a vision of a flaming cross appeared to him with the inscription, "In this sign conquer." He therefore authorized his mostly pagan soldiers to place **a cross** on their shields, and went on to win the battle. Believing the Christian God to be his secret to military success and the key to uniting his empire, Constantine adopted Christianity as the official religion of Rome in 324 A.D. His life continued to be marred by bloodshed and political intrigue until his death, but through his influence the bishops of Rome gained rapid ascendancy to political and temporal power.

Sun Worship

The real secret of Constantine and the bishops of Rome is their cunning introduction of **sun worship and paganism into Christianity**. It was done so shrewdly that, incredibly, it has been veiled within the faith for centuries. Through Constantine, paganism and Christianity joined hands during the Roman Empire.

History readily records that Constantine was a sun-worshiper. In one decree he declared, "**On the venerable Day of the Sun, let the magistrates and people residing in cities rest, and let all workshops be closed**". He made this decree in honor of the sun after his supposed conversion to Christianity! Constantine, even after his "conversion," remained a pagan.

HIStory or OUR Story   **Chapter 9**

Constantine and Rome changed world history. Believing in the Most High and the Bible as His infallible Word are the only ways to safely combat error and ground ourselves in truth. Through the Dark Ages, these facts were eclipsed and paganism took over the church. Thank the Most High that today we have ready access to the Bible, the ultimate resource, and to the throne of grace. **God's truth will always prove stronger than the world's fiction.**

It was prophesied that Rome would change **times** and **laws**.

Daniel 7:25
And he shall speak great words **against the most High**, and shall <u>wear out</u> (persecute) the saints of the most High, and think to <u>**change times and laws**</u>: and they shall be given into his hand until a time and times and the dividing of time

But Yahuah did not want His people, the Yahsraelites to be like the other nations, we were different see scripture reference:

Esther 3: 8
Then Haman said to King Ahasuerus, "There is a **certain people** scattered and dispersed among the peoples in all the provinces of your kingdom; **their laws are different** <u>from those of all other people</u> and they do not observe the king's laws, so it is not in the king's interest to let them remain"

Jeremiah 10: 2-5
2 Thus says Yahuah, "<u>Learn not</u> the way of <u>the heathen</u> (the nations/non-Hebrews), and be not <u>dismayed</u> (in awe of) at the <u>signs of heaven</u> (sun, moon, stars **Genesis 1:14**); for <u>the heathen</u> (the nations/non-Hebrews) are <u>dismayed</u> (in awe of) at them.
3 For the customs of the people are vain: for one cutteth a tree out of the forest, the work of the hands of the workman, with the axe.
4 They **deck it** with **silver** and with **gold**; they fasten it with nails and with hammers, that it move not.
5 They are upright as the **palm tree**, but speak not: they must **needs be borne** (must be carried), because they cannot go. Be not afraid of them; for they cannot do evil, neither also is it in them to do good"

Leviticus 18: 1-5
1 And Yahuah spoke to Musa/Moses, saying,
2 "Speak to the children of Yahsrael, and say to them, I am Yahuah your God.
3 After the doings of the land of Egypt, wherein you dwelt, shall you not do: and after the doings of the land of Canaan, where I bring you, shall you not do: neither shall you walk in their ordinances.
4 You shall do **My judgments**, and keep **My ordinances**, to walk therein: I am Yahuah your God.
5 You shall therefore keep My statutes, and **My judgments**: which if a man do, he shall live in them: I am Yahuah"

HIStory or OUR Story   Chapter 9

We as children of Yahuah were commanded to keep His Commandments and Laws. One of the chief ways of doing that was by keeping his weekly Sabbath and His feasts. We have forcefully forgotten Yahuah's Feasts as to how to keep them, when to keep them and and we have no idea what they mean. We also have forgotten Yahuah's true 7th day Sabbath , how to keep it, and when to keep it. I will provide you an overview of this from here.

Have you ever wondered what the Father has planned for your life? It seems that you are not the only one to ponder this age old question. Yahuah has a system for His creation and you are a part of that system. In Genesis, the first and second chapter, we find the creation of the universe and of man. With the creation of the universe, God set up a system to dictate reoccurring events. With the creation of man, He set up a design of worship.

It is awesome to know we have a Creator who cares enough to work out all of the details of our lives. The creations in the heavens are Yahuah's for all of mankind. If we take the time to discover His plan for us, then we can appreciate the beauty behind it. We were given two "great lights" in the beginning: the sun and the moon. One was to rule over the day, and the other, the night. The sun not only gives us warmth and daylight, it lets us know our years and seasons. The moon is multi-purpose as well. Not only does it help us to see at night, but it tells us when to begin a new month in our yearly cycle and when to begin our days.

This brings me to the topic of our discussion: the Feasts or "Appointed Times" of Yahuah. In **Leviticus 23**, Yahuah instructed Musa to tell the people about His (set apart) days. Yahuah began His instruction to Musa by calling these days **"The Appointed Times of Yahuah."** That is very significant in two ways. First, because this lets us know that they are **Yahuah's Holy Days**, not *'jewish holidays'* as some like to proclaim. And second, as stated in **Genesis 1:14**, He put in place a system to tell us when these signs, Appointed Times, days and years were to begin.

HIStory or OUR Story   Chapter 9

The first Appointed Time which was to be proclaimed as a "holy" set apart gathering is the **Sabbath Day**

It is a weekly day of observance. Six days of work is done, but the seventh day is a Sabbath of rest. It is a day of rest with Yahuah our God. Prophetically, Sabbath represents our eternal rest from sufferings. Those called by The Name of Yahuah, will spend eternity resting in His presence. What a blissful thought to know in Him there is perfect rest. I've heard someone say, "It doesn't matter what day of the week the Sabbath is on, everyday is a Sabbath." Sounds good, but this is a false teaching and **CANNOT** be found anywhere in the Word of Yahuah. I understand we are to worship Him everyday, but He *specifically* set apart the *seventh* day as a day of rest. It is mentioned and practiced throughout all of the scriptures. There is no justification for a "Sunday" being reflected as Sabbath. Yahuah's day was changed by an Emperor named Constantine in the late third or early fourth century. The first day of the week is not what day we were commanded to observe. Man changed times and laws, not Yahuah. Satan wants to steal the worship of Yahuah. It has been his ploy since the very beginning. It is the trick of the enemy to deceive people into believing the "Lord's Day" theory. Yes; they teach the Savior was raised early in the morning of the first day of the week, but where is it in Yahuah's commands that we were to change His set apart day because of it? The Sabbath is a sign between Yahuah and His people. It is very important that you study this out and make a decision on whose report you are going to believe, man's or Yahuah's?

There are some Appointed times given by Yahuah that contain additional Sabbaths besides the weekly one. They are called "High Sabbaths" or a "high" day. They are annual days of rest. If a particular festival contains a commanded day of rest, even if its in the middle of the week, it is still a Sabbath day. There are a total of seven commanded "High" days in a year.

The second Appointed Time of Yahuah is Pesach or "**Passover**" as it is commonly known. It falls in the Spring, along with three other feasts. They are known as the "Spring Festivals." In the first month, on the fourteenth day of the month, between the evenings, is when it begins. Before the children of Yahsrael were brought out of Egypt, they were instructed by Yahuah to kill a perfect lamb and place its blood over each of their door posts. The blood was to be a sign. It was to protect and cause the Death Angel to "passover" them later that night to kill all of the first born of their oppressors.

If they had not obeyed, they too would have experienced the plague of death. It is to be observed throughout all the generations, an everlasting Law. Prophetically, this day represents the Messiah being the perfect Lamb given for slaughter. Through His sacrificial blood, we are able to escape **eternal** death. As with the door posts, if we do not have the blood of the Lamb covering our heart, we will not be protected when the judgment of sin comes.

On the next day after Passover is the **Feast of Unleavened Bread.**" It is the fifteenth day of the first month on Yahuah's Biblical calendar. The first and the last day of this Festival is a Sabbath. This Feast represents Yahushua being the "unleavened" or sin-free Bread. The people were instructed not to eat anything made with leaven for seven days. *Eating unleavened bread was to remind them how they were brought out of captivity.* They were bought out so quickly by night, that they did not even have time to put any leaven in their bread for baking. Yahuah spoke to the people and said "If anyone eats what is leavened, that same being shall be **cut off** from the congregation of Yahsrael, whether **sojourner** or **native**." Exodus 12:19

Leaven was not even to be found in the home for seven days. Prophetically, leaven is represented as sin. When sin is present, it affects all of its surroundings, just as leaven does. We were freed from the bondage of sin so we are to remove sin from our lives or "houses", to be acceptable to the Father. If we do not remove the sin, we will be cut off. Yahushua was cut off when He took on the sins of the world and was buried for three days and three nights. Yahushua's death purified our hearts. When we celebrate the Feast of Unleavened bread, we in turn are rejoicing for the sins of man being taken away by Yahushua the Messiyah!

Next on the list is **First fruits**. It is a wave offering and first portion specifically dedicated to God. They were to bring a sheaf of the first-fruits of their harvest to the priest. It is on the day following the weekly Sabbath during the Feast of Unleavened bread. "And the priest shall wave the sheaf before Yahuah, for your acceptance. On the morrow after the Sabbath, the priest waves it." This feast was just a foreshadow of our Messiah being the "First-fruits" of resurrection.

When the Apostles went to the tomb of the Messiyah, they found it empty. He had risen from the dead! His resurrection gives us victory over death. When we are in Him, death has no power over us! We are promised that we, too, will be raised from the dead. Yahushua is our High Priest and was able to be our acceptable "wave offering" to the Father. HalleluYah!

HIStory or OUR Story   Chapter 9

Counting fifty days, starting from the day of First Fruits and you will arrive at the feast called "**Pentecost**." The count is seven full weeks or "completed Sabbaths" plus one day. Pentecost is a Sabbath day to Yahuah. It is also another agricultural feast. The people were to bring Yahuah the first-fruits of that particular harvest time as well to Him. They were also instructed not to reap the harvest of their land completely, but to leave the corners of the land for the poor and the stranger. Yahuah was teaching them to show kindness to anyone who is in need, because He, too, would show kindness to anyone in need, regardless of them being of the children of Ashamedly or not.

Prophetically, the kindness that was shown by Yahuah, was the gift of the (Holy Spirit). He was given as a comforter and helper to show us the way to be pleasing to the Most High. In the Messiyah **Acts 2:1-4** we see the gift of the Holy Spirit being poured out on the Followers of the Messiyah as divided tongues of fire.

He gave them the ability to speak in different languages in order to proclaim the Good News of the Messiyah. What a wonderful gift from God! There is nothing impossible with Yahuah our God!

All of the above Spring Feasts were fulfilled to the very day and hour at the first coming of the Messiyah Yahushua. They were all apart of Yahuah's Time Plan for the redemption of mankind. It is a Law throughout all of our generations to keep or "guard" these Appointed Times. They allow us to practice and remember Yah's Plan for us.

Now on to the Fall feasts. The first of the Fall feasts is called " **The Feast of Trumpets**." It simply means "the day of noise/blasts". It comes on the first day of the seventh month of the year. It is the only festival that no one knows the exact day or hour when it begins. In Yahuah's calendar, there are 29 to 30 days in each month; depending on the cycle of the moon. On the "Dark Phase"of the moon, begins the first day of a new month. {See **Psalms 81:3** left off "concealed" or "covered" moon and just put "new"}
Due to Feast of Trumpet's falling on the first day of the month, we have to wait on the 29th day at the end of the sixth month to know if there will be 30 days or not. That is why during this festival time, some believe Yahushua will return for His "church." He said in **Matthew 24:36** " But concerning that day, the hour no one knows, not even the Angels of heaven, but My Father only."

The Father gave us these days as a sign. If we pay close attention and learn from His Feasts, we can say with some assurity that The Messiyah will return with a "loud shout" on one of His Fall days. Just something to think about. Anyway, Yom Kippur begins a ten-day period leading up to the holiest day of Yahuah's calendar, "Day of Atonement." A shofar or "ram's horn" is blown as a loud wake up call to remind us that the Day of Atonement is just around the corner. It is a day of rest or Sabbath, a remembrance of blowing of trumpets, a gathering. Below is a picture of a shofar.

HIStory or OUR Story   Chapter 9

On the tenth day of the seventh month is the "**Day of Atonement**." It is a day of gathering for us. No work is to be done. Yahuah instructed the people to "afflict their beings", or what we know as fasting. No food or water for one complete day. From sundown on the ninth to sundown on the tenth, the seventh month is a time of reflection. It is written in **Leviticus 23:29-31** "For any being who is not afflicted on that same day, he shall be cut off from his people. "And any being who does any work on that same day, that being I shall destroy from the midst of of his people. "You do no work- a Law forever throughout your generations in all your dwellings." Yahuah is serious when He says something and means exactly what He says. It is only through Yahushua that we are able to be pleasing to Him.

As we reflect on our past or current sins in the year, we are to repent of any wrong doings. The blood of Yahushua was placed on the mercy seat as an atonement for our sins. Without His sacrifice, we would be doomed to the sentence of death due to sin. Sin brings death. Obedience brings life, and life more abundantly!

This Day is considered the Holiest day of the year. It is the day of remembrance of our redemption through Yahushua the Messiyah!
The last of the Fall feasts is the "**Feast of Tabernacles.**" It is on the fifteenth day of the seventh month. It is another seven day festival. On the first and the last day is a Sabbath. No matter what days the festivals fall on during the year, they are still on a Sabbath. An offering made by fire was to be brought to Yahuah each day of the seven days of Sukkoth. On the eighth day was the day of gathering. (**Leviticus. 23:36**) Yahuah no longer accepts burned offerings, because The Lamb of God, Yahushua was the Last acceptable offering. Anything now would be an abomination and stink in His nostrils. There are some who don't believe that Yahushua is the Anointed One sent to save us. Those, who are of disbelief, still do things according to tradition.

All who are native Yahsraelites were also commanded to dwell in a booth for seven days. They did this to remember how Yahuah made the children of Yahsra'el dwell in booths or tents when they were brought out of Egypt. Today, we spend the seven days rejoicing and dwelling with the Father and loved ones. This festival represents the prophesied fulfillment of the coming Kingdom of God, which Yahushua taught about during His ministry. We will forever dwell with our Master and Savior Yahushua the Messiyah! No matter what your nationality or denomination is, Yahuah loves you. If you believe that Yahushua is the Son of the Most High, Yahuah, and that He was raised from the dead, you shall be saved, and dwell with Him eternally!

HIStory or OUR Story   **Chapter 9**

Yahuah devised His plan for mankind in His Feasts. This is why it is written in

Colossians 2:16-17 "Let no man therefore judge you in **meat**, or in **drink**, or in respect of an **holy day**, or of the **new moon**, or of the **sabbath days**: Which <u>are</u> a shadow of things <u>to come</u>; but the body is of Christ.

Here is a overview of what the Sabbath means as well as the Feast Days of Yahuah and they are His Feast days, not Jewish Days, or Christians days, but **God's Feasts.**

Leviticus 23: 2 "Speak to the children of Yahsrael, and say to them, Concerning the feasts of Yahuah, which you shall **proclaim to be holy** convocations, even these are <u>My feasts</u>.
1. **Weekly 7th Day Sabbath**- Day of rest. Signifying eternal rest with the Father and Him resting from His works.
2. **"Passover"**- First of the Spring Festivals. Represents the death and sacrifice of the Sacrificial Lamb, Yahushua. **{fulfilled}**
3. Festival of **"Unleavened Bread"**- It's the next Spring Festival. No leaven is eaten for one week. Represents the burial of our spotless, sin free Messiyah. **{fulfilled}**
4. **First Fruits**- Giving the first portion of your harvest or "gain" dedicated to Yahuah. Represents the resurrection of the' Messiyah and being dedicated or given to Yahuah as the first in resurrection of the dead . **{fulfilled}**
5. **"Pentecost"**- Counting off days till the next harvest. Remembering those in need. Represented by Yahuah remembering the needs of man and giving the "Holy Spirit" as a gift to help and guide the people of Yahuah. **{fulfilled}**
6. **"Feast of Trumpets"**- Blowing of the shofar to make a loud noise from the people. A day of shouting and rejoicing. Represents the "Rapture" of the Body of the Messiah. **{waiting to be fulfilled}**
7. **"Day of Atonement"**- A day of reflection and repentance. A complete fast. A time to remember the covering of the sins of man. Represented by the Second Coming of Yahushua the Messiyah. Forgiving and Restoring His chosen, the people of Yahsra'el. **{waiting to be fulfilled}**
8. **"Feast of Tabernacles"**- A time to dwell with the Father. A reminder of being brought out of bondage. Represents the "Millennial Reign" or thousand years with Yahushua without the interference or influence of Satan.

HIStory or OUR Story   Chapter 9

Constantine sought to unite his kingdom's pagan and Christian worshippers, in order to promote stability and ensure that his empire lasted. The easiest way to bring harmony would be to blend sun worship and Christianity. History shows that the Church of Rome did not object; indeed, it had been engaging in the practice for nearly two centuries!

The bishops at Rome also claimed Peter as the head of the church, instead of Christ (**Ephesians 4: 15**). Developing a non-biblical doctrine of "apostolic succession," they claimed that the authority conferred on Peter was transferred to themselves. The "Saint Peter" that was created was actually a combination of pagan idolatry and Christian veneration. Even today, the statue in St. Peter's Cathedral in Rome includes a solar disk above his head. Tradition has it that this was actually a statue of Jupiter taken from a pagan temple and simply renamed "St. Peter"! Sun worship, which appears in nearly every pagan religion in the world, soon appeared in Christian art, imagery, and theology. The halo often seen on Christ and Mary is actually a symbol of sun worship. Madonna ("Mary") was depicted holding sun disks.

At the Council of Nicaea, Constantine also persuaded those in attendance that only one Easter "Resurrection" day should be kept. "Our Savior has left us only one festival day … and he desired to establish only one Catholic Church," he argued. Then he added this significant statement. "You should consider … that we should have nothing in common with the Jews."

Constantine felt that the Jews were "murderers of the Lord," and therefore desired to blot out any links between Christianity and Judaism. For this reason, he persuaded the Christian church to drop the ancient biblical Sabbath, given at Creation, and replace it with Sunday worship. "The Church made a sacred day of Sunday … largely because it was the weekly festival of the sun; for it was a definite Christian policy to take over the pagan festivals endeared to the people by tradition, and to give them a Christian significance." Pope Sylvester I finally made Christian Sunday keeping official by decreeing that "the rest of the Sabbath should be transferred to the Lord's day Sunday."

Also America will have you believe that "Thanksgiving" should be a joyous time. A time of celebration and laughter. A time when we honor the Native Americans by saying, "Thanks for GIVING" us this land, but that could not be farther from the truth. Here is a depiction of what they teach us, trying to brainwash us like children as to what happened.

HIStory or OUR Story Chapter 9

In January, they observed the Kalends of January, which represented the triumph of life over death. This whole season was called Dies Natalis Invicti Solis, "the Birthday of the Unconquered **SUN**", also instituted by Rome.

Therefore, brothers and sisters, getting dressed for a night of fornicating, getting drunk/getting high, honoring superstitions and making fake vows that you never keep, is traditionally done in the name of Winter solstice Honoring the so called god of "New beginnings AKA Janus. But have you considered the One you say you believe in? Of course you haven't! You don't even know when the Most High's New Year actually begins. But because you are programmed to follow the schedule of the beast (the man-made calendar of Rome created and named by Pope Gregory III) thus our calendar is called the Gregorian calendar.

Columbus Day is a U.S. holiday that commemorates the landing of Christopher Columbus in the **New World** on October 12, 1492. It was unofficially celebrated in a number of cities and states as early as the 18th century but did not become a federal holiday until the 1937. For many, the holiday is a way of both honoring Columbus' achievements and celebrating **Italian**-American heritage. Throughout its history, Columbus Day and the man who inspired it have generated controversy, and many alternatives to the holiday have appeared in recent years.

But we all know the truth! Christopher Columbus did not discover America! How can you discover a place where people already lived???? No one ever questioned that! These are the same people who claimed they discovered NEWFOUNDLAND. They had the audacity to call a land New-Found-Land where the land was already FOUND, the Beothuk already lived there.

HIStory or OUR Story **Chapter 9**

The Most High wouldn't begin the New Year in the driest and most dead season...

Deuteronomy 16:1 Observe the month of ABIB, and keep the passover to Yahuah God: for in the month of ABIB Yahuah your God brought you forth out of Egypt by night.

"ABIB" means "Ear of Corn" associated with April or spring season. This is MONTH when Musa (Moses) led the Yahsraelites out of Egypt by night...

Exodus 12:1,2 And Yahuah spoke to Musa and Ahron (Aaron) in the land of Egypt saying, "This month shall be to you the **BEGINNING of MONTHS**: it shall be the **FIRST MONTH** of the YEAR to you."

So the month of ABIB is the FIRST MONTH of the YEAR for us. The month was later changed to Nisan after the exile. Nisan (ABIB) is symbolized by fertility, offspring, life, growth, etc. January comes from ancient Roman god, Janus, the god of Beginnings or Transitions,. **Two sided face depicting that he tells the future and past.** We're living in modern day Rome. Get right or stay wrong.

Lent

Lent is a word which we employ to denote the forty days of fasting preceding Easter. This practice is common in much of Christendom, being celebrated by Catholics, Episcopalians, Lutherans, Methodists, Presbyterians, Anglicans, etc. The word "Lent" comes from a Germanic root meaning "Spring" but is more often associated with the 40 days from Ash Wednesday to Easter Sunday. **It originated in the Babylonian pagan religion**, but was adopted into Christianity when the Roman Empire adopted Christianity as its official religion.

Search the scriptures diligently, from Old Testament to New, and you will find no mention of any Hebrew Yahsraelites or any followers of Yahushua (Christ) observing an annual period of 40 days of fasting and abstinence preceding the festival of the Passover, yet today most of the Christian world observes a 40 day period called Lent, which precedes the festival of Easter Sunday.

So what is Lent's origin according to the Catholic Church?

"For we have not a high priest who is unable to sympathize with our weaknesses, but one who in every respect has been tested as we are, yet without sinning" [**Hebrews 4:15**]. By the solemn forty days of Lent, the Church unites herself each year to the mystery of Yahushua in the desert.

Source: The Catechism of the Catholic Church, copyright 1994 by the United States Catholic Conference, Inc., published by Liquori Publications.

So according to Catholics, Lent is derived from the 40 days Yahushua spent fasting in the wilderness, but it is admitted that the observance of Lent was unknown to the disciples and it did not find its way into the church until several centuries after the time of Yahushua..

NOTE: Lent is a moveable observance, connected to and preceding the festival of Easter. Easter is celebrated on a day specified only by the Roman Catholic Church, and not the Bible, and is fixed based on the sun and the Spring/Vernal equinox.

HIStory or OUR Story Chapter 9

Here's how it began. According to tradition Semeramis, the wife of Nimrod the King of Babylon, claimed she had been supernaturally impregnated by the Sun god and gave birth to Tammuz. One day while hunting, Tammuz was killed by a wild boar. Semeramis mourned for 40 days, at the end of which Tammuz was supposedly brought back from the dead. She proclaimed herself Queen of Heaven. She founded a celibate priesthood to worship her son and declared its chief priest infallible, and memorialized her mourning in an annual 40 day period of denial. It was the world's first counterfeit of the Biblical story of the Redeemer and grew into a mother-child cult that was duplicated in almost every pagan mythology.

If you feel that Yahuah is leading you into a 40 day period of self-deprivation to draw nearer to Him, more power to you. But if you're just observing a tradition of man's religion, it won't serve any purpose except to prove that you can go without something for 40 days.

HIStory or OUR Story   Chapter 9

CHRISTMAS

Instituted by Rome, the Winter Solstice was celebrated many years before the birth of Yahushua. The Romans called their winter holiday "Saturnalia", honoring Saturn, the God of Agriculture. The pagan origins of Christmas are rooted in ancient Babylon, the feast of the Son of Isis (Goddess of Nature) was celebrated on December 25. Raucous partying, gluttonous eating and drinking, and gift-giving were traditions of this feast. Many other pagan gods are celebrated on this date. Remember Yule logs? Well they were burned in honor of the **SUN**. The word Yule itself means "wheel," the wheel being a pagan symbol for the sun. Mistletoe was considered a sacred plant, and the custom of kissing under the mistletoe began as a fertility ritual. Pope Julius I declared that Yahushua's birth would be celebrated on December 25. He was trying to make it as painless as possible for pagan Romans (who remained a majority at that time) to convert to Christianity by uniting the two through pagan feasts.
Deities "born, celebrated and honored" on December 25:
Horus c. 3000 BCE, Osiris c. 3000 BCE, Attis of Phrygia c.1400 BCE, Krishna c. 1400 BCE, Mithra of Persia c. 600 BCE, Buddha c. 563 BCE, Heracles c. 800 BCE, Dionysus c. 186 BCE, Tammuz c. 400 BCE, Adonis c. 200 BCE. There is Oris and Saturn and of course Jesus Christ and many more. So, what is wrong with this picture? Why is almost every pagan deity celebrated on December 25th?

The entire purpose of joining everyone to Dec 25 is to bring everyone under pagan Roman festivals by marking the 'birthday of the unconquered sun.'" In winter when the sun seemed weakest, pagans held ceremonies to get this source of warmth and light to come back from its distant travels. December 25 was thought to be the day that the sun began its return. In an effort to convert pagan's religious leaders, they allowed them to bring in their deities and also celebrate them on this day. So that everyone would adopt this festival which really pays homage to the Sun god (no matter what you call him).
So everyone goes out and drags a tree into their house; they put up wreaths & mistletoe; they put gifts under the tree and get ready to partake in the rites of Saturnalia worship (pagan festival). This entire holiday is wicked to its core. Don't think that the Most High is okay with us offering up this wicked celebration to him, because He has already said "I hate your appointed feasts" **(Isaiah 1:14)**

Yule Log

EXPOSING WICKEDNESS! "YULE TIDE" - PLEASE UNDERSTAND WHAT YOU CELEBRATE!

Christmas is the pagan day of the god "Yule". Yule or Yuletide ("Yule time") is a pagan religious festival observed by the historical Germanic peoples, later being absorbed into and equated with the Christian festival of Christmas.

The yule log is in reality the "sun log." "Yule" means "wheel," a pagan symbol of the sun. Yet today, professing Christians speak of the "sacred YULETIDE" season as a wonderful time of year. But they don't know that it originally had a lot to do with dedicating children as gifts. Bonfires were lit in the fields, and crops and trees were "wassailed" with toasts of spiced cider. Children were escorted from house to house with gifts of clove, spiked apples and oranges, which were laid in baskets of evergreen boughs and wheat stalks dusted with flour. "Living infants and children were BURNED IN THE FIRE to the god Molech during this time. This was the time of the winter solstice (December 25th) when those heathen were dismayed at the signs of heaven (**Isaiah 41:10**)!"

The Fact is: These phallus/penis worshiping, child sacrificing pagans, who decorated their trees, didn't steal the holiday from "Christians". It is the other way around! Christmas has a very strange and wicked past. But in spite of this, have we heeded the commandments of Yahuah? He has said, "You shall not do so to Yahuah your God: for every abomination to Yahuah, which he hates, have they done to their gods; for even their sons and their daughters they have burned in the fire to their gods (**Deuteronomy 12:31**). You shall not let any of your children pass through the fire to Molech, neither shall you profane the name of your God for I am Yahuah" (**Leviticus 18: 21**). Yet we continue in these wicked practices stating that Christmas is for the kids, no matter what the origin of it was before.

The evidence is clear that human sacrifice and the December 25th winter solstice go hand in hand. Human sacrifice originated during the winter solstice, which we now call Christmas. "The giving of presents, particularly candles and dolls, originated from human sacrifice at this time of year." The gifts under the trees, for the ancient pagans, were their first born children, which they sacrificed to bring peace and to ensure the return of the sun. Here is what Yahuah has said, "You pollute yourselves with idols under every green tree, slaying the children in the valleys under the clefts of the rocks" (**Isaiah 57:5**).

If you had lived 3000 years ago to keep this holiday, people now call "Christmas", you might be bringing your firstborn child to be sacrificed and sent through the fire of Molech.

Archaeologists have found 6000 children's urns in Carthage alone and the remains involved fire. Your precious child would have been the gift under the tree to Yule. These children were sacrificed in a grove of evergreen trees, it saluted the sun god, therefore, the sun would return again and thus, there would be peace and good will to all men...so the pagans thought! This practice of sacrificing children under the "green" tree (evergreen) was a worldwide phenomenon of old that was even practiced by Israel in the valleys of Ben Hinnom (Gehenna). See **Isaiah 57:5.** COME OUT OF HER MY PEOPLE!!

Sunrise Sunday Service

The New Book of Knowledge (1978) states, "The custom of a sunrise service on Easter Sunday can be traced to ancient spring festivals that celebrated the rising sun. Sunday worship has pagan origins, and is found to be directly linked to ancient Sun-worship found in Babylonian, Egyptian, Greek, Roman, Teutonic-German, Hindu, and Persian cultures. Sunday was the day set aside in the Mithra (Roman) cult as its official day to assemble together to worship its Sun-deity. Roman Emperor Constantine legislated Sun-day as a day of rest dedicated to the Greek and Roman **SUN-god**, Helios. Constantine worshipped "Christos Helios" which means "Christ-The-True-Sun." The Roman Catholic Church venerates Sun-day as its Sabbath even today, and has handed it down to Christianity. Sunday keeping was introduced directly from paganism during the second century.

There are three strong Bible reasons against sunrise services. First, the great and terrible Yahuah has already very plainly condemned sunrise services (**Ezekiel 8:15-18**). Second, He also condemned any other form of worship of the heavenly bodies (**II Kings 23:5**). Third, YAHUSHUA did not rise on Easter Sunday morning; He rose the night before at the end of His prophesied three days and three nights. When the women arrived at His tomb in the dark of the morning, He was already long gone.

The Name Jesus versus Yahushua

In the Hebrew alphabet, there was no "J". Originally, the name of the Messiah was Yahushua. When the Gentiles tried to transliterate His name into Greek, they came up with Iesus or "Iesous". When Iesous was transliterated into Latin, it became "Iesus", which was then carried over into English. The name "Iesus" became our modern day "Jesus" when the letter "J" developed 400 years ago, but in reality "Iesus" (Hail Zeus) was the Greek god Zeus, supreme god of the Olympians. In Greek mythology, Zeus was the father of Perseus and Heracles, the latter of whom once wrestled him to a draw. Zeus was the youngest son of the Titans' Cronus and Rhea. When he was born, his father Cronus intended to swallow him as he had all of Zeus's siblings: Poseidon, Hades, Hestia, Demeter and Hera. Based on this historical background, calling the Messiah Jesus is idolatry:

Exodus 23:1 "Be careful to do everything I have said to you. DO NOT invoke the names of other gods; do not let them be heard on your lips",

These days, most females claim to be very **independent**, but can't go grocery shopping without their EBT card. They can't go to a doctor without their Medicaid Card, and can't get their own place without Government Section 8 housing. Some even act like they're crazy to get a SSI check. The last time I checked, being **INDEPENDENT** was having the ability to do everything on your own, NOT with the help of those who pay their Taxes. I suggest YOU re-evaluate the definition of the word if this happens to be YOU:

Independent
adjective
1. Not subject to another's authority or jurisdiction; autonomous; FREE.

"THE GOOD FRIDAY JOKE

How in the world could Jesus have died on Good Friday afternoon, risen from the dead on Easter Sunday morning, and still have been in the ground the three days and three nights that He prophesied and promised (**Matthew 12:38-40**)? This common tradition only allows one day and two nights. If you count parts of Friday and Sunday as whole days, you still only have three days and two nights. The math does not work! There are only two nights! Of course, once Constantine and the religious compromisers at the council of Nicea in 325 A.D. had subscribed to **SUN** and **MOON** worship for setting the date, it was not difficult to further reject the words of Yahushua the Messiyah and create their Good Friday - Easter Sunday combination. Simply put, saints that believe the Bible can rejoice over their arrogant persecutors with seminary degrees and worldly education, just as Yahushua had promised (**Matthew 11:25-27; I Corinthians 1:19-20; 1Corinthians 3:19-20**). He had declared that the only sign he left us of his authenticity was knowing he would be in the heart of the earth **three days and three nights**. (**Matthew 12:38-40**).

FISH ON FRIDAY

This tradition is a form of Venus sex worship. Rome has long demanded that her followers abstain from meat at certain times, especially during Lent, on Fridays, and particularly on Good Friday. Even elementary Bible readers know that this abstinence from meat is a doctrine of the devil, which Paul foretold to Timothy (**I Timothy 4:1-3**). Where did this pagan custom originate? Friday, the English name of the sixth day of the week, is the Germanic translation of "dies Veneris" or "Day of Venus." Venus was the Roman goddess of sexual love. A fertility symbol associated with Venus is the fish, because fish can produce more rapidly than any other creature. A single cod can spawn 9,000,000 eggs in a year! Eating fish on Friday is an act of adoration to Venus and her cohorts, and it celebrates the principles of fertility and reproduction.

HOT CROSS BUNS are to the Queen of Heaven. What in the world are hot cross buns? They are a definite custom and tradition of Easter. They are special buns made only in the Spring with a cross of icing on the top for eating around Easter. Did Kafa (Peter), Yamase (James), and Yahonon (John) make such buns to celebrate YAHUSHUA'S death, burial, and resurrection? **Of course not!** Similar buns had been baked during the Spring for hundreds of years before Yahushua, by most cultures and nations in the world. Some of the buns were very similar to modern hot cross buns, and their ancient history among pagan peoples can be found in the links below. But the true God had already condemned this pagan custom in the Holy Scriptures, when Yahsrael picked it up from the Phoenicians and Babylonians and their families made cakes to the Queen of Heaven (**Jeremiah 7:18; 44:19**).

THE SNARE OF TRADITIONS

The traditions of men stand in opposition of the word of Yahuah. People love their traditions over the truth. Daily they draw near to him with their mouths, and they honor him on their lips but their hearts are far away from him. So in vain, they continue to worship him teaching as doctrines the commandments of men (**Matthew 15:7-9**). Their traditions shall be a snare to them because they have not considered Yahuah's commandments. **Exodus 22:20** says, "make no covenant with them because if you do, it will surely be a snare unto you." What people don't realize is that these traditions are linked to other gods and they are worshipping them when they celebrate their days. What has happened is: men have exchanged the truth for lies and began to worship created things instead of the Creator (**Romans 1:25**).

There is no biblical instruction or commandment to celebrate or worship the birth of the Messiyah period. However millions, if not billions, of people create all kinds of wicked revised customs, and traditions to do around pagan feasts. They erect trees, place lavish decorations, exchange gifts, hang mistletoe, and burn Yule logs, etc. All to honor pagan deities surrounding fertility gods. They ignore what the scriptures say concerning these practices.

The Most High has said that He HATES our wicked traditions and He doesn't want us coming before him with this wicked stuff (**Isaiah 1:12-15**). Instead, He told us what He expects of us. He said, "You shall observe to do therefore as the Most High have commanded you: you shall not turn aside to the right hand or to the left. You shall walk in all the ways which Yahuah your Power has commanded you, that ye may live, and that it may be well with you, and that you may prolong your days in the land which you shall possess" **He said do not add or subtract ANYTHING!! (Deuteronomy 5:32-33** and **Deuteronomy 12:30:32**). So anything outside of what he commanded is not things that we should be following. He commanded us to withdraw from them and come out from honoring this stuff (**2Thesselonians 3:6**). It is a **snare** (trap) to those who think it's harmless. When you continue in these traditions you are practicing idolatry. Those who love to honor this stuff use many different excuses. They say, "Well, I am doing it for the kids" "It doesn't matter where something came from, he knows my heart and why I do it" Others say, "don't judge me!! The scriptures say " Let no man therefore judge you in meat, or in drink, or in respect of a holiday, or of the new moon etc. (**Colossians 2:16**). So you can't judge me on this" They go all out to honor these traditions over the commandments. Even the Messiah said, "Why do you also transgress the commandment of Yahuah by your tradition? He said, "by doing this you have you made the commandment of Yahuah of none effect by your tradition (**Matthew 15:3, 6**).

People! You really need to get this. The Most High is no longer winking at our ignorance anymore (**Acts 17:30**). We can't continue to let people spoil us through philosophy and vain deceit, after the tradition of men, after the rudiments of the world, and not after the Messiyah (**Colossians 2:8**). We are commanded to withdraw ourselves from every brother that walks disorderly, and not after the tradition which we have been given (**2Thessolonians 3:6**). If you call yourself "dead to the world", why are you living like you are still subject to its ordinances (**Colossians 2:20-22**)? WHY????? Don't you know that a friend of the world is an enemy to the Most High (**James 4:4**)? Time to get free People. Stop loving the world as if you are still a part of it. Take no part in the deeds of darkness anymore. It's time to renew your minds (**I John 2:15-17, Ephesians 5:11**, and **Romans 2:2**). Once you walk away from these things, and come out of wickedness, you will begin to see. And then, the truth shall set you free (**John 8:32**)!!!

LOVING THE **HEATHEN** (nations) AND THEIR WAYS, we embraced everything that our European Masters told us!! We refuse to let go of their pagan ways!!! We love them so deeply that we will part company with family over them. Every holiday, we act like robots!When they say jump, our people say how high? You can tell our people over and over again why we should not do certain things and they look at you with this blank look, like..."What do you mean?" Then they turn right back around and continue on thinking that they can serve the Most High by offering him up pagan traditions. He told our people before saying, "You must not do as they do in Egypt, where you used to live, and you must not do as they do in the land of Canaan, where I am bringing you. Do not follow their practices." That was way back then. Now Fast forward>>.What are our people doing today? Many of them are still looking to the ways of Egypt. They want to go back to Egypt, study about their ways, look to the strength of Egypt, and seek out their hidden knowledge. Even though the Most High warns them not do this mess. He said, "Woe to them that go down to Egypt for help; and stay on horses, and trust in chariots, because they are many; and in horsemen, because they are very strong; but they look not unto the Holy One of Yahsrael, neither seek Yahushua (**Jeremiah 31:1**)!
He told us not to learn the ways of the heathens around us (**Jeremiah 10:2**), and he told us not to inquire as to how they serve their gods, thinking that we can do the same (**Deuteronomy 12:30**). But, do we listen? Have we taken these words to heart? Absolutely not! Everything they (the nations) do, we want to create a replica of the same thing.

Leviticus 20:23 says, "You must not live according to the customs of the nations I am going to drive out before you." Because they did all kinds of wicked things and Yahuah has said, " I abhorred (Hated) them" But, have these words provoked our people to change?

HIStory or OUR Story   **Chapter 9**

Not at all! Yahsrael is a stiff neck, hard headed nation who have ears and hear not; they have eyes and still can't see (**Isaiah 6:9, 42; 20** and **Matthew 13:13**). "You stiff-necked people! Your hearts and ears are still uncircumcised. You are just like your ancestors. You always resist the set apart Spirit! (**Acts 7:51**).

We are a people that have not learned how to function without the influence of other nations. When you tell our people that the promises in this book are for us, what is the first thing that they do? They say, "He loves everyone". They instantly try to find folks in scripture that they "think"upholds other nations, so they can justify bringing Massa (the slave mindset) along. I have had folks get downright angry when I tell them who this book is really about. They look for reasons to save the seed offspring of our oppressors. The mentality of some of our people is really sad to watch. But as we all know, you can't save everyone! There shall only be a remnant of our people that will get this truth (**Isaiah 10:22**). It has been decreed that two-thirds of our people shall be cut off (**Zechariah 13: 8**). He is coming back for the remnant, not the church and all of its masters. He is coming back for Yahsrael, not our oppressors. He is coming back for the obedient. Not those who continue to follow the ways of the Heathens. It's time to come out of her, and let go of Massa! LET THEM GO!

The 4th of July our 'so called' Independence Day

Where were your ancestors on the fourth of July in **1776** black man/woman??? Oh, that's right! They were in the fields still slaves and NOT free. The so called 'black' people of America were not emancipated until **1865**. 1776 is when the Europeans declared their independence from a province in their homeland, Great Britain. The 4th of July had nothing to do with us and has nothing to do with us! It was never made for, nor established by us or for us. Our ancestors were still slaves in the field picking cotton during this time. So why we feel the need to celebrate it is **BEYOND ME**!! And at this point, it should be **BEYOND YOU too**. Remember we were never Americans in their minds. Being an 'American' IS NOT a nationality for us, it is a citizenship. Obviously you should know, the 4th of July/Independence Day was **NOT FOR YOU, the SO CALLED 'BLACK MAN/WOMAN'**!!

HIStory or OUR Story   Chapter 10

We Did It- They Hid It

To this day, the so-called 'black man and woman' have contributed so much to modern society but our oppressors do not like to acknowledge this fact. They do not give proper credit. You see the truth is, slavery was just a blip on our radar screen. Slavery is just a bug that flew out onto the highway and got smashed by our big boy truck as we continued to drive down the highway of time. I'm not saying slavery doesn't matter, what I am saying is that our oppressors centralize slavery in our history, as if slavery is our beginning but as you can see, it could not be further from the truth. You can't limit 'black history' to one month and think that all of our history can be learned and taught in 28 days!! Then leave the other 11 remaining months for us to learn European or 'white history'. It's disproportionate! The European Caucasians, so called 'white people", have only been on the earth for a little over 6,000 plus years. The Hametic and Shemetic so called 'black races' have been here for millions of years.

Anyway, without any further ado, here are some accomplishments by us that we did, that they hid.

- **Air Conditioner Unit Design** Frederick Jones
- **Art Museum Design (Philadelphia)** Julian Abele Born

Abele (pronounced "able") was the Chief Designer at the prestigious Horace Trumbauer and Associates architectural firm from 1938-50. He attended the Institute for Colored Youth, which has since been transformed into Cheyney University, and in 1904 was the first African to graduate from the University of Pennsylvania School of Architecture. (Refer below to the section captioned "Library.")

- **Baby Carriage — Safety Leveler** William Richardson

This essential invention ended the constant and serious problem of babies falling out of carriages, most of which were inherently defective because they were built without a leveler to keep the carriage safely balanced.

- **Bicycle Frame — Folding/Separating Version** Isaac Johnson
- **Blimp (Air Ship) — Modern Version** John Pickering

This blimp (i.e., air ship) was the first to be powered by an electric motor and to have directional controls.

- **Blood Bank** Dr. Charles Drew 1940
- **Bridge Safety Gate** Humphrey Reynolds
- **Chair — Folding** John Purdy (& Daniel Sadgwar)
- **Clock (Refer Below To Watch)** Benjamin Banneker 02/6/1753
- **Clothes Drier — Modern Forerunner** George Samson 06/7/1892

- **Computer — World's Fastest** Philip Emeagwali 1989

Emeagwali is the world's leading supercomputer expert. Also, he actually invented an *inter*national *net*work system that predated the current Internet. CNN called him "A father of the Internet," and President Bill Clinton described him as "one of the great minds of the information age." He holds several undergraduate and graduate degrees and has an IQ so high that it cannot be measured on conventional tests. He is a prolific inventor, so far having submitted 41 inventions to the U.S. Patent and Trademark Office. One of those inventions makes oil fields so productive that it has saved the U.S. hundreds of millions of dollars each year. (Refer below to the section captioned "Weather Fore-casting.")

- **Curtain Rod** Samuel Scottron 08/30/1892
- **Dry Cleaning Process** Thomas Jennings 03/3/1821

Jennings is the first African to receive a U.S. patent. After earning money from his patent, he used those funds to buy his enslaved family's freedom and to support the abolition movement. Also, in 1831, he served as the Assistant Secretary for the First Annual Convention of The People of Color (which, by the way, was held in Philadelphia).

- **Elevator — Automatic Electric Shaft Closing** Alexander Miles 10/11/1887

This invention has saved hundreds of thousands of lives by drastically improving upon pre-existing and quite dangerous ascending/descending contraptions. Those contraptions (i.e., primitive elevators), when stopped on a floor other than that desired by a passenger, required that passenger to manually shut a door to cut off access to the shaft, which often caused that passenger to fall into that deep shaft.

- **Fire Escape — Portable** Daniel McCree 11/11/1890
- **Fire Extinguisher Improvement** Thomas Martin 03/26/1872
- **Firemen's Mobile Ladder** Joseph Winter 05/7/1878
- **Gas Mask** Garrett Morgan 10/13/14
- **Golf Tee** Dr. George Grant 12/12/1899

Prior to this invention by Dr. Grant (who, by the way, graduated from and later taught at Harvard Dental School), golfers had to use their hands to make a mound of sand and then place the ball on top of that mound. Despite his innovative genius that greatly benefited golfers worldwide, he was barred — and still would be barred — from many country clubs because of his race.

HIStory or OUR Story   **Chapter 10**

- **Heart (Open Heart) Surgery** Dr. Daniel Hale Williams 07/9/1893

Dr. Williams performed this miraculous feat by removing a knife from the heart of a victim that had been stabbed, after which he sutured the wound and the patient recovered. He also founded the Provident Hospital and Medical Center in Chicago, IL, which is the oldest free standing Black-owned hospital in the country.

- **Heating Furnace — Ventilation System** Alice Parker 12/19/19

This invention provided a mechanism for routing heat to various rooms throughout a building.

- **Ice Cream — Method and Recipes** Augustus Jackson 1832

Jackson, a Philadelphian and a former White House chef, uniquely used ice mixed with salt to lower and control the temperature of his special mix of ingredients, which proved to be a major breakthrough in the creation of ice cream as we know it today. He also created various ice cream flavors. However, he never applied for a patent.

- **Ice Cream Scooper — Spring Loaded** Alfred Cralle 02/2/1897
- **Ironing Board — Improvement** Sarah Boone 04/26/1892

This invention, which was a narrowed, curved, and reversible appliance, made it possible for the first time in history to easily and efficiently press and crease parts of clothing like sleeves and types of clothing like uniquely tailored women's garments.

- **Lawn Mower — Improved, Rotary Blade** John Burr 05/9/1899
- **Lawn Sprinkler — Swiveling** Joseph Smith 05/4/1897
- **Library Design (Free Library — Philadelphia.)** Julian Abele 04/21/1881 Born

Refer above to the section captioned "Art Museum."

- **Light Bulb — Electric Lamp Improvement** Lewis Latimer 09/13/1881

Latimer, the son of parents who had escaped slavery, was an inventor, draftsman, engineer, and scientist, as well as an author, poet, musician, and philanthropist. It is a little known fact that he was the person who actually drew the blueprints for Alexander Graham Bell's telephone in 1878. Three years later, in 1881, he and assistant Joseph Nichols were the first persons to receive a patent for the direct forerunner to today's commonly used light bulb. Prior to this, the electric lamp by Thomas Edison and others had no real practical use because it could not emit light for an extended period. But the new light bulb by Latimer (with assistant Nichols) used a revolutionary method of manufacturing carbon filaments that produced light for effectively extended periods. It was because of this ingenious invention that Latimer was asked by numerous countries, states, and cities — including Philadelphia — to write an instruction manual (which he did in 1890) and to supervise the installation of incandescent light plants. In addition, it is quite interesting that he was the original draftsman for Edison (inventor of the 1879 temporary electric lamp) who relied on Latimer as the expert witness in Edison's patent infringement suit.

- **Lock — Modern** Washington Martin 07/23/1889

The innovative lock invented by Martin is precisely what made today's locks possible. It creatively included a cylinder and spiral spring coiled around a metal pin, thereby frustrating thieves and burglars throughout the country.

- **Mail Box** Phillip Downing 10/27/1891

This invention is also known as a letter box and a letter drop.

- **Overnight Delivery Package Receptacle** Folarin Sosan 1997

Sosan, through his Package Park (Maita) company, made it possible for overnight and next day package delivery providers such as Federal Express, United Parcel Service, and the U.S. Postal Service (as well as other major and small businesses) to have all of their deliveries immediately received by customers and then accurately tracked by computer.

- **Pants — Modern Suspenders** Archia Ross 11/28/1899

These suspenders, called "trouser supports and stretchers," included practical and stylish features such as metal clasps.

- **Pencil Sharpener** John Love 11/23/1897
- **(The) "Real McCoy"** Elijah McCoy,

The term "The Real McCoy" is used to describe anything that is of excellent quality. People began using that term about 130 years ago in honor of one of the most talented and skillful inventors in American history, a man with more than 50 patents beginning in 1872. (Although his year of birth is often listed as 1843, it might be 1844. The exact year is unknown because his records, like the records of most Africans during that period, were often inaccurate because of the indifference of slave-holding and other racist whites.)

- **Refrigeration Transport System** Frederick Jones 07/12/49

Although he patented it in 1949, he actually invented it in 1935.

- **Security System — Home** Marie Brown 12/2/69

This home protection system was the first to include television and video surveillance.

HIStory or OUR Story   Chapter 10

- **Statue of Liberty — A Black Female** 1875

French historian Edourd de Laboulaye, who was the chairman of the French Anti-Slavery Society, proposed to the French government that the people of France present to the people of United States, through the American Abolitionist Society, the gift of a Statue of Liberty (with construction beginning in 1875) in recognition of the abolition of American slavery and also therefore obviously in recognition of the major role played by the approximately 150,000 Black soldiers who helped abolish slavery by winning the Civil War. When the statue, sculpted by de Laboulaye's close friend and fellow French Anti-Slavery Society member Frederic Auguste Bartholdi, was presented in 1884 to a U.S. official, its color was black and it had broken chains at the feet and left hand of the female-modeled sculpture. Later, the hand chain was removed. It must be noted that the original design of this statue was for a lighthouse project in Egypt (meaning Kemet) and it featured an Egyptian (meaning Kemetic) female with broken chains of slavery at her feet.

- **Thermostat and Temperature Control System** Frederick Jones 2/23/60
- **Toilet — Modern Bathroom Features** Thomas Elkins 01/9/1872

This invention, which was called a "chamber commode," featured all of today's creature comforts such as a toilet stool, wash stand, mirror, bureau, and book rack.

- **Traffic Signal** Garrett Morgan 11/20/23

After he saw a crash between a car and a horse-drawn carriage, Morgan decided that it was absolutely essential for him to invent some type of traffic safety device. As a result, he was the first person to apply for and receive a patent for an inexpensive "hand-cranked semaphore traffic management" mechanism that would control vehicular and pedestrian traffic, thereby protecting humans from injury and even death and protecting cars from damage. This led directly to today's red, yellow, and green light signals. General Electric bought his patent for $40,000 and in 1963 the U.S. government awarded Morgan a citation for his invention that has saved millions of lives and body parts and has avoided billions in property damage. (He also had this invention patented in Britain and Canada.)

- **Trolley — Electric Railway** Elbert Robinson 09/19/1893

Robinson creatively used electricity in overhead wires to propel passenger-carrying vehicles.

- **Typewriter — Improvement** Lee Burridge (& Newman Marshman) 4/7/1885
Unlike previous bulky and exclusively upper case "letter-writing machines" that were described as a cross between "a small piano and a kitchen table" and that blocked the user from being able to see what he was typing as he was typing, the novel invention by Burridge and Marshman was quite practical. It printed both upper and lower case letters, was a much smaller device, and allowed the user to see what he was typing as he was typing. Also, it required fewer parts and movements to operate and allowed for the use of any paper length.
- **Watch — U.S. (Refer Above To Clock)** Benjamin Banneker 02/6/1753
Benjamin's grandmother (who was an English indentured servant) married an indigenous African whose name was "Banna Ka." Later, white people began calling him "Bannaky" and thereafter started spelling his name "Banneker." Benjamin's invention was not really a clock but instead was an ingenious wooden pocket watch. In addition to his status as an inventor, municipal surveyor, almanac author, mathematician, scientist, mechanical engineer, and astronomer, he also was a vocal anti-abolitionist who on August 19, 1791 petitioned slaveholder Thomas Jefferson to end the "absurd and false ideas" of white supremacy.
- **Weather Forecasting — Computerized** Philip Emeagwali 1989
Using the Hyperball Computer that he invented in 1975, this pre-eminent scientist solved the world's largest mathematical equations that produced meticulously accurate weather forecasting worldwide. (Refer above to the section captioned "Computer.")
- **Wrench — Updated** Jack Johnson 04/18/22
This is the very same Jack Johnson who became the world's first Black heavyweight champ by winning "The Heavyweight Championship of The World" in 1908 and who had won "The *Colored* Heavyweight Championship of The World" in 1903. His updated wrench was a tool designed specifically to tighten or loosen fastening devices. This wrench was important not only because of its practical use and not only because of the person who conceived it, but also because it was invented while he was in Leavenworth Prison on trumped up racist charges involving a 1912 alleged violation of the Mann Act stemming from his out-of-state trips with his white girlfriend. (The Mann Act made it illegal to cross state lines to engage in "immoral activity" with white women.) It should be noted that in addition to his wrench invention, Johnson also received a patent (number 1,438,709) for a car theft protection device on December 12, 1922.

- **Trolley — Electric Railway** Elbert Robinson 09/19/1893
  Robinson creatively used electricity in overhead wires to propel passenger-carrying vehicles.
- **Wheelchair — Stair Climbing** Rufus Weaver 11/19/68
- The **Cellular Phone**: Henry T. Samson, July 6, 1971
  To the Egyptians (Kemites), a circle, which has no beginning and no end, signified eternity, just as marriage signifies an eternal bond.
- The **Patent Act of 1793 and 1836** barred enslaved Africans from obtaining patents because they were not considered citizens.
- In 1861, Jefferson Davis, president of the Confederate States of America, enacted a patent law that allowed enslaved Africans to receive patent protection for their inventions, according to *Bloomberg.com*.
- In **1870**, the U.S. government passed a patent law giving all American men, including Blacks, the rights to their inventions.

The Patent Act of 1793 and 1836 barred enslaved Africans from obtaining patents because they were not considered citizens.

Can you believe it!! They barred the very architects of humanity from being able to obtain a patent!! This means everything that they did in America, they could not get credit for it!! They were not even counted citizens in a land where they actually existed first!! Amazing, right?!!

In 1861, Jefferson Davis, president of the Confederate States of America, enacted a patent law that allowed enslaved Africans to receive patent protection for their inventions, according to Bloomberg.com.

In 1870, the U.S. government passed a patent law giving all American men, including Blacks, the rights to their inventions.

So that means that every invention by a so called 'black man' in this country prior to 1870, a white man is getting credit for it today. Even if a so called 'black man' got an honorable mention for his/her own invention, he didn't get paid for it. Neither is the black man/woman's family getting royalties for these inventions to this day. There are countless inventions the so called 'black man' has invented, but the white man is being financially compensated for it to this day.

The Residual Slave Mentality

Are We Still Slaves?? Are we still confined to the chains of slavery? Many people believe that the enslavement of Black men, women and children is a thing of the past. The world believes that AmeriKKKa has set her black slaves free, from the bondage of their white slavemasters. Even some Black people in AmeriKKKa, believe that they are actually free from the oppression and control of their white oppressors.

In fact, most black people in AmeriKKKa today have been psychologically duped into believing that they actually operate according to their own will. These misled perceptions cannot be further from the actual truth. The slavemasters don't have to chain you down or whip you anymore. You have freedom in name, but not in definition. You are not a slave in name, but you are in definition! The definition of the word slave means, "One who is dominated by some outside influence and having no personal rights or freedom." The MessiYah defined freedom as "knowing the truth" and that "the truth sets us free".

So ask yourself: have your oppressors ever told you the truth about who you are nationality wise or historically? Have they told you what nation you come from or what your ancestors' tribe was? The answer is NO! We are orphans and fatherless. We don't know our forefathers, which is just like a child today who doesn't know his biological father. The child is clueless and vulnerable. He doesn't know much about himself. We are clueless as a people. Do you really know what true freedom is all about? What do you know other than what white people have told you? Nothing! What do you know other than what black folks have told you that they heard from white folks? Nothing!!

Yes, the physical slavery is "somewhat" over, but what about the biological slavery? What about the economical slavery? What about the sociological slavery? What about the spiritual slavery? What about the psychological slavery? The physical chains were just one aspect amidst the many horrors of slavery! The chains are off of our hands, but we aren't producing anything! The chains are off of our feet, but we aren't going anywhere! Why? This is because the physical chains were the least of our worries! We still have the biggest chain of all wrapped around our minds, hearts, and souls! Your mind is still locked down, and it is your mind that controls your hands and your feet! That's like having a brand new shiny car, but the engine is locked up! Having a car that can't go anywhere is just like not having a car at all! The white man took the chains off of our hands and feet because we stopped swinging and we stopped kicking! So why not take the chains off?!

HIStory or OUR Story   **Chapter 11**

We have been in the chains for so long, that we have forgotten why the white slave master put the chains on us in the first place! We have forgotten the original reason and purpose for the physical chains! The chains were to hold you down, but if you aren't trying to get up, then the chains have outlived their purpose! Initially, we were physically and mentally strong. They kept us physically strong to be good workers for their benefit, but they have made us mentally weak over time.

They took **Willie Lynch**'s idea, "**Let them keep the body, but take the mind**". Ladies and Gentlemen, the real reason that they put chains on your ancestors' hands was because your ancestors had hands. They were skilled warriors, masters in the martial arts. Martial arts were not primarily used for war but for exercise and balance. It was a man's means of taking care of himself, his family and his tribe. When it comes to the chains on the feet they chained your feet to keep them from running or fighting back. The feet are the vehicles that one uses when he's going places. Feet also represent freedom to come and go as you please. The chains held them down. Get up. The neck controls the head, whether you look straight, left, right, up or down. And the head controlled the body. Psychologically, the belly chain around the stomach signifies controlled birth, and our nutrition.

Today if a person is a professional boxer, their hands are considered deadly weapons. It would be a felony if they punched a civilian--unless it was in self-defense. Furthermore if it came to a use of force situation, that professional would have to use the minimal amount of force necessary because of the stigma that comes with that. It was a part of our culture which they wanted to make sure that those skills to defend 'self' wasn't passed on to the offspring. The Europeans strategically separated the children from their parents and kept them busy in the cotton fields using their hands to pick cotton, instead of training daily and studying the universe as their parents did when they were children.

It's time for a resurrection from our destruction. Although we have suffered destruction, we have never been taught self-construction. **We are free in name, but not in definition**. A born slave doesn't know he is a slave. He believes he is free, and life as he knows is okay because it's considered normal to him.

Do you see something wrong with that backward, wayward thinking? This is your world. Shape it or someone else will. A slave is dominated by an outside influence more than an internal influence. In this case, the outside influence is someone that is not you, and does not consider you or your people's best interest.

HIStory or OUR Story   Chapter 11

We (so called 'black people') are dominated by an outside influence more than an internal influence. What do you know about freedom other than what white people have told you? Nothing! What do you know other than what black folks have told you, which they heard from white folks? Nothing!

Here is a hypothetical example:

The relationship between a dog and its master can be directly paralleled to the relationship between black people and their white slave masters for the past four centuries with AmeriKKKa. Suppose that tomorrow, for some reason, you became interested in getting a pet dog for your family or household. Suppose that you then go to the pet store to look around, and you find a dog that you are interested in buying. You then purchase the dog and bring it back to your home. Now once you get home you notice that this dog is a bit active and untamed, so you purchase a collar for the dog and chain the dog to a tree in the backyard. Since the dog is untamed, you have to begin training the dog to obey your commands. You can eventually train this dog to do everything, from catching a frisbee to attacking an enemy of yours, at a single command. But before you train your new dog to do all of these other things, you must first train your dog to not run away from you and to return to you at your immediate command. You have to keep tugging the dog with the collar until the dog stops trying to run away from you.

You also have to give the dog food and water on a daily routine schedule to ensure its physical and nutritional survival. The dog will forget how to independently hunt and find food for itself. Therefore persuading the dog away from any desires to flee you, or do for itself.

Also I must add that anytime the dog does anything to disobey you, you will reprimand it. Anytime the dog is extra obedient to your wishes, you will give the dog extra food and a pat on the head. This psychological training is absolutely necessary to gain total control over your animal. You must break down its free spirit, tame it, and make it totally dependent upon you. This is the only way to win your animal's obedience permanently.

After a while, you will have your dog so obedient, and so well trained, that you can take the collar off the dog, and un-chain the dog. The dog can now roam freely because you have it so well trained, that it will run to you at your very command! The dog isn't going anywhere!

HIStory or OUR Story   **Chapter 11**

The dog now loves you! The dog loves you because you feed it every day! It is happy and satisfied to get dog slop and water every day, even though you may be in the house eating a full steak dinner every day! The dog believes that it deserves nothing better than dog slop. The dog is so grateful to you. The dog has forgotten how to provide for itself, like in the days of its independence. The dog loves you because it remembers when it was chained to that tree in the backyard, and it also remembers the day that you unchained its neck from the tree! So the dog licks your hand every time it remembers that you set it free!!

But, what the dog has failed to remember is that you were the same no-good devil that chained it to the tree in the first place!! Yes, the dog has totally forgotten that you were the one who purchased it from the bondage of one man to be under your bondage. The dog has been psychologically tricked by you. So the dog does not recognize you for who you really are. The dog has forgotten that you are the no-good bastard that originally locked him up!!
So you had better not let that dog remember that fact! Because as soon as that dog is reminded of that fact, that will be the same day that the dog bites you in your ass!! That dog will then proceed to bite everybody's ass, in the family, that has been smiling at it for all these years! The dog will then leave your house, never to come back again! Do you understand what I'm saying? Do you really understand what is being said to you? Think about it. Now if your dog does leave you one day, how will you handle it? How will you react? Will you react violently and chase the dog like pharaoh did the children of Israel when they were let go? Will you mourn over the fact that your dog has left you? After all, "a dog is man's best friend." If your dog leaves you, will you miss the way it used to curl up around your feet and lick your boots clean? Will you miss the way it used to do anything just to get you to pat its head? It just loved your attention.

Will you miss the way it used to dance and wag its tail, for your entertainment? Will you miss the dog's protection? Will you miss the way it would attack any of your enemies, even if the enemies were other dogs that looked just like it! You would not even have to break a sweat. The dog would fight all of your fights for you. Will you miss the loyal service of your well trained dog?

I wonder will white folks miss us so-called 'Negroes' once we get smart enough to leave them! I wonder will we ever start remembering how we got here in the first place! I wonder if we will start remembering who put the chains on us in the first place, and will we ever realize why they took them off!! They did not take the chains off of us because they felt ashamed of the horrible crimes they committed against us!! Don't be a fool to believe that!! They took the chains off because we Negroes were so psychologically trained, that we were not going anywhere anyway! So now we live our entire lives running around his backyard doing what we have been trained to do and hoping for a proverbial dog biscuit, a pat on the head, or some left over scraps from the slave master's table! Moral of story: the first loyalty of a dog is to protect its master, even to its own detriment.

HIStory or OUR Story — Chapter 11

Even after reading all of this I know that some of you out there will still love' massa'. You will love 'massa' more than yourself and more than your own kind. It really is a shame. 'Uncle Tom' loved him some 'Uncle Sam' (the government) and I'm afraid that still has not changed even to this day.

Take note of this passage from the late great Malcolm X. He gave a great illustration of the social dynamics of the so called 'black man in America'. What's frightening is that even though he said that over 50 years ago, what he said still applies today!!

"Message to The Grassroots" speech by Malcolm X, delivered November 10, 1963

"We want to have just an off-the-cuff chat between you and me — us. We want to talk right down to earth in a language that everybody here can easily understand. We all agree tonight, all of the speakers have agreed, that America has a very serious problem. Not only does America have a very serious problem, but our people have a very serious problem. America's problem is us. We're her problem. The only reason she has a problem is she doesn't want us here. And every time you look at yourself, be you black, brown, red, or yellow — a so-called Negro — you represent a person who poses such a serious problem for America because you're not wanted. Once you face this as a fact, then you can start plotting a course that will make you appear intelligent, instead of unintelligent. What you and I need to do is learn to forget our differences. When we come together, we don't come together as Baptists or Methodists. You don't catch hell 'cause you're a Baptist, and you don't catch hell 'cause you're a Methodist. You don't catch hell 'cause you're a Methodist or Baptist. You don't catch hell because you're a Democrat or a Republican. You don't catch hell because you're a Mason or an Elk. And you sure don't catch hell 'cause you're an American; 'cause if you was an American, you wouldn't catch no hell. You catch hell 'cause you're a black man. You catch hell, all of us catch hell, for the same reason.

HIStory or OUR Story   **Chapter 11**

So we are all black people, so-called Negroes, second-class citizens, ex-slaves. You are nothing but a ex-slave. You don't like to be told that. But what else are you? You are ex-slaves. You didn't come here on the "Mayflower." You came here on a slave ship — in chains, like a horse, or a cow, or a chicken. And you were brought here by the people who came here on the "Mayflower." You were brought here by the so-called Pilgrims, or Founding Fathers. They were the ones who brought you here.

We have a common enemy. We have this in common: We have a common oppressor, a common exploiter, and a common discriminator. But once we all realize that we have this common enemy, then we unite on the basis of what we have in common. And what we have foremost in common is that enemy — the white man. He's an enemy to all of us. I know some of you all think that some of them aren't enemies. Time will tell.

In Bandung back in, I think, 1954, was the first unity meeting in centuries of black people. And once you study what happened at the Bandung conference, and the results of the Bandung conference, it actually serves as a model for the same procedure you and I can use to get our problems solved. At Bandung all the nations came together. Their were dark nations from Africa and Asia. Some of them were Buddhists. Some of them were Muslim. Some of them were Christians. Some of them were Confucianists; some were atheists. Despite their religious differences, they came together. Some were communists; some were socialists; some were capitalists. Despite their economic and political differences, they came together. All of them were black, brown, red, or yellow.

The number one thing that was not allowed to attend the Bandung conference was the white man. He couldn't come. Once they excluded the white man, they found that they could get together. Once they kept him out, everybody else fell right in and fell in line. This is the thing that you and I have to understand. And these people who came together didn't have nuclear weapons; they didn't have jet planes; they didn't have all of the heavy armaments that the white man has. But they had unity. They were able to submerge their little petty differences and agree on one thing: That though one African came from Kenya and was being colonized by the Englishman, and another African came from the Congo and was being colonized by the Belgian, and another African came from Guinea and was being colonized by the French, and another came from Angola and was being colonized by the Portuguese. When they came to the Bandung conference, they looked at the Portuguese, and at the Frenchman, and at the Englishman, and at the other — Dutchman — and learned or realized that the one thing that all of them had in common: they were all from Europe, they were all Europeans, blond, blue-eyed and white-skinned. They began to recognize who their enemy was. The same man that was colonizing our people in Kenya was colonizing our people in the Congo. The same one in the Congo was colonizing our people in South Africa, and in Southern Rhodesia, and in Burma, and in India, and in Afghanistan, and in Pakistan. They realized all over the world where the dark man was being oppressed. He was being oppressed by the white man; where the dark man was being exploited, he was being exploited by the white man. So they got together under this basis — that they had a common enemy.

HIStory or OUR Story Chapter 11

And when you and I here in Detroit and in Michigan and in America who have been awakened today look around us, we too realize here in America we all have a common enemy, whether he's in Georgia or Michigan, whether he's in California or New York. He's the same man: blue eyes and blond hair and pale skin — same man. So what we have to do is what they did. They agreed to stop quarreling among themselves. Any little spat that they had, they'd settle it among themselves, go into a huddle. Don't let the enemy know that you got a disagreement.

Instead of us airing our differences in public, we have to realize we're all the same family. And when you have a family squabble, you don't get out on the sidewalk. If you do, everybody calls you uncouth, unrefined, uncivilized, savage. If you don't make it at home, you settle it at home; you get in the closet — argue it out behind closed doors. And then when you come out on the street, you pose a common front, a united front. And this is what we need to do in the community, and in the city, and in the state. We need to **stop airing our differences in front of the white man**. Put the white man out of our meetings, number one, and then sit down and talk shop with each other. That's all you gotta do.

I would like to make a few comments concerning the difference between the black revolution and the Negro revolution. There's a difference. Are they both the same? And if they're not, what is the difference? What is the difference between a black revolution and a Negro revolution? First, what is a revolution? Sometimes I'm inclined to believe that many of our people are using this word "revolution" loosely, without taking careful consideration of what this word actually means, and what its historic characteristics are. When you study the historic nature of revolutions, the motive of a revolution, the objective of a revolution, and the result of a revolution, and the methods used in a revolution, you may change words. You may devise another program. You may change your goal and you may change your mind.

Look at the American Revolution in 1776. That revolution was for what? For land. Why did they want land? Independence. How was it carried out? Bloodshed. Number one, it was based on land, the basis of independence. And the only way they could get it was bloodshed. The French Revolution — what was it based on? The land-less against the landlord. What was it for? Land. How did they get it? Bloodshed. Was no love lost; was no compromise; was no negotiation. I'm telling you, you don't know what a revolution is. 'Cause when you find out what it is, you'll get back in the alley; you'll get out of the way. The Russian Revolution — what was it based on? Land. The land-less against the landlord. How did they bring it about? Bloodshed. You haven't got a revolution that doesn't involve bloodshed. And you're afraid to bleed. I said, you're afraid to bleed.

As long as the white man sent you to Korea, you bled. He sent you to Germany, you bled. He sent you to the South Pacific to fight the Japanese, you bled. You bleed for white people. But when it comes time to seeing your own churches being bombed and little black girls be murdered, you haven't got no blood. You bleed when the white man says bleed; you bite when the white man says bite; and you bark when the white man says bark.

HIStory or OUR Story   Chapter 11

I hate to say this about us, but it's true. How are you going to be nonviolent in Mississippi, as violent as you were in Korea? How can you justify being nonviolent in Mississippi and Alabama, when your churches are being bombed, and *your* little girls are being murdered, and at the same time you're going to violent with Hitler, and Tojo, and somebody else that you don't even know?
If violence is wrong in America, violence is wrong abroad. If it's wrong to be violent defending black women and black children and black babies and black men, then it's wrong for America to draft us and make us violent abroad in defense of her. And if it is right for America to draft us, and teach us how to be violent in defense of her, then it is right for you and me to do whatever is necessary to defend our own people right here in this country.

The Chinese Revolution — they wanted land. They threw the British out, along with the Uncle Tom Chinese. Yeah, they did. They set a good example. When I was in prison, I read an article — don't be shocked when I say I was in prison. You're still in prison. That's what America means: prison. When I was in prison, I read an article in Life magazine showing a little Chinese girl, nine years old; her father was on his hands and knees and she was pulling the trigger 'cause he was an Uncle Tom Chinaman. When they had the revolution over there, they took a whole generation of Uncle Toms — just wiped them out. And within ten years that little girl became a full-grown woman. No more Toms in China. And today it's one of the toughest, roughest, most feared countries on this earth — by the white man. 'Cause there are no Uncle Toms over there.

Of all our studies, history is best qualified to reward our research. And when you see that you've got problems, all you have to do is examine the historic method used all over the world by others who have problems similar to yours. And once you see how they got theirs straight, then you know how you can get yours straight. There's been a revolution, a black revolution, going on in Africa. In Kenya, the Mau Mau were revolutionaries; they were the ones who made the word "Uhuru" [Kenyan word for "freedom"]. They were the ones who brought it to the fore. The Mau Mau, they were revolutionaries. They believed in scorched earth. They knocked everything aside that got in their way, and their revolution also was based on land, a desire for land. In Algeria, the northern part of Africa, a revolution took place. The Algerians were revolutionists; they wanted land. France offered to let them be integrated into France. They told France: to hell with France. They wanted some land, not some France.
And they engaged in a bloody battle.
So I cite these various revolutions, brothers and sisters, to show you — you don't have a peaceful revolution. You don't have a turn-the-other-cheek revolution. There's no such *thing* as a nonviolent revolution. The only kind of revolution that's nonviolent is the Negro revolution. The only revolution based on loving your enemy is the Negro revolution. The only revolution in which the goal is a desegregated lunch counter, a desegregated theater, a desegregated park, and a desegregated public toilet; you can sit down next to white folks on the toilet. That's no revolution. Revolution is based on land. Land is the basis of all independence. Land is the basis of freedom, justice, and equality. The white man knows what a revolution is. He knows that the black revolution is world-wide in scope and in nature. The black revolution is sweeping Asia, sweeping Africa, is rearing its head in Latin America.

HIStory or OUR Story   **Chapter 11**

The Cuban Revolution — that's a revolution. They overturned the system. Revolution is in Asia. Revolution is in Africa. And the white man is screaming because he sees revolution in Latin America. How do you think he'll react to you when you learn what a real revolution is? You don't know what a revolution is. If you did, you wouldn't use that word.
A revolution is bloody. Revolution is hostile. Revolution knows no compromise. Revolution overturns and destroys everything that gets in its way. And you, sitting around here like a knot on the wall, saying, "I'm going to love these folks no matter how much they hate me." No, you need a revolution. Whoever heard of a revolution where they lock arms, as Reverend Cleage was pointing out beautifully, singing "We Shall Overcome"? Just tell me. You don't do that in a revolution. You don't do any singing; you're too busy swinging. It's based on land. A revolutionary wants land so he can set up his own nation, an independent nation. These Negroes aren't asking for no nation. They're trying to crawl back on the plantation.

When you want a nation, that's called nationalism. When the white man became involved in a revolution in this country against England, what was it for? He wanted this land so he could set up another white nation. That's white nationalism. The American Revolution was white nationalism. The French Revolution was white nationalism. The Russian Revolution too — yes, it was — white nationalism. You don't think so? Why do you think Khrushchev and Mao can't get their heads together? White nationalism. All the revolutions that's going on in Asia and Africa today are based on what? Black nationalism. A revolutionary is a black nationalist. He wants a nation. I was reading some beautiful words by Reverend Cleage, pointing out why he couldn't get together with someone else here in the city because all of them were afraid of being identified with black nationalism. If you're afraid of black nationalism, you're afraid of revolution. And if you love revolution, you love black nationalism.

To understand this, you have to go back to what the young brother here referred to as the house Negro and the field Negro — back during slavery. There was two kinds of slaves. There was the house Negro and the field Negro. The house Negroes – they lived in the house with master, they dressed pretty good, they ate good 'cause they ate his food — what he left. They lived in the attic or the basement, but still they lived near the master; and they loved their master more than the master loved himself. They would give their life to save the master's house quicker than the master would. The house Negro, if the master said, "We got a good house here," the house Negro would say, "Yeah, we got a good house here." Whenever the master said "we," he said "we." That's how you can tell a house Negro. If the master's house caught on fire, the house Negro would fight harder to put the blaze out than the master would. If the master got sick, the house Negro would say, "What's the matter, boss, we sick?" We sick! He identified himself with his master more than his master identified with himself. And if you came to the house Negro and said, "Let's run away, let's escape, let's separate," the house Negro would look at you and say, "Man, you crazy. What you mean, separate? Where is there a better house than this? Where can I wear better clothes than this? Where can I eat better food than this?" That was that house Negro. In those days he was called a "house nigger." And that's what we call him today, because we've still got some house niggers running around here.

This modern house Negro loves his master. He wants to live near him. He'll pay three times as much as the house is worth just to live near his master, and then brag about "I'm the only Negro out here." "I'm the only one on my job." "I'm the only one in this school." You're nothing but a house Negro. And if someone comes to you right now and says, "Let's separate," you say the same thing that the house Negro said on the plantation. "What you mean, separate? From America? This good white man? Where you going to get a better job than you get here?" I mean, this is what you say. "I ain't left nothing in Africa," that's what you say. Why, you left your mind in Africa.
On that same plantation, there was the field Negro. The field Negro — those were the masses. There were always more Negroes in the field than there was Negroes in the house. The Negro in the field caught hell. He ate leftovers. In the house they ate high up on the hog. The Negro in the field didn't get nothing but what was left of the insides of the hog. They call 'em "chitlins" nowadays. In those days they called them what they were: guts. That's what you were — a gut-eater. And some of you all still gut-eaters.

The field Negro was beaten from morning to night. He lived in a shack, in a hut; He wore old, castoff clothes. He hated his master. I say he hated his master. He was intelligent. That house Negro loved his master. But that field Negro — remember, they were in the majority, and they hated the master. When the house caught on fire, he didn't try and put it out; that field Negro prayed for a wind, for a breeze. When the master got sick, the field Negro prayed that he'd die. If someone come to the field Negro and said, "Let's separate, let's run," he didn't say "Where we going?" He'd say, "Any place is better than here." You've got field Negroes in America today. I'm a field Negro. The masses are the field Negroes. When they see this man's house on fire, you don't hear these little Negroes talking about "our government is in trouble." They say, "*The* government is in trouble." Imagine a Negro: "Our government"! I even heard one say "our astronauts." They won't even let him near the plant — and "our astronauts"! "Our Navy" — that's a Negro that's out of his mind. That's a Negro that's out of his mind.

Just as the slavemaster of that day used Tom, the house Negro, to keep the field Negroes in check, the same old slavemaster today has Negroes who are nothing but modern Uncle Toms, 20th century Uncle Toms, to keep you and me in check, keep us under control, keep us passive and peaceful and nonviolent. That's Tom making you nonviolent. It's like when you go to the dentist, and the man's going to take your tooth. You're going to fight him when he starts pulling. So he squirts some stuff in your jaw called novocaine, to make you think they're not doing anything to you. So you sit there and 'cause you've got all of that novocaine in your jaw, you suffer peacefully. Blood running all down your jaw, and you don't know what's happening. 'Cause someone has taught you to suffer — peacefully.

HIStory or OUR Story   Chapter 11

The white man do the same thing to you in the street, when he want to put knots on your head and take advantage of you and don't have to be afraid of your fighting back. To keep you from fighting back, he gets these old religious Uncle Toms to teach you and me, just like novocaine, suffer peacefully. Don't stop suffering, just suffer peacefully. As Reverend Cleage pointed out, "Let your blood flow In the streets." This is a shame. And you know he's a Christian preacher. If it's a shame to him, you know what it is to me. Our religion teaches us to be intelligent. Be peaceful, be courteous, obey the law, respect everyone; but if someone puts his hand on you, send him to the cemetery. That's a good religion. In fact, that's that old-time religion. That's the one that Ma and Pa used to talk about: an eye for an eye, and a tooth for a tooth, and a head for a head, and a life for a life: That's a good religion. And doesn't nobody resent that kind of religion being taught but a wolf, who intends to make you his meal.
This is the way it is with the white man in America. He's a wolf and you're sheep. Any time a shepherd, a pastor, teach you and me not to run from the white man and, at the same time, teach us not to fight the white man, he's a traitor to you and me. Don't lay down our life all by itself. No, preserve your life. it's the best thing you got. And if you got to give it up, let it be even-steven.

The slavemaster took Tom and dressed him well, and fed him well, and even gave him a little education — a little education; gave him a long coat and a top hat and made all the other slaves look up to him. Then he used Tom to control them. The same strategy that was used in those days is used today, by the same white man. He takes a Negro, a so-called Negro, and make him prominent, build him up, publicize him, make him a celebrity. And then he becomes a spokesman for Negroes — and a Negro leader.
I would like to just mention just one other thing else quickly, and that is the method that the white man uses, how the white man uses these "big guns," or Negro leaders, against the black revolution. They are not a part of the black revolution. They're used against the black revolution.

When Martin Luther King failed to desegregate Albany, Georgia, the civil-rights struggle in America reached its low point. King became bankrupt almost, as a leader. Plus, even financially, the Southern Christian Leadership Conference was in financial trouble; plus it was in trouble, period, with the people when they failed to desegregate Albany, Georgia. Other Negro civil-rights leaders of so-called national stature became fallen idols. As they became fallen idols, they began to lose their prestige and influence, local Negro leaders began to stir up the masses. In Cambridge, Maryland, Gloria Richardson; in Danville, Virginia, and other parts of the country, local leaders began to stir up our people at the grassroots level. This was never done by these Negroes, whom you recognize, of national stature. They controlled you, but they never incited you or excited you. They controlled you; they contained you; they kept you on the plantation.

HIStory or OUR Story   **Chapter 11**

As soon as King failed in Birmingham, Negroes took to the streets. King got out and went out to California to a big rally and raised about — I don't know how many thousands of dollars. He come to Detroit and had a march and raised some more thousands of dollars. And recall, right after that [Roy] Wilkins attacked King, accused King and the CORE (Congress Of Racial Equality) of starting trouble everywhere and then making the NAACP (National Association for the Advancement of Colored People) get them out of jail and spend a lot of money; and then they accused King and CORE of raising all the money and not paying it back. This happened; I've got it in documented evidence in the newspaper. Roy started attacking King, and King started attacking Roy, and Farmer started attacking both of them. And as these Negroes of national stature began to attack each other, they began to lose their control of the Negro masses. And Negroes were out there in the streets. They were talking about how we were going to march on Washington. By the way, right at that time Birmingham had exploded, and the Negroes in Birmingham — remember, they also exploded. They began to stab the crackers in the back and bust them up 'side their head — yes, they did. That's when Kennedy sent in the troops, down in Birmingham. So, and right after that, Kennedy got on the television and said "this is a moral issue." That's when he said he was going to put out a civil-rights bill. And when he mentioned civil-rights bill and the Southern crackers started talking about how they were going to boycott or filibuster it, then the Negroes started talking — about what? We're going to march on Washington, march on the Senate, march on the White House, march on the Congress, and tie it up, bring it to a halt; don't let the government proceed. They even said they was going out to the airport and lay down on the runway and don't let no airplanes land. I'm telling you what they said. That was revolution. That was revolution. That was the black revolution.

It was the grass roots out there in the street. It scared the white man to death, scared the white power structure in Washington, D. C. to death; I was there. When they found out that this black steamroller was going to come down on the capital, they called in Wilkins; they called in Randolph; they called in these national Negro leaders that you respect and told them, "Call it off." Kennedy said, "Look, you all letting this thing go too far." And Old Tom said, "Boss, I can't stop it, because I didn't start it." I'm telling you what they said. They said, "I'm not even in it, much less at the head of it." They said, "These Negroes are doing things on their own. They're running ahead of us." And that old shrewd fox, he said, "Well If you all aren't in it, I'll put you in it. I'll put you at the head of it. I'll endorse it. I'll welcome it. I'll help it. I'll join it."

A matter of hours went by. They had a meeting at the Carlyle Hotel in New York City. The Carlyle Hotel is owned by the Kennedy family; that's the hotel Kennedy spent the night at, two nights ago; it belongs to his family.

HIStory or OUR Story   Chapter 11

A philanthropic society headed by a white man named Stephen Currier called all the top civil-rights leaders together at the Carlyle Hotel. And he told them that, "By you all fighting each other, you are destroying the civil-rights movement. And since you're fighting over money from white liberals, let us set up what is known as the Council for United Civil Rights Leadership. Let's form this council, and all the civil-rights organizations will belong to it, and we'll use it for fund-raising purposes." Let me show you how tricky the white man is. And as soon as they got it formed, they elected Whitney Young as the chairman, and who [do] you think became the co-chairman? Stephen Currier, the white man, a millionaire. Powell was talking about it down at the Cobo Hall today. This is what he was talking about. Powell knows it happened. Randolph knows it happened. Wilkins knows it happened. King knows it happened. Everyone of that so-called Big Six — they know what happened.

Once they formed it, with the white man over it, he promised them and gave them $800,000 to split up between the Big Six; and told them that after the march was over they'd give them $700,000 more. A million and a half dollars — split up between leaders that you've been following, going to jail for, crying crocodile tears for. And they're nothing but Frank James and Jesse James and the what-do-you-call-'em brothers.
As soon as they got the setup organized, the white man made available to them top public relations experts; opened the news media across the country at their disposal; and then they begin to project these Big Six as the leaders of the march. Originally, they weren't even in the march. You was talking this march talk on Hastings Street — Is Hastings Street still here? — on Hastings Street. You was talking the march talk on Lenox Avenue, and out on — What you call it? — Fillmore Street, and Central Avenue, and 32nd Street and 63rd Street.

That's where the march talk was being talked. But the white man put the Big Six [at the] head of it; made them the march. They became the march. They took it over. And the first move they made after they took it over, they invited Walter Reuther, a white man; they invited a priest, a rabbi, and an old white preacher. Yes, an old white preacher. The same white element that put Kennedy in power — labor, the Catholics, the Jews, and liberal Protestants; the same clique that put Kennedy in power, joined the march on Washington.

HIStory or OUR Story   Chapter 11

It's just like when you've got some coffee that's too black, which means it's too strong. What you do? You integrate it with cream; you make it weak. If you pour too much cream in, you won't even know you ever had coffee. It used to be hot, it becomes cool. It used to be strong, it becomes weak. It used to wake you up, now it'll put you to sleep. This is what they did with the march on Washington. They joined it. They didn't integrate it; they infiltrated it. They joined it, became a part of it, took it over. And as they took it over, it lost its militancy. They ceased to be angry. They ceased to be hot. They ceased to be uncompromising. Why, it even ceased to be a march. It became a picnic, a circus. Nothing but a circus, with clowns and all. You had one right here in Detroit — I saw it on television — with clowns leading it, white clowns and black clowns. I know you don't like what I'm saying, but I'm going to tell you anyway. 'Cause I can prove what I'm saying. If you think I'm telling you wrong, you bring me Martin Luther King and A. Philip Randolph and James Farmer and those other three, and see if they'll deny it over a microphone.

No, it was a sellout. It was a takeover. When James Baldwin came in from Paris, they wouldn't let him talk, 'cause they couldn't make him go by the script. Burt Lancaster read the speech that Baldwin was supposed to make; they wouldn't let Baldwin get up there, 'cause they know Baldwin's liable to say anything. They controlled it so tight — they told those Negroes what time to hit town, how to come, where to stop, what signs to carry, what song to sing, what speech they could make, and what speech they couldn't make; and then told them to get out town by sundown. And everyone of those Toms was out of town by sundown. Now I know you don't like my saying this. But I can back it up. It was a circus, a performance that beat anything Hollywood could ever do, the performance of the year. Reuther and those other three devils should get a Academy Award for the best actors 'cause they acted like they really loved Negroes and fooled a whole lot of Negroes. And the six Negro leaders should get an award too, for the best supporting cast"

"Message to The Grassroots" speech by Malcolm X, delivered November 10, 1963

HIStory or OUR Story   **Chapter 11**

It might come as a surprise to most people that sagging dates back centuries; not just within the past decade or so. But at that time, sagging was not a fashion statement! During slavery, slaves were forced to wear oversized clothing to discourage escapes. By the pants being three sizes too big, it made it harder for slaves to run. It was believed that escape attempts would be prevented or minimized if the slaves couldn't run.

Sagging has since gone from physical captivity to mental enslavement! If we took time to educate our young men that slaves were deprived of the well-fitting pants that we take for granted today, they might start to take more pride in their appearance and want to pull their pants up!

Today's sagging is a symptom of incarceration. Although there is some truth to the age-old rumor of sagging being a 'sexual signal' in prison, it is still a symptom of a greater problem. Before prison jumpsuits, inmates were issued uniforms based on what was available and in many cases, those uniforms were oversized. Prisoners also weren't issued belts as a deterrent for murder and suicide.

Gang bangers continued to 'sag' their pants after being released from prison to signify that they had 'done time'. Over time, rappers glorified the 'gang' look and the sagging fad was born.
Some young men don't even know the sexual signals they're sending to men who are attracted to saggers, which is much more widespread than many of us think! Your son probably doesn't even realize that he's the silent focus of lustful eyes as he walks down the street with his jeans sagging.

On the other hand, there are young men who actually do realize the sexual implications of wearing the sagging style.

HIStory or OUR Story   Chapter 12

KNOW THY ENEMY

The 8 rules of wars

1. The first rule of war is to know your enemy
2. The second rule of war is that everyone is your enemy until proven otherwise
3. The third rule of war is never trust your enemy
4. The fourth rule of war is to keep your enemy in front of you at all times
5. The fifth rule of war is to never give audience to your enemy
6. The sixth rule of war is to remember that all friends have the ability to one day become your enemy
7. The seventh rule of war is if they are not your friend, then they are your enemy
8. Before you can defeat the enemy without you must defeat the enemy within

I know there are some of you out there who are still brainwashed by this American society and you don't believe that the European 'white man' is your enemy. Well, let's examine this. First off, I am not saying that *every* Euro-white person is your enemy, but I am saying that the vast majority of them are indeed your enemies. They are your historical enemy. They have been so for a long time, and that has not changed. First, let's revisit the definition of the word enemy.

Enemy: people who dislike you, hold you back, do not have your best interest in mind, people who <u>hate</u> you (**Leviticus 26:17**)

- 1619 On Wednesday August 20, 1619 Dutch Ship called "Jesus" lands in Jamestown, Virginia, carrying the first enslaved people to what would become the United States

- 1630 Virginia Assembly sentences Hugh Davis, a white man, to be "soundly whipped" before an assembly of black people for engaging in a relationship with a black woman

- 1667 Virginia Assembly enacts a law declaring that enslaved Africans who convert to Christianity will not be freed from bondage

- 1740 South Carolina enacts Negro Act of 1740, allowing masters to whip and kill slaves who violate the law by growing their own food, learning to read, assembling in groups, or earning money

- 1796 President George Washington offers $10.00 reward for return of Oney Judge, an enslaved black woman who fled after learning that Mrs. Washington planned to give her away as a wedding gift

- 1804 Virginia legislature passes law outlawing all night-time meetings of enslaved people; such unlawful assemblies are made punishable by up to 20 lashes

- 1804 New Jersey passes gradual Emancipation act, becoming the last Northern state to abolish slavery

- 1807 Congress bans import of slaves, effective January 1, 1808, but establishes no punishment for Africans illegally smuggled into the country after enactment of the ban

- 1811 Largest slave insurrection in U.S. history begins in Louisiana territory; after their defeat, many of the 500 rebelling slaves are mutilated, decapitated, and burned alive

- 1822 Denmark Vesey, a free black man in South Carolina, is accused of planning a large slave insurrection and later hanged along with over 30 alleged co-conspirators

- 1829 Cincinnati, Ohio, paper prints notice that law requires black residents to post $500 bond signed by two white men, leading to mob violence that drives out over half of the city's black population

- 1831 Choctaw people begin "Trail of Tears," a forced march from Mississippi to Oklahoma, during which nearly a third of the Choctaw nation perishes

- 1831 Nat Turner, the black leader of an anti-slavery revolt, is hanged in Jerusalem, Virginia

- 1834 Alabama legislature passes law that effectively bans any freed black person from residing in the state

HIStory or OUR Story   **Chapter 12**

- 1842 Maryland law provides for punishment of up to 20 years in prison for any African American found with an anti-slavery publication in his or her possession

- 1844 After slavery is declared illegal in Oregon, the state passes its first laws prohibiting black people from living there and authorizing whipping of black people found living in Oregon

- 1847 Missouri outlaws education of black people in the state and bans immigration of free black people into the state

- 1851 Southern physician Samuel Cartwright claims discovery of "Drapetomania," a disease that makes African Americans want to run from slavery, and prescribes whipping and amputation as treatment

- 1855 Celia, a 19-year-old enslaved black woman whose middle-aged white "owner" repeatedly raped her since she was only 14, kills him during an attempted rape and is later convicted and hanged

- 1857 U.S. Supreme Court in Dred Scott v. Sandford rules that people of African descent cannot be U.S. citizens, and are not protected by the Constitution, and have no standing to sue in federal courts

- 1863 In the midst of the Civil War, Confederate Congress declares black Union soldiers criminals and authorizes their enslavement or execution

- 1863 President Abraham Lincoln signs Emancipation Proclamation abolishing slavery in Confederate states but not in non-rebelling slave states (Delaware, Maryland, Kentucky)

- 1865 Kentucky refuses to ratify Thirteenth Amendment abolishing slavery; but finally does so in 1976

- 1865 Mississippi requires local sheriffs to round up black orphans and sell them to whites as laborers

- 1865 Mississippi makes it a crime punishable by fines and imprisonment for free black adults to be unemployed or to assemble, and for whites to associate with free blacks

- 1865 South Carolina passes law that requires black "servants" to enter into labor contracts with white "masters", to work from dawn to dusk, and to maintain a "polite" demeanor

- 1866 White mob attacks blacks and Radical Republicans at a convention for black voting rights in New Orleans, Louisiana, killing more than 40 people and wounding hundreds

- 1866 Texas passes law providing that black people cannot testify in court unless the defendant is black or the crime charged was committed against a black person

- 1869 White mob kidnaps and whips black Georgia legislator Abram Colby for promoting equal rights for African Americans

- 1871 President Ulysses Grant declares martial law in South Carolina due to widespread Ku Klux Klan violence

- 1875 Tennessee passes laws authorizing racial discrimination in hotels, public transportation, and amusement parks

- 1883 U.S. Supreme Court in U.S. v. Harris refuses to permit Congress to criminalize acts of the terrorist group, the Ku Klux Klan

- 1883 In Pace v. Alabama, U.S. Supreme Court upholds constitutionality of criminalizing sex and marriage between black and white people after interracial couple is sentenced to two years in prison

- 1890 Benjamin Tillman, a white supremacist who advocated violence against black voters and opposed education for African Americans, is elected governor of South Carolina

- 1896 Mob of 20 sets fire to Jefferson Parish, Louisiana, home of Patrick (white) and Charlotte (black) Morris, who are burned to death; their son, Patrick Morris Jr., escapes with his life

- 1900 Harvard professor Albert Bushnell Hart tells American Historical Association of Detroit, Michigan, that states where lynchings are prevalent should legalize lynching to maintain order

HIStory or OUR Story   **Chapter 12**

- 1901 After having rejected it in 1865, Delaware ratifies Thirteenth Amendment, which abolishes slavery

- 1901 White woman and black man are arrested in Atlanta for walking and talking together on the street

- 1902 A 14 year old black boy is buried alive for allegedly blowing a kiss at a white girl

- 1908 After failed lynching attempt, crowd of more than 5000 whites storms black neighborhoods, burns black businesses and homes, and kills black citizens in Springfield, Illinois, riots

- 1909 Colored Alabamian reports that an African American wagon driver in Montgomery, Alabama, was shot dead because he did not "drive as far to the right as white man thought he should"

- 1910 African American boxer Jack Johnson defeats "Great White Hope" James Jeffries in what is called the fight of the century; Johnson is later persecuted by government officials

- 1913 President Woodrow Wilson's cabinet begins government-wide segregation of workplaces, rest-rooms, and lunchrooms

- 1915 Alabama legislature bars white female nurses from treating black male patients

- 1917 Four days of attacks on African Americans in East St. Louis, Illinois, leaves 200 dead and cause 6,000 black residents to flee the city

- 1919 White mob massacres over 100 black people in Elaine, Arkansas, after black sharecroppers organize to demand fair prices for their products

- 1919 An African American teenager drowns in Lake Michigan after being stoned by whites because he drifted into unofficial "white" section of the water

- 1919 Chicago, Illinois, race riot ends, leaving 38 dead, 537 injured, and 1000 black people homeless

- 1920 Three black circus workers are accused of raping a white woman and lynched by a mob of 10,000 in Duluth, Minnesota

- 1921 Up to 300 people are dead after whites attack prosperous black community in Tulsa, Oklahoma, and burn it to the ground during two days of rioting

- 1922 Harvard University President Albert Lowell defends ban of black student from residence halls and dining rooms, saying "we do not owe to them inclusion in a social setting with white people"

- 1923 After a white woman falsely accuses a black man of rape, a white mob attacks the thriving black town of Rosewood, Florida, in a multi-day riot that destroys the town and leaves up to 80 dead

- 1923 Bullet-riddled body of black farmhand Ben Hart found in Jacksonville, Florida, after he was accused of peeping into a white woman's room

- 1939 Lloyd Gaines, a black man, disappears months after U.S. Supreme Court orders him admitted to University of Missouri School of Law; family suspects he was murdered

- 1940 Jesse Thornton, a black man in Luverne, Alabama, is lynched for referring to a white police officer by his name, without using "Mr."

- 1942 White mob abducts Cleo Wright, accused of assaulting a white woman in Sikeston, Missouri, from jail as church lets out, drags him behind a car, and sets him on fire in front of two black churches

- 1942 Mob of more than 1,000 white people riot outside Detroit public housing project to prevent black families from moving in

- 1943 White workers at Packard Motor Company in Detroit, Michigan, strike to protest promotion of black workers

HIStory or OUR Story   Chapter 12

- 1944 Reverend Isaac Simmons, a black man, is buried three days after he is murdered by six white men who wanted to steal his family's land in Mississippi; his family is threatened and flees the county in fear

- 1944 George Sidney, a 90-pound, black, 14-year-old boy, is electrocuted in South Carolina after being wrongly convicted of rape and murder, becoming the youngest person electrocuted in 20th-century America

- 1944 In Philadelphia Pennsylvania, 6000 white transit employees strike after eight black men begin training to become motormen on street cars, a job that had been reserved for white men only

- 1944 William James Howard, a black 15-year old, is lynched by three white men in Swan County, Florida, after one of the men accuses Howard of writing a love note to his daughter

- 1945 White House Correspondents' Association denies access to President Franklin Roosevelt's funeral for a black reporter to whom Roosevelt had issued credentials despite the association's "whites-only" policy

- 1946 Navy veteran Davis Knight marries a white woman in Eligible, Mississippi, and is later sentenced to five years in prison for miscegenation based on testimony that his great-grandmother was black

- 1946 All-white jury in Holmes County, Mississippi, takes ten minutes to acquit three white men of lynching Leon McAtee, a black man they flogged for allegedly stealing a saddle

- 1947 Civil rights activist Bayard Rustin is arrested for sitting with a white man on a public bus in Chapel Hill, North Carolina, and spends 22 days on a prison chain gang

- 1947 Mob of white men brutally beats Willie Earle, slashing chunks of flesh from his body before blasting him with a shotgun, in Greenville, South Carolina; 28 men charged with the murder are later acquitted

- 1955 Rosa Parks is arrested for refusing to give up her seat to a white passenger on a city bus in Montgomery, Alabama

- 1955 Black WWI veteran Lamar Smith is shot and killed in front of the Brookhaven, Mississippi, courthouse for urging blacks to vote; no one is arrested or charged despite numerous witnesses

- 1955 Roy Bryant and J.W. Milam, white members of the Ku Klux Klan, abduct 14-year-old Emmett Till from his great-uncle's cabin in Mississippi and murder him

- 1955 White male jurors acquit Roy Bryant and J.W. Milam in Emmett Till's murder and later explain they knew the men were guilty but felt life imprisonment or death was too harsh for killing a black boy

- 1955 In Belzoni, Mississippi, NAACP member Rev. George Lee is fatally shot after angering local whites when he attempted to register to vote

- 1956 Montgomery County grand jury indicts more than 85 bus boycott leaders and charges them with violating a statute barring boycotts without just cause

- 1956 Four white men rape Annette Butler, a black 16-year-old, in Tylertown, Mississippi and are never charged

- 1956 After enrollment of black high school students in Mansfield, Texas, triggers rioting, Governor Allan Shivers calls in the Texas Rangers to prevent school desegregation

- 1956 Civil rights leader Rev. Fred Shuttlesworth survives bombing of his Birmingham, Alabama, home by the Ku Klux Klan, the first of five attempts on his life over the next seven years

- 1956 Rosa Jordan, a pregnant African American resident of Montgomery, Alabama, is shot in both legs while riding a desegregated bus

- 1956 After paying $4,000 for their story, Look magazine publishes confession of two white men acquitted of killing 14-year old Emmett Till in 1955, they never faced prosecution

HIStory or OUR Story Chapter 12

- 1956 African American singer Nat King Cole is attacked on stage by four white men while performing for an all-white audience in Birmingham, Alabama

- 1957 Ku Klux Klan members force Willie Edward Jr., a black resident of Montgomery, Alabama, to jump to his death from a bridge over the Alabama River; they never faced prosecution for his murder

- 1957 In Montgomery, Alabama, the congregations of four black churches gather for Sunday services three days after their churches and two homes were bombed

- 1958 Citizens of Little Rock, Arkansas, vote to close public schools rather than integrate; schools remain closed for one year

- 1958 After refusing to accept black lawyers as members, District of Columbia Bar Association votes to change policy

- 1959 Richard and Mildred Loving plead guilty to violating Virginia law against interracial marriage and receive one-year sentences in prison unless they leave the state for 25 years

- 1960 Escorted by U.S. Marshals, six-year-old Ruby Bridges integrated William Frantz Elementary School in New Orleans, Louisiana, as mobs protest outside

- 1961 Mobs of white students riot, forcing school officials to suspend Charlayne Hunter and Hamilton Holmes after they become the first black students to integrate the University of Georgia

- 1961 Freedom Rider John Lewis, future U.S. Congressman from Georgia, is assaulted for attempting to enter white waiting room at Greyhound bus terminal in rock Hill, South Carolina

- 1961 Freedom Riders arrive in Montgomery, Alabama, where local police allow mob of angry whites to attack; several people are severely injured, including a U.S. Justice Department representative

- 1961 Ten Interfaith Riders go on trial after being arrested for seeking service at segregated airport restaurant in Tallahassee, Florida, and face $500 fine or 30 days in jail

- 1961 White mob sets fire to bus carrying Freedom Riders, an interracial group challenging segregation, near Anniston, Alabama, and attacks riders with clubs, bricks, iron pipes, and knives

- 1962 President John F. Kennedy orders an end to racial discrimination in federally financed housing

- 1963 More than 700 black children protesting racial segregation in Birmingham, Alabama, are arrested, blasted by fire hoses, clubbed by police, and attacked by police dogs

- 1963 Four young black girls attending Sunday school are killed when a bomb explodes at the 16th Street Baptist Church, a popular location for civil rights meetings in Birmingham, Alabama

- 1965 Dr. Martin Luther King Jr. and more than 200 others are arrested and jailed after a voting rights march in Selma, Alabama

- 1966 Vernon Dahmer, black businessmen and voting rights activist, dies after his Hattiesburg, Mississippi, home is fire-bombed

- 1968 Dr. Martin Luther King Jr. is assassinated in Memphis, Tennessee, on the balcony of the Lorraine Motel

- 1972 Washington Star reports on Tuskegee Syphilis Experiment in which U.S. Centers for Disease Control and Prevention studied the disease's effect on hundreds of poor black Alabama sharecroppers even after the cure was discovered

- 1973 Two young black girls, Minnie (14) and Mary Alice Relf (12), sue Montgomery, Alabama, health clinic for sterilizing them without their knowledge or consent

- 1981 After a Mobile, Alabama, jury acquits a black man of killing a white police officer, Ku Klux Klan members randomly kidnap and kill 19-year old Michael Donald, a black man, and hang his body from a tree

HIStory or OUR Story   **Chapter 12**

- 1986 Michael Griffith, a 23-year old black man, is hit by a car and killed after being chased onto a highway by a white mob in Howard, Beach, New York

- 1989 Yusef Hawkins, a 16-year-old black boy, is murdered in Bensonhurst, New York, by a mob of 30 whites who wrongly believe he is visiting a white girl in their neighborhood

- 1991 Severe beating of Rodney King, a black man, by Los Angeles police officers during a traffic stop is caught on tape; the officers are acquitted of criminal charges

- 1994 Denny's restaurant chain agrees to pay largest-ever settlement to African Americans who sued after being refused service, made to wait longer, or charged more than white customers

- 1994 U.S. Department of Justice files suit against Randolph County, Alabama, school principal who refuses to permit racially integrated prom

- 2005 U.S. Congress formally apologizes for failure to pass any of the 200 anti-lynching bills introduced from 1882 to 1968

- 2007 Turner County High School in Ashburn, Georgia, holds its first racially integrated prom; in prior years, parents had organized private, segregated proms for white and black students

- 2009 Justice of the peace in Louisiana refuses to marry an interracial couple because of their race and later acknowledges he denied marriage licenses to interracial couples for years

- 2010 Police officer Johannes Mehserle is sentenced to two years for fatally shooting black 22-year-old Oscar Grant III in the back while he was face down on an Oakland, California, train platform

- 2012 U.S. Department of Justice files civil rights law-suit against Meridian, Mississippi, officials for incarcerating black children for dress code violations and talking back to teachers

- 2012 Trayvon Benjamin Martin, an unarmed 17-year old African American, was fatally shot in Sanford, Florida by George Zimmerman, a neighborhood watch volunteer. George Zimmerman was never charged.

- 2012 Jordan Davis, an unarmed 17-year old African American male, was fatally shot in Jacksonville, Florida for playing loud music with his friends. Michael Dunn, a white man, was later convicted of first-degree murder and sentenced to life in prison

HIStory or OUR Story   **Chapter 12**

- 2014 Mike Brown, an unarmed 18 year old black man, was fatally shot by a Ferguson Missouri police officer Darren Wilson. The police officer was never indicted.

- 2014 Eric Garner died in Staten Island, New York, after a police officer put him in a chokehold. The New York City Medical Examiner's Office concluded that Garner died partly as a result of the chokehold. New York City Police Department policy prohibits the use of chokeholds. Mr. Garner repeated multiple times "I can't breathe, I can't breathe", but the police officer Panteleo did not let go. Officer Panteleo was never charged.

- **2015 a black male Otis Bird, was found hanging from a tree in Mississippi**

HIStory or OUR Story   **Chapter 12**

President Barack Obama and First Lady Michelle Obama are extremely accomplished Ivy League trained individuals. They represent the best of the black family and, yet and still, their treatment has been nothing short of inflammatory and down right disrespectful. If these wicked people cannot respect us when we reach the highest office in the land, what makes you think they have an iota of respect for you, if you shine?

As Christ said in **Luke 21:23** "If they do these things to the green tree, what will they do to the dry?" In the above sentence, Christ was the green tree and the women of Yahrushalom was the dry. President Barack Obama and Michelle Obama are the green tree of our day, and we are the dry.

HIStory or OUR Story   Chapter 12

Abraham Lincoln said, "**I will say, then, that I am not, nor ever have been, in favor of bringing about in any way the social and political equality of the white and black races**—that **I am not, nor ever have been, in favor of making voters or jurors of Negroes, nor of qualifying them to hold office, nor to intermarry with white people;** and I will say in addition to this, that **there is a physical difference between the white and black races** which I believe will forever forbid the two races living together on terms of social and political equality. And inasmuch as they cannot so live, while they do remain together there must be the position of **superior** and **inferior**, and **I**, as much as any other man, **am in favor of having the superior position assigned to the white race.**"

- **Henry Barry** <u>a member of the Virginia House of Delegates</u>, who said on January 20, 1832, 183 years ago

"Pass as severe laws as you will to keep these **unfortunate creatures in ignorance**. It is in vain unless you can **extinguish that spark of intellect which God has given them**. Sir, we have as far as possible **closed every avenue by which light may enter their minds**. We only have to go one step further to **extinguish their capacity to see the light** and our work will be completed. And **they would then be reduced to the level of the beasts of the field** and **we should be safe. Sir, a death struggle must come between the two classes or races in which one or the other will be extinguished forever**."

- It has been well documented that during slavery and into the 20th Century, **black babies were used as alligator bait** in North and Central Florida.
  The black slaves would have their young babies stolen during the course of the day, during times when their mothers weren't watching. Some would be infants, some would be **a year old and some would be toddlers**. Slavemasters would grab these **children** and take them down to the swamp and leave them in pens, little chicken coops. They would go down there at night, take these **babies and tie them up**, put a **rope around their neck** and around their torso, and around head, tie it tight. They would throw the babies in, tied to this rope and in a matter of minutes the alligators were on them. The alligator would **clamp his jaws on that child**. As a matter of fact, once clamped, the alligator swallowed. There would be nothing left but the rope! Again, some would be infants, some would be a year old, and others would be toddlers.

During slavery, if they didn't give us good **education**, good **housing**, good **food** or good **clothes**, have you ever asked: Why did they give us such 'good religion'?" Thus we are deceived. **Deuteronomy 33:29** "Happy are you, O **Yahsrael**: who is like to you, O people saved by Yahuah, the shield of your help, and who is the sword of your Excellency! And **your enemies** shall be found **liars to you** and you shall trample down their high places."

Why do you think the black Hamites, the Africans, have never fought for us Shemites/black Hebrews? They never said "Return them?" They never told us where we came from, or told us any African country was the land of our origin! The reason is because we are not from them. The **Africans** were and are our **enemies,** just as the **Arabs** and **Europeans**. All of them have tried to hide the truth from us.

HIStory or OUR Story   Chapter 12

Willie Lynch Letter

This speech was said to have been delivered by **Willie Lynch** on the bank of the James River in the colony of Virginia in 1712. Lynch was a British slave owner in the West Indies. He was invited to the colony of Virginia in 1712 to teach his methods to slave owners there.

Greetings,

Gentlemen. I greet you here on the bank of the James River in the year of our Lord one thousand seven hundred and twelve. First, I shall thank you, the gentlemen of the Colony of Virginia, for bringing me here. I am here to help you solve some of your problems with slaves. Your invitation reached me on my modest plantation in the West Indies, where I have experimented with some of the newest, and still the oldest methods for control of slaves. Ancient Rome would envy us if my program is implemented. As our boat sailed south on the James River, named for our illustrious King, whose version of the Bible we cherish, I saw enough to know that your problem is not unique. While Rome used cords of wood as crosses for standing human bodies along its highways in great numbers, you are here using the tree and the rope on occasions. I caught the whiff of a dead slave hanging from a tree, a couple miles back. You are not only losing valuable stock by hangings, you are having uprisings, slaves are running away, your crops are sometimes left in the fields too long for maximum profit , you suffer occasional fires, your animals are killed. Gentlemen, you know what your problems are; I do not need to elaborate. I am not here to enumerate your problems, I am here to introduce you to a method of solving them. In my bag here, **I HAVE A FULL PROOF METHOD FOR CONTROLLING YOUR BLACK SLAVES**. I guarantee every one of you that, if installed correctly, **IT WILL CONTROL THE SLAVES FOR AT LEAST 300 HUNDRED YEARS**. My method is simple. Any member of your family or your overseer can use it. **I HAVE OUTLINED A NUMBER OF DIFFERENCES AMONG THE SLAVES; AND I TAKE THESE DIFFERENCES AND MAKE THEM BIGGER. I USE FEAR, DISTRUST AND ENVY FOR CONTROL PURPOSES**. These methods have worked on my modest plantation in the West Indies and it will work throughout the South. Take this simple little list of differences and think about them. On top of my list is "AGE," but it's there only because it starts with an "A". The second is "COLOR" or shade. There is **INTELLIGENCE, SIZE, SEX, SIZES OF PLANTATIONS, STATUS** on plantations, **ATTITUDE** of owners, whether the slaves live in the valley, on a hill, East, West, North, South, have fine hair, course hair, or is tall or short. Now that you have a list of differences, I shall give you an outline of action, but before that, I shall assure you that **DISTRUST IS STRONGER THAN TRUST AND ENVY STRONGER THAN ADULATION, RESPECT OR ADMIRATION**. The Black slaves after receiving this indoctrination shall carry on and will become self-refueling and self-generating for **HUNDREDS** of years, maybe **THOUSANDS**. Don't forget, you must pitch the **OLD** black male vs. the **YOUNG** black male, and the **YOUNG** black male against the **OLD** black male.

You must use the **DARK** skin slaves vs. the **LIGHT** skin slaves, and the **LIGHT** skin slaves vs. the **DARK** skin slaves. You must use the **FEMALE** vs. the **MALE**, and the **MALE** vs. the **FEMALE**. You must also have white servants and overseers [who] distrust all Blacks. But it is **NECESSARY THAT YOUR SLAVES TRUST AND DEPEND ON US. THEY MUST LOVE, RESPECT AND TRUST ONLY US**. Gentlemen, these kits are your keys to control. Use them. Have your wives and children use them, never miss an opportunity. **IF USED INTENSELY FOR ONE YEAR, THE SLAVES THEMSELVES WILL REMAIN PERPETUALLY DISTRUSTFUL**. Thank you gentlemen."

LET'S MAKE A SLAVE

It was the interest and business of slave holders to study human nature, and the slave nature in particular, with an emphasis on practical results...They had to deal not with earth, wood and stone, but with men and, by every regard, they had for their own safety and prosperity, they needed to know the material on which they were to work, conscious of the injustice and wrong they were perpetuating every hour, and knowing what they themselves would do. Were they the victims of such wrongs? They were constantly looking for the first signs of the dreaded retribution. They watched therefore with skilled and practiced eyes, and learned to read with great accuracy, the state of mind and heart of the slave, through his sable face. Unusual sobriety, apparent abstractions, sullenness and indifference indeed, any mood out of the common was ground for suspicion and inquiry. Frederick Douglas' LET'S MAKE A SLAVE is a study of the scientific process of man-breaking and slave-making. It describes the rationale and results of the Anglo Saxons' ideas and methods of ensuring the master/slave relationship. **LET'S MAKE A SLAVE:** "The Original Development of a Social Being Called **'The Negro.'**" Let us make a slave. What do we need? First of all, we need a black nigger man, a pregnant nigger woman and her baby nigger boy. Second, we will use the same basic principle that we use in breaking a horse, combined with some more sustaining factors. What we do with horses is: we break them from one form of life to another; that is, we reduce them from their natural state in nature. Whereas nature provides them with the natural capacity to take care of their offspring, we break that natural string of independence from them and thereby create a dependency status so that we may be able to get from them useful production for our business and pleasure.

CARDINAL PRINCIPLES FOR MAKING A NEGRO

For fear that our future generations may not understand the principles of breaking both of the beast together, the nigger and the horse. We understand that short range planning economics results in periodic economic chaos; so to avoid turmoil in the economy, it requires us to have breadth and depth in long range comprehensive planning, articulating both skill and sharp perceptions. We lay down the following principles for long range comprehensive economic planning. Both horse and niggers [are] no good to the economy in the wild or natural state. Both must be **BROKEN** and **TIED** together for orderly production. For an orderly future, special and particular attention must be paid to the **FEMALE** and the **YOUNGEST** offspring.

Both must be **CROSSBRED** to produce a variety and division of labor. Both must be taught to respond to a peculiar new **LANGUAGE**. Psychological and physical instruction of **CONTAINMENT** must be created for both. We hold the six cardinal principles as truth to be self-evident, based upon following the discourse concerning the economics of breaking and tying the horse and the nigger together, all inclusive of the six principles laid down above. NOTE: Neither principle alone will suffice for good economics. All principles must be employed for the orderly good of the nation. Accordingly, both a wild horse and a wild or natural nigger is dangerous even if captured. For they will have the tendency to seek their customary freedom, and in doing so, might kill you in your sleep. You cannot rest. They sleep while you are awake, and are awake while you are asleep. They are **DANGEROUS** near the family house and it requires too much labor to watch them away from the house. Above all, you cannot get them to work in this natural state. Hence, both the horse and the nigger must be broken; that is breaking them from one form of mental life to another. **KEEP THE BODY, TAKE THE MIND!** In other words, break the will to resist. Now the breaking process is the same for both the horse and the nigger, only slightly varying in degrees. But, as we said before, there is an art in long range economic planning. **YOU MUST KEEP YOUR EYE AND THOUGHTS ON THE FEMALE and the OFFSPRING** of the horse and the nigger. A brief discourse in offspring development will shed light on the key to sound economic principles. Pay little attention to the generation of original breaking, but **CONCENTRATE ON FUTURE GENERATION**. Therefore, if you break the **FEMALE** mother, she will **BREAK** the offspring in its early years of development; and when the offspring is old enough to work, she will deliver it up to you, for her normal female protective tendencies will have been lost in the original breaking process.

For example, take the case of the wild stud horse, a female horse and an already infant horse and compare the breaking process with two captured nigger males in their natural state, and a pregnant nigger woman with her infant offspring. Take the stud horse, break him for limited containment. Completely break the female horse until she becomes very gentle, whereas you or anybody can ride her in her comfort. Breed the mare and the stud until you have the desired offspring. Then, you can turn the stud to freedom until you need him again. Train the female horse whereby she will eat out of your hand, and she will in turn train the infant horse to eat out of your hand also. When it comes to breaking the uncivilized nigger, use the same process, but vary the degree and step up the pressure, so as to do a complete reversal of the mind. Take the meanest and most restless nigger, strip him of his clothes in front of the remaining male niggers, the female, and the nigger infant, tar and feather him, tie each leg to a different horse faced in opposite directions, set him afire and beat both horses to pull him apart in front of the remaining niggers. The next step is to take a bullwhip and beat the remaining nigger males to the point of death, in front of the female and the infant. Don't kill him, but **PUT THE FEAR OF GOD IN HIM**, for he can be useful for future breeding.

HIStory or OUR Story   Chapter 12

Dr. MARTIN LUTHER KING'S "Burning House Speech"

Dr. Martin Luther King Jr.'s last speech echoed in my head as I watched the Ferguson aftermath put the country in a tailspin:

"I've come upon something that **disturbs me deeply**. We have fought hard and long for integration, as I believe we should have, and I know we will win. But I have come to believe that **we are integrating into a burning house**. I'm afraid that America has lost the moral vision she may have had. And I'm afraid that even as we integrate, we are walking into a place that does not understand that this nation needs to be deeply concerned with the plight of the poor and disenfranchised. Until we commit ourselves to ensuring that the underclass is given justice and opportunity, we will perpetuate the anger and violence that tears the soul of this nation. **I fear I am integrating my people into a burning house.**"

HIStory or OUR Story Chapter 12

What is happening today with Dr. Bill Cosby is nothing more than a modern day lynching. In the space of only one month, Cosby went from a well-respected public figure to Public Enemy Number One. None of it would have been possible without the Internet. What we are now seeing right before our eyes is the media lynching of Dr. Bill Cosby. The tree and the rope they are now using today are the Internet and the television. What's worse is nobody is saying anything about it. You know back in the days of physical slavery, they would tie the black man down, beat him, and then lynch him in front of the entire plantation of slaves. Even though the slaves had the power in numbers, the slave masters still did what they wanted because the slaves were mentally weak and afraid. The slaves made excuses to themselves: "He must have done something"; "He must have deserved it"; "If Massa say so, it must be so boss"; If all these good white folks say he raped her ,then he did". These sentiments were entertained, instead of the slaves saying: "He's one of us, no more".

Dr. Bill Cosby has not been to court and the law says that a man is "innocent until proven guilty". Instead the media has decided to put out propaganda suggesting that he is already guilty. What's even worse is that we are just standing around watching it in silence like our ancestors did. We are the ones that have the power. We have the money, and we control the ratings. We make shows, and we can break shows. Don't forget the sit-ins and boycotts of yesteryear. The truth is we have the power to control the media. The media plays off of us. After all that Dr. Cosby has done for us and given to the black community, the least we can do is to take up for his constitutional right to be "innocent unless proven guilty". Dr. Cosby had a new show that was coming out around the time 'Empire' was released. Empire is about homosexuals, murder, infidelity, profanity, deceit, lust, fornication and greed. A show like Empire, we should have boycotted!

As a result of these allegations, they pulled the Cosby show off the air without due process. The Cosby show exemplified hard work, success, integrity, honesty, black love, and positive black images. The show displayed Mr. Huxtable: a Black man in the home; a highly educated doctor; a well-spoken, well-dressed, family man of integrity. The Cosby show showed us Claire Huxtable a lawyer, as well as a mother, and a great wife who did submit herself to her husband in a godly fashion.
 I have heard it said regarding the allegations that, "If Cosby didn't do it, why doesn't he come out and say something and defend himself." Some actually believe that silence is a sign of guilt. I disagree.

Even Christ Himself, when accused of many things did not say a word, but nobody says, "Oh he's guilty because he did not speak up when they falsely accused him.
Read: **Matthew 27:12-14**
12: And when He was accused of the chief priests and elders, **He ANSWERED NOTHING**.
13 Then said Pilate to Him, "Do you not hear **HOW MANY THINGS they WITNESS against You**?"
14 And He answered him **NOT A WORD**: insomuch that the governor was greatly amazed.
And also you'll notice that they sought **false witnesses** against Him. From the beginning they looked for people who would lie.
Read Matthew 26: 59-60
59 The chief priests and the whole Sanhedrin were looking for false evidence against Yahushua so that they could put him to death.
60 But they did not find any, though many false witnesses came forward. Finally two came forward.

HIStory or OUR Story **Chapter 12**

We all know that Judas was paid off, so do not put it past these big media companies that they would not pay off these women to come forward and accuse Dr. Bill Cosby just the same. The scriptures say, "There is nothing new under the sun". **Ecclesiastes 1:9-10**.

Here is a little enlightenment. A lie told a thousand times does make it the truth. Just like **Rosewood and Black Wall Street, Dr. Bill Cosby** is black, prominent, powerful, successful, economically independent, conscious, ambitious, and very intelligent. In all three cases, rape and a white woman were the common denominators used as an excuse to tear down and destroy all of these three powerful entities. Two out of the three, we already know were bogus claims. In Cosby's case, let's use common sense.

The **FYM** (Free Your Mind) website published the following account on November 15, 2014 by a Wilhelmina model who claims that she was offered a total of $15,000 to set up and frame Dr. Bill Cosby:

"**I wasn't going to send this email to FYM,** but, the feeding frenzy on Bill Cosby's character made my response necessary. In 1982, I had a photographer named Choice. Choice was contacted by a casting agent, I was told to meet the client at the Ritz Carlton for lunch in New York in the summer of 82'. This client wanted to talk to me about a film project. I arrived at the Ritz Carlton at 11:30 AM. Two male clients arrived: a Caucasian male (late 30s) and an Asian male (early 50s). They indicated that I'd be perfect for a film project.

HIStory or OUR Story Chapter 12

I was told the project paid $5,000 cash. I thought that was strange, who pays $5,000 cash for a modeling job? The job was to meet Bill Cosby and to try to seduce him; it would be a part of the script. I was confused by this job request. They told me I would be recording the session to see if I was successful and believable. My response to them, "I would like to meet Mr. Cosby first and discuss the script." They said "no, it wasn't necessary to meet him." They said it was "a spontaneous casting call." I have never in my life heard of a "spontaneous casting call".

As a legitimate model, this seemed strange and unethical. I immediately turned down the job. The Asian man continued speaking and offered me $10,000 cash up front and $5,000 upon delivery of some seductive photos and some of his sperm. Sperm? (I was in shock when they said sperm??) I then realized that these two men had unethical intentions. I excused myself, went to the bathroom, and then I left the hotel and went home. Now, as a model in New York, I've been offered drugs, trips around the world, films, videos, money from rich men, and the list is endless.

As a naive model you're offered many compromising projects, but, this blew my mind. I was offered $15,000 to seduce and destroy Bill Cosby. Why else would they need suggestive photos and sperm? I also realized that America has a history of oppressing, killing and destroying successful and poor people of color.

I wasn't going to send this letter to FYM, but, the media lynching of one of our global icons (Bill Cosby), is simply unacceptable. Also after watching Nightline, Associated Press, CNN, CBS, NPR, Fox, and many other news outlets blatantly misconstrue and lie about old dismissed allegations of Bill Cosby, I'm shocked by the lack of integrity of our major news media. Why would CNN, ABC, CBS, Associated Press and the like lie about 30-year-old untrue news?

Nightline simply cut, deleted and distorted the Cosby interview– making him appear guilty. What has happened to the integrity of our nation?

I was offered $15,000 cash to discredit and ruin Bill Cosby's good name. I'm 100% convinced that all the women coming forward have been paid off to discredit Bill Cosby as well. Why? He is simply too powerful, his intentions are to empower people of color and his net worth would anger any weak man."

So in closing what are you going to do? I have exercised my voice in this book, and I speak up for justice for Mr. Bill Cosby whenever I hear anyone speak prematurely against him. So, that's what I do. Ask yourself: In the midst of this media lynching and the bottom dwellers trying to discredit Dr. Bill Cosby, what will you do???

He is being lynched right now in front of your eyes, what will you do?

Remember the power is NOT in the Pulpit, but in the Pew.

The power is not with a favored few, but with the miraculous many. The power is not with the President, but with the people. We are the people, you are the people!

The Rosewood massacre was a racially motivated attack on African Americans and their neighborhood, which was committed by a white mob in Florida during January 1–7, 1923. The town of Rosewood, a majority-black community, was abandoned and destroyed in what contemporary news reports characterized as a race riot (with the implication blacks had broken out in violence). The great majority of victims were black males. Prior to the massacre, the town of Rosewood had been a quiet, primarily black, self-sufficient whistle stop on the Seaboard Air Line Railway. Trouble began when white men from several nearby towns lynched a Rosewood resident because of unsupported accusations that a white woman (Fanny Taylor) in nearby Sumner had been sexually assaulted by a black man in her home. A group of white men, believing this rapist to be a recently escaped convict named Jesse Hunter, who was hiding in Rosewood, assembled to capture this man. When the town's African-American citizens rallied together to defend themselves against further attacks, a mob of several hundred whites formed in reaction and started combing the countryside hunting down black people. They attacked and destroyed the community, burning almost every structure within Rosewood. Survivors from the town hid for several days in nearby swamps until they were evacuated by train and car to larger towns. Although state and local authorities were aware of the violence, no arrests were made for what happened in Rosewood. The town was abandoned by its black residents; none ever returned. No one was ever charged with any of the Rosewood murders.

HIStory or OUR Story Chapter 12

"If the soil of the <u>United States</u> could speak, before one word is spoken, it would cough up <u>blood</u> first."

N
 E
  V
   E
    R

 F
  O
   R
    G
     E
      T
       !

The Recovery Of His People

This is the point in history where we are right now. We have been scattered all over the world today and Yahuah has been pouring out His Spirit upon us waking us up. As it is written in:

Joel 2: 25-32
"So I will **restore to you the years** that the locust has eaten, the cankerworm, and the caterpillar, and the palmerworm
My great army which I sent among you.
You shall eat in plenty and be satisfied,
And praise the name of Yahuah your <u>God</u>,
Who has dealt wondrously with you;
And My people shall never be put to shame.
Then you shall know that I am in the midst of Yahsrael:
I am Yahuah your God
And there is no other.
My people shall never be put to shame.
God's Spirit Poured Out
And it shall come to pass afterward
That I will pour out My Spirit on all flesh;
Your sons and your daughters shall prophesy,
Your old men shall dream dreams,
Your young men shall see visions.
And also on My menservants and on My maidservants
I will pour out My Spirit in those days.
And **I will show wonders in the heavens and in the earth:**
Blood and **fire** and **pillars of smoke.**
The **sun shall be turned into darkness,**
And **the moon into blood,**
<u>Before</u> the coming of the great and awesome day of Yahuah
And it shall come to pass
That whoever calls on the name of Yahuah
Shall be saved
For in Mount Zion and in Yahrushalom there shall be deliverance,
As Yahuah has said,
Among the remnant whom Yahuah calls"

HIStory or OUR Story   **Chapter 13**

It was prophesied early on that the **blessings** and the curses of **Deuteronomy Chapter 28** <u>WOULD BE poured out upon us</u>, but afterward we would remember and return.

Read
Deuteronomy 30: 1-8

"And when all these things come upon you, **the blessing** and **the curse**, which I have set before you, and **you** <u>call them to mind</u> among all the nations where Yahuah your God has driven you,
And return to Yahuah your God, you and your children, and obey His voice in all that I command you today, with all your heart and with all your soul
Then **Yahuah your God will restore your fortunes and have mercy on you**, and He will **gather you again from all the peoples** where <u>Yahuah your God has scattered you</u>.
If **your outcasts** are in the uttermost parts of heaven, **from there** Yahuah your God will gather you, and **from there He will take you.**
And **Yahuah your God will bring you into the land that your fathers possessed,** that you may possess it. And **He will make you more prosperous and numerous than your fathers.**
And Yahuah your God will circumcise your heart and the heart of your offspring, so that you will love Yahuah your God with **all your heart and with all your soul,** that you may live.
And **Yahuah your God will put all these curses on your foes and enemies who persecuted you**. And you shall again obey the voice of Yahuah and keep all His commandments that I command you today."

2Chronicles 7:14
"**If My people which are called by My name** shall humble themselves, and pray, and seek My face, and turn from their wicked ways; then will I hear from heaven and will forgive their sin, and will heal their land."

So now we have to identify His People, and the people called by His name.

Joel 3:2 " I will gather all nations and bring them down to the Valley of <u>Yahoshaphat</u> (Yah's judgement). There I will put them **on trial** for what they did to **My people and for My heritage,** because they scattered **My people** among the nations and **divided up My land**"

The Bible says that those who are sealed for protection before the Most High brings His final plagues on the earth will be the children of Yahsrael

Read Revelation 14:4 "And I heard the number of them which were sealed: and there were sealed a **hundred and forty and four thousand** of <u>all the tribes</u> **of the children of Yahsrael.**

HIStory or OUR Story   **Chapter 13**

Were the other nations of the earth called by Yahuah's name??

Read Isaiah 63: 17-19
"O YAHUAH, why have you made us to error from your ways, and hardened our heart from your fear? Return for Your Servants' sake, **the tribes** of Your inheritance.
The people of Your holiness have possessed it but a little while: **OUR** adversaries have trodden down Your sanctuary. We are Yours: **You <u>NEVER bore rule over them</u>**; they WERE NOT called by Your Name."

Also see scriptures in **Psalms 79** also. So as you can see the nations (the Gentiles) **were not called by His name**, but the children of Yahsrael was.

Read Numbers 6:22-27
"And Yahuah spoke to Musa (Moses) saying "Speak to Aaron and to his sons saying, on this wise you shall bless the **children of Yahsrael**, saying to them, Yahuah bless you and keep you, Yahuah make His face shine upon you, and be gracious to you: Yahuah lift up His countenance upon you, and give you peace. And they shall **put My name upon the children of Yahsrael**; and I will bless them."

So as you can see by the scriptures, it is Yahsrael that Yahuah is referring to in **2 Chronicles 7:14** who are the people **called by His name**.

Right now in this current day and time, we Hebrew Yahsraelites are waking up and coming together. We are becoming conscious and aware of where we are and who we are. We are Yahsrael and we are in **our enemies' lands**, but Yahuah is going to bring us back to our own land. Take note of the prophesies concerning us.

Isaiah 40: 1-2
1   "Comfort you, comfort you My people, says your God.
2   Speak you comfortably to Yahrushalom (Jerusalem), and cry to her, that her hard service is accomplished, that her iniquity is **pardoned**: for she has **received of Yahuah's hand DOUBLE FOR ALL OF HER SINS**."

HIStory or OUR Story   Chapter 13

Malcolm X "Dry Bones Speech" 1963 NY Unity Rally

"**We believe in the truth that is in the Bible.** We do not believe in the lies that the white man has put in the Bible. We believe in the prophets and the scriptures that they wrote to the people. We believe in the resurrection of the dead. Not in the physical resurrection, but in mental resurrection. We believe that the so-called negroes are most in need of a mental resurrection therefore they will be resurrected first. We believe in the resurrection of the dead, but not when you're physically dead. When you stop breathing and your heart stop beating and that man sticks you in the ground that's all she wrote! You are not going anywhere. Your soul isn't going anywhere, your body isn't going anywhere, nothing is happening after that. When you are dead you are done. That's it! You can forget it! **Negroes are dead! Walking zombies! You're the one that the book is talking about who is dead. Dead to the knowledge of yourself, dead to the knowledge of your own people, dead to the knowledge of your own God**. Dead to the knowledge of the devil. You don't even know who the devil is. You think the devil is someone down inside the ground and is going to burn you after you're dead. When the devil is right here on top of this earth, he got blue eyes, blonde hair, white skin, and he's giving you hell every day. You're still too dead to see it. We believe in the resurrection of the dead. **We believe that the 20 million black people in America in the last days will be taught the truth**. The **trumpet of truth** will sound in your ear, as its being sounding today. The trumpet of truth, and as truth strikes your ear, it strikes your heart, it will open your eyes, it will open your ears, it will make you stand up, it will do the same thing for you that truth did for the dry bones in the valley, because **the picture of dry bones in the valley is talking about you**, the picture of Lazarus laying dead four days is talking about you, you are Lazarus, you are the dry bones, you are the prodigal son, **you are the lost sheep**. You are the people about whom the Bible is speaking who will stand up in the last days when the trumpet is sounded. Black people are waking up, black people are standing up, black people are rising up! And are installing fright into that knee-shaking white man. **We believe we are the people of Gods choice**. That's what we believe. We believe **we're the chosen people. We don't believe that the Jews are the chosen people**. We don't believe that Jews are going to the promised land. We don't think the Jews are apart of God; **no Jews are nothing but another part of that same race of devils that come out of Europe. They didn't even come out of the holy land.** They come out of the caves of Europe. A Jew, a Frenchmen, or an Irishmen, okay all of them are the same thing, a race of devils. They got different kinds, Germans, Irish, all of them the same thing. Just like you got a german shepherd, a Irish setter, a French poodle, Chihuahua, but they all dogs. Furthermore, we believe we are the people of God's choice. As it is written that, **"God would choose a rejected and despised"**, and we can find no other persons fitting this description in these last days more than the so-called negroes in America. We believe in the resurrection of the righteous. We believe in the judgment. We believe this first judgement, as God revealed, will take place right here in America. The resurrection will take place in America. The judgment will take place in America. The separation will take place in America. And the destruction will take place in America. Doom will take place in America. Doomsday will take place right here. This is the place the Bible was talking about, when the Bible mentions Babylon it means America. When the Bible mentions Sodom and Gomorrah it means America. When the Bible mentions Egypt it means America. This is Rome, this is Babylon, this is that wicked kingdom that God is going to come and set flame to in the last days and you're living in that day right now. And I'm glad."

-Malcolm X
Unity Rally Speech in Harlem, NY 1963

HIStory or OUR Story   Chapter 13

Ezekiel 37 1-28

1. The hand of Yahuah was upon me, and carried me out in the Spirit of Yahuah, and set me down in the midst of the **valley** (low area/depression/place of gloom and fear) which was full of **bones** (remains of a body)
2. And caused me to pass by them round about: and, behold there were many in the open valley; and, lo, they were very **dry** (thirsty/unproductive/plain)
3. And He said to me, "Son of **man** (a human), can these bones live? And I answered, O Yahuah God, You know.
4. Again He said to me, "Prophesy (foretell/predict/declare by divine inspiration/speak as a mediator between God and man) upon these bones, and say to them, O you dry bones, hear the word of Yahuah
5. Thus says Yahuah God to these bones, Behold, I will cause **breath** (life) to enter into you, and you shall live
6. And I will lay **sinews** (strength/a piece of tough fibrous tissue uniting muscle to bone or bone to bone) upon you, and will bring up flesh upon you, and cover you with skin, and put breath in you and you shall live; and you shall know that I am Yahuah"
7. So I **prophesied** as I was commanded: and as I prophesied, there was a noise, and behold a noise, and behold a shaking, and the bones came together, bone to his bone
8. And when I **beheld** (looked), lo, the sinews and the **flesh** (outer covering of skin) came upon them; and the skin covered them above: but there was no **breath** (life) in them.
9. Then He said to me, "Prophesy to the wind, prophesy son of **man** (a human), Thus says Yahuah God, Come from the **four winds** (four corners of the earth/the whole earth)", O breath, and breathe upon these **slain** (dead/lifeless) that they may live"
10. So I prophesied as He commanded me, and the **breath** (life) came into them, and they lived, and stood up upon their feet, and **exceeding** (extremely) **great army** (military force).
11. Then He said to me, "Son of man, these bones are the **whole** (entire) **house of Yahsrael:** behold, they say, **Our bones** (remains of our body) are **dried** (thirsty/unproductive/plain), and **our hope** (strong desire/goal) is lost: we are cut off from **our parts** (the rest of our family)
12. Therefore prophesy and say to them, Thus says Yahuah God; Behold **O My people**, I will open **your graves** (your enemies lands/deep darkness), and cause you to come up out of your graves, **and bring you into the land of Yahsrael**

13. And you shall know that I am Yahuah, when I have opened your graves, O **My People**, and brought you up out of your <u>graves</u> (your enemies' lands/deep darkness),
14. And shall put My Spirit in you, and you shall live (enjoy life/thrive), and **I shall place you in your own land**: then shall you know that I Yahuah have spoken it, and performed it", **says Yahuah**
15. **The word of Yahuah came again to me, saying,**
16. "Moreover, you son of <u>man</u> (a human) take you one stick, and write upon it, For **Yahudah**, and for **the children of Yahsrael** his companions, then take another stick, and write upon it, For Yosef, the stick of E'phrayim, and for **all the house of Yahsrael** his companions:
17. And join them one to another into one stick; and **they shall become one** in your hand
18. And when the children of your people shall speak to you, saying, "Will you not show us what you mean by these"?
19. Say to them, Thus says Yahuah God; Behold, I will take the stick of Yosef, which is in the hand of Ephrayim, and **the tribes of Yahsrael** his fellows, and **will put them with him**, even with the stick of **Yahudah**, and **make them one** stick, and **they shall be one in My hand**
20. And the sticks whereon you write shall be in your hand before **their eyes**
21. And say to them, Thus says Yahuah God; Behold, **I will take the children of Yahsrael** from among <u>the heathen</u> (the nations) where they be gone, and will gather them **on every side**, and bring them into **their own land**:
22. And I will make them **one nation** in the land upon the mountains of Yahsrael; and **one king** shall be king to them all: and they shall be **no more** two nations, **neither shall they be divided** into two kingdoms **any more at all**:
23. **Neither shall they defile themselves any more** with their <u>idols</u> (man-made gods), nor with their detestable things, <u>nor with any of their transgressions</u>; but **I will <u>save them</u>** <u>out of all their dwelling places</u>, wherein they have sinned, and will <u>cleanse</u> them: so shall they be **My people**, and I will be their God

Isaiah 11: 9-16

"They shall not hurt nor destroy in all My holy mountain: for the earth shall be full of the knowledge of Yahuah, as the waters cover the sea.
10 And in that day there shall be a root of Yishai, which shall stand for an ensign of the people; to it shall the Gentiles seek: and His rest shall be glorious.
11 And it shall come to pass in that day, that Yahuah shall s**et His hand AGAIN the SECOND TIME to recover the remnant of His people**, which shall be left, from Assyria, and from Egypt, and from Pathros, and from Cush, and from Elam, and from Shinar, and from Hamath, and from the islands of the sea.
12 And He shall set up an ensign for the nations, and shall **ASSEMBLE THE OUTCAST OF YAHSRAEL**, and gather together the dispersed of Yahudah **from the four corners of the earth**.
13 The envy also of Ephraim shall depart, and the adversaries of Yahudah shall be cut off: Ephraim shall not envy Yahudah, and Yahudah shall not vex Ephraim.
14 But they shall fly upon the shoulders of the Philistines toward the west; they shall spoil them of the east together: they shall lay their hand upon Edom and Moab; and the children of Ammon shall obey them.
15 And Yahuah shall utterly destroy the tongue of the Egyptian sea; and with His mighty wind shall **He shake his hand over the river,** and shall strike it in the **seven streams**, and make men go over dryshod.
16 And there shall be **a highway for the remnant of His people**, which shall be left, from Assyria; **like as it was to Yahsrael in the day that he came up out of the land of Egypt**.

Amos 9:9-15

9   "For behold, I will command,
and shake the house of Yahsrael among all the nations
as one shakes with a sieve,
but no pebble shall fall to the earth.
10   All the sinners of My people shall die by the sword,
who say, 'Disaster shall not overtake or meet us.'

The Restoration of Yahsrael

11   "In that day I will raise up
the booth of Daud that is fallen
and repair its breaches,
and raise up its ruins
and rebuild it as in the days of old,
12   that they may possess the remnant of Edom
and all the nations who are called by My name,"
declares Yahuah who does this.
13   "Behold, **the days are coming**," declares Yahuah,
"when the plowman shall overtake the reaper
and the treader of grapes him who sows the seed;
the mountains shall drip sweet wine,
and all the hills shall flow with it.
14   **I will restore the fortunes of My people Yahsrael,**
and they shall rebuild the ruined cities and inhabit them;
they shall plant vineyards and drink their wine,
and they shall make gardens and eat their fruit.
15   I will plant them on their land,
and they shall never again be uprooted
out of the land that I have given them,"
says Yahuah your God."

HIStory or OUR Story   **Chapter 13**

Jeremiah Chapter 30

1. The word that came to Yeremiyahu from Yahuah, saying,
2. Thus speaks Yahuah, the God of Yahsrael, saying, Write you all the words that I have spoken to you in a book.
3. For, lo, the days come, says Yahuah, that I will return the captives of **My people Yahsrael** and **Yahudah**, says Yahuah; and **I will cause them to return to the land that I gave to their fathers**, and they shall possess it.
4. And these are the words that **Yahuah spoke concerning Yahsrael and concerning Yahudah**.
5. For thus says Yahuah: We have heard a voice of trembling, of fear, and not of peace.
6. Ask you now, and see whether a man does travail with child: why do I see every man with his hands on his loins, as a woman in travail, and all faces are turned into paleness?
7. Alas! for that day is great, so that none is like it: it is even the time of Yahkob's trouble; but <u>HE SHALL BE SAVED OUT OF IT</u>
8. And it shall come to pass in that day, says Yahuah of hosts, that **I will break his yoke from off your neck, and will burst your bonds**; and strangers shall no more make him their slaves;
9. but they shall serve Yahuah their God, and Daud their king, whom I will raise up to them.
10. Therefore fear you not, O Yahkob my servant, says Yahuah; neither be dismayed, O Yahsrael: for, lo, <u>I WILL SAVE YOU FROM AFAR</u>, and your seed **FROM THE LAND OF THEIR CAPTIVITY**; and Yahkob shall return, and shall be quiet and at ease, and none shall make him afraid.
11. For <u>I am with you</u>, says Yahuah, to <u>SAVE YOU</u>: for **I WILL MAKE A FULL END OF ALL THE NATIONS** where I have scattered you, but **I WILL NOT MAKE A FULL END OF YOU**; but I will correct you in measure, and will in no wise leave you unpunished.
12. For thus says Yahuah, Your hurt is incurable, and your wound grievous.
13. **There is none to plead your cause**, that you may be bound up: you have no healing medicines.
14. All your lovers have forgotten you; they seek you not: for I have wounded you with the wound of an enemy, with the chastisement of a cruel one, for the greatness of your iniquity, because your sins were increased.
15. Why do you cry for your hurt? your pain is incurable: for the greatness of your iniquity, because your sins were increased, **I HAVE DONE THESE THINGS TO YOU**.

HIStory or OUR Story   **Chapter 13**

16 Therefore **ALL THEY THAT DEVOUR YOU SHALL BE DEVOURED**; and **ALL YOUR ADVERSARIES, EVERY ONE OF THEM SHALL GO INTO CAPTIVITY**, and they that spoil you shall be a spoil, and **ALL THAT PREY UPON YOU WILL I GIVE FOR A PREY**

17 For **I will restore health to you**, and **I will heal you of your wounds**, says Yahuah; because they have called you an OUTCAST saying, "IT IS ZION, WHOM NO MAN SEEKS AFTER"

18 Thus says Yahuah: Behold, **I WILL RETURN THE CAPTIVES** of Yahkob's tents, and have compassion on his dwelling-places; and the city shall be builded upon its own hill, and the palace shall be inhabited after its former manner.

19 And out of them shall proceed thanksgiving and the voice of them that make merry: and I will multiply them, and they shall not be few; I will also glorify them, and they shall not be small.

20 Their children also shall be as aforetime, and their congregation shall be established before Me; and I will punish all that oppress them.

21 And **their prince shall be of themselves**, and **their ruler shall proceed from the midst of them**; and I will cause him to draw near, and he shall approach to Me: for who is he that had boldness to approach Me? says Yahuah

22 And you shall be My people, and I will be your God.

23 Behold, the tempest of Yahuah, even His wrath, is gone forth, a sweeping tempest: it shall burst upon the head of the wicked.

24 The fierce anger of Yahuah shall not return, until He have executed, and till He have performed the intents of His heart: in the LAST DAYS you shall understand it."

Jeremiah 31:1-4

1" At that time," declares the Yahuah "I will be the God of all the families of Yahsrael, and they will be My people."

2 This is what YAHUAH says:
"The people who survive the sword
will find favor in the wilderness;
I will come to give rest to Yahsrael."

3 **YAHUAH appeared to us in the past, saying:**
"I have loved you with an everlasting love;
I have drawn you with unfailing kindness.

4 I will build you up again,
and you, Virgin Yahsrael, will be rebuilt.
Again you will take up your tambourines
and go out to dance with the joyful"

HIStory or OUR Story Chapter 13

Luke 21: 24-28

24 "They will fall by the sword and will **be taken** as SLAVES TO ALL NATIONS. YAHRUSHALOM will be trampled on by the nations until the times of the nations are fulfilled.
25 "There will be signs in the **sun**, **moon** and **stars**. On the earth, nations will be in anguish and perplexity at the roaring and tossing of the sea.
26 People will faint from terror, apprehensive of what is coming on the world, for the heavenly bodies will be shaken.
27 At that time **they will see the Son of Man coming** in a cloud **with power** and **great glory**.
28 When these things begin to take place, STAND UP and LIFT UP YOUR HEADS, because YOUR REDEMPTION is drawing near."

Matthew 24: 27-31

27 For as the lightning cometh forth **from THE EAST**, and is seen even to the west; so shall be the coming of the Son of man.
28 Wheresoever the carcass (Yahsrael's dead body) is, there will the eagles (gentiles/nations preying upon us **Lamentations 4: 18-19**) be gathered together.
29 But immediately after the tribulation of those days **the sun shall be darkened**, and the **moon shall not give her light**, and the **stars shall fall from heaven**, and the powers of the heavens shall be shaken:
30 and then shall appear the sign of the Son of man in heaven: and then shall **all the tribes of the earth mourn**, and **they shall see the Son of man coming** on the clouds of heaven with **power** and **great glory**.
31 And **He shall send forth His messengers** with a great sound of a trumpet, and they shall gather together His elect **(Isaiah 45:4)** from the four winds, **from one end of heaven to the other.**"

So from the following scriptures as you can see that we scattered Yahsraelites are the dry bones in the valley. We are God's elect scattered to the four corners of the earth. But as promised in **Deuteronomy 30:4** Yahuah would gather us from even the farthest parts of the earth, so we must patiently wait for Him, spread the **Gospel** (good news), and turn back to His laws.

HIStory or OUR Story   **Chapter 13**

It has been prophesied to us that in the future the world will not reminisce about how Yah brought them out of Egypt anymore. Today we still discuss that. That's Yahuah's last time He intervened and personally delivered His people thresher Yahsraelites. Scripture teaches us that Yahuah will do it one more last time, from all of the lands where Yahsrael has been scattered to.

Jeremiah 23:1-8

1 **WOE BE TO THE PASTORS** that **destroy** and **scatter the sheep** of My pasture! **says Yahuah**.
2 Therefore thus says Yahuah God of Yahsrael against the pastors that feed My people; You have scattered My flock, and driven them away, and have not visited them: behold, I will visit upon you the evil of your doings, **says Yahuah.**
3 And I will gather **the remnant** of My flock out of all countries where **I have driven them**, and will bring them again to their folds; and **they shall be fruitful and increase**.
4 And I will set up shepherds over them which shall feed them: and **they shall fear no more, nor be dismayed, neither shall they be lacking**, <u>says Yahuah</u>.
5 Behold, the days come, **says Yahuah**, that I will raise to Daud a righteous Branch, and a King shall reign and prosper, and shall execute judgment and justice in the earth.
6 In his days Yahudah shall be saved, and Yahsrael shall dwell safely: and this is His name whereby He shall be called, Yahuah Our Righteousness.   pronounced(Yah-oo-ah-staddadick)
7 Therefore, behold, the days come, **says Yahuah**, that they shall **NO MORE say**, Yahuah lives, which brought up the children of Yahsrael out of the land of Egypt;
8 But, Yahuah lives, which brought up and which led the seed of the house of Israel out of the north country, and **from all countries** where I had driven them; and they shall dwell in their own land"

Jeremiah 16: 10-15

10 And it shall come to pass, when you shall show this people all these words, and they shall say to you, Why has Yahuah pronounced all this great evil against us? or what is our iniquity? or what is our sin that we have committed against Yahuah our God?
11 Then shall outstay to them, Because your fathers have forsaken me, **says Yahuah**, and have walked after other gods, and have served them, and have worshipped them, and have forsaken me, and have not kept My law;
12 And you have done worse than your fathers; for, behold, you walk every one after the imagination of his evil heart, that they may not listen to Me:
13 Therefore will I cast you out of this land into a land that you know not, neither you nor your fathers; and there shall you serve other gods day and night; where I will not show you favor.
14 Therefore, behold, the days come, says Yahuah, that it shall **NO MORE** be said, Yahuah lives, that brought up the children of Yahsrael out of the land of Egypt;
15 But, Yahuah lives, that brought up the children of Yahsrael from the land of the north, and from all the lands where He had driven them. and I will bring them again into their land that I gave to their fathers.

THE TWO WITNESSES OF REVELATION EXPLAINED

There have been numerous theories about who the TWO WITNESSES of **Revelation 11** are. Some have said that they are Musa and Yahonon the Baptist, while others have proposed that's its Enoch and Elijah. After much careful studying of the Scriptures and a variety of Batman & Robin combos, have "WE" all gotten it **WRONG**? YES!!! Many of us have filled in what we think (from our own understanding and theories). But does scripture clearly state that they, meaning the 2 witnesses, are TWO "literal men?" No! We have only assumed that they are.

To answer this question, one would have to revisit the word of prophecy in **the fourth chapter of Zechariah**. Remember we must search the scriptures for His secret things.

Important Fact: The two witnesses were described as the **"two olive trees"** and the **"two candlesticks"** in **Revelation 11:4**. So this tells us that we need to seek the Scriptures to see if this prophecy is mentioned anywhere else in the word to better understand who these "Two Witnesses" are and surprisingly it does! Zekariyah (Zechariah) and Yeshayahu (Isaiah) are the prophets who spoke of the **two olive trees** and the **two candlesticks** that are being revealed as the **Two Witnesses** of **Revelation 11**.

Zechariah 4:2-4 says, "And said to me, "What do you see? And I said, I have looked, and behold a candlestick all of gold, with a bowl upon the top of it, and his seven lamps thereon, and seven pipes to the seven lamps, which are upon the top thereof: And **two olive trees** by it, one upon the right side of the bowl, and the other upon the left side thereof. So I answered and spoke to the angel that talked with me, saying, "What are these, my Master?"'

Zechariah 4:11-14
"11 Then answered I, and said to him, What are these two olive trees upon the right side of the candlestick and upon the left side thereof?
12 And I answered again, and said to him, "**What be these two olive branches which through the two golden pipes empty the golden oil out of themselves?**"
13 And he answered me and said, "Do you not know what these be?" And I said, "No, my master".
14 Then said he," **These are the two anointed ones, that stand by the Most High of the whole earth.**"

In **Zechariah 3:9**, The Most High told Yoshua (Joshua), "For, behold, I will bring forth MY SERVANT, the BRANCH. So the question is, "Who are the natural branches of the Most High Yahuah that serve Him?"

Zechariah 4:14 says that the **Two Witnesses = Two Anointed Ones**

Anoint- to ordain, to set apart, approve, appoint, accept, witness, and to **choose**.

With that being said, **who has the Most High anointed, set apart, appointed, ordained and CHOSEN to be His WITNESSES in the Earth**? Let's allow Scripture to once again reveal His truth.

Enlightenment: Yahuah has **chosen** the entire house of **Yah'kob (12 Tribes of Yahsrael)** as the **two witnesses** to bear His testimony before all the nations of the earth. He divided the twelve tribes into two houses, **Yahudah** and **Yahsrael.** However, these two houses are prophesied in **Ezekiel 37** to become ONE again!

Now, let us go back to Revelation 11:3-4 to see what Scripture reveals concerning these Two Witnesses.

Revelation 11:3-4
"3 And I will give power to my **two witnesses**, and they shall prophesy a thousand two hundred and threescore days, clothed in sackcloth.
4 These are the **two olive trees**, and the **two candlesticks** standing before the Most High Yahuah of the earth.

We see that the two witnesses are symbolically called "two olive trees" and also "two lampstands." We'll examine each of these symbols in turn and see what the Scriptures have to say about them.

First, let's see what the Scriptures says about the "two olive trees." Are these olive trees spoken of anywhere else in the Word of the Most High Yahuah? Let's continue reading and find out!

Zechariah 4:2-4 "And he said to me, "What do you see?" And I said, I have looked, and behold a candlestick all of gold, with a bowl upon the top of it, and his seven lamps thereon, and seven pipes to the seven lamps, which are upon the top thereof: And **two olive trees** by it, one upon the right side of the bowl, and the other upon the left side thereof. So I answered and spoke to the angel that talked with me, saying, "**What are these, my Master?**"

Zechariah 4:5-6, "Then the angel that talked with me answered and said to me, "Do you know not what these are?" And I said, "No, my master". Then he answered and spoke to me, saying, "This is the word of the Most High Yahuah to Zerubbabel, saying, "Not by might, nor by power, but by My spirit", says the Most High of hosts."

Zechariah 4:11-14
11 "Then answered I, and said to him, What are these two olive trees upon the right side of the candlestick and upon the left side thereof?
12 And I answered again, and said to him, **What be these two olive branches which through the two golden pipes empty the golden oil out of themselves?**
13 And he answered me and said, "Do you not know what these be? And I said, "No, my master".
14 Then said he, **"These are the two anointed ones, that stand by the Most High of the whole earth."**

Hebrew Roots Bible: *14* Then said he," **These are the two SONS of Fresh Oil, who stand by the Master of the whole earth."**

In **Zechariah 4** we see the same symbols that are used in Revelation 11 for the olive trees and the lampstand. The two olive trees are said to be "the anointed ones" (literally "**sons of the oil**") who stand beside the Most High of the whole earth" (**Zechariah. 4:14**). However, the angel doesn't give Zekariyah (or us) a direct answer regarding the identity of these two trees. Therefore, we must look in the book of Jeremiah to find the identification of the olive trees.

Jeremiah 11:16-17
"16 The Most High called your name, A green **olive tree**, fair, and of goodly fruit: with the noise of a great tumult he has kindled fire upon it, and the **branches of it are broken**.
17 For the Most High of hosts, that planted you, has pronounced evil against you, for the evil of the **house of Yahsrael** and of the **house of Yahudah**, which they have done against themselves to provoke Me to anger in offering incense to the Lord."

Remember, in **Zechariah 3:9**, The Most High told Yoshua, "For, behold, I will bring forth MY SERVANT, the BRANCH.

So, we see that **Jeremiah 11** refers to **both** houses of Yahsrael a "**green olive tree.**" They were planted and named by **Yahuah** the Father Himself. However, can we still be certain from Scripture that both the House of Yahudah and the House of Yahsrael are symbolically labeled as olive trees? Or, is there more? Since Scriptures always repeat themselves, let's take a look at another clue to the House of Yahsrael being the Two Olive Trees.

HIStory or OUR Story   **Chapter 14**

Hosea 14:5-6
"5 I will be as the dew to **Yahsrael**: he shall grow as the lily, and cast forth his roots as Lebanon.
6 His **branches** shall spread, and his beauty shall be as the **olive tree**, and his smell as Lebanon.

Jeremiah 11:16 Yahuah called your name, a green **olive tree**, fair, and of goodly fruit: with the noise of a great tumult he has kindled fire upon it, and the **branches** of it are broken

Isaiah 43:1;10-12
1 "But now thus says the Most High that created you, **O Yah'kob**, and He that formed you, **O Yahsrael**, Fear not: for I have redeemed you, I have called you by your name; **you are mine**.

10 **You are My witnesses, says Yahuah, and My servant whom I have chosen**: that you may know and believe Me, and understand that I am He: before Me there was no God formed, neither shall there be after Me.
11 I, even I, am the Most High; and **beside Me there is no saviour.**
12 I have declared, and have saved, and I have showed, when there was no strange god among you: **therefore you are My witnesses**, says the Most High, that I am Yahuah.

Isaiah 44:1-2; 7-8
1 "Yet now hear, **O Yah'kob My servant**; and Yah**srael, whom I have chosen**:
2 Thus says the Most High that made you, and formed you from the womb, which will help you; Fear not, **O Yah'kob, My servant**; and you, Yeshurun (Yahsrael), whom I have chosen.

7 Who is like Me? **Let them proclaim it, let them declare and set it forth before Me.** Who has announced from of old the things to come?
8 Fear not, neither be afraid: **have not I told you from that time, and have declared it? You are even My witnesses.** Is there a God beside Me? Yes, there is no God I know not any."

Recap: Revelation 11:3-4

"3 And I will give power to My **two witnesses**, and they shall prophesy a thousand two hundred and threescore days, clothed in sackcloth."
4 These are the **two olive trees**, and the **two candlesticks** standing before God of the earth.

Remember we have this charge from Yahuah
Isaiah 58:1 "Cry aloud, spare not, lift up your voice like a trumpet, and show My people their transgression, and the house of of Yahkob their sins."

The candlesticks here depict the seven assemblies. The seven assemblies listed in **Revelation 1:11** literally mean "an assembly of called out ones." We can see that in the book of Revelation, a candlestick represents a called out **group** of people. The symbolism fits perfectly with the House of Yahudah and the House of Yahsrael, who were at first called out of Egypt together to be Yahuah's people. At the end of this age, they will be called out once more to **witness** against the people of this earth when they forsake **YAHUAH** and worship the Anti-messiah.

The scriptures are overwhelmingly evident that the two witnesses, who are symbolically called the **two olive trees** and **two candlesticks,** are in fact the House of Yahudah and the House of Yahsrael.

Revelation 7:1-4
1 And after these things I saw four angels standing on the four corners of the earth, holding the four winds of the earth, that the wind should not blow on the earth, nor on the sea, nor on any tree.
2 And I saw another angel ascending from the east, having the seal of the living Yahuah: and he cried with a loud voice to the four angels, to whom it was given to hurt the earth and the sea,
3 Saying, "Hurt not the earth, neither the sea, nor the trees, till we have sealed the servants of our Yahuah in their foreheads".
4 And I heard the number of them which were sealed: **and there were sealed an hundred and forty and four thousand of all the tribes of the children of Yahsrael**

Verses 5-8 lists the twelve tribes, 12,000 from each tribe.

The 144,000 sealed from the tribes of Yahsrael have long been a mystery, but now the purpose and mission of these witnesses should be understood. These 144,000 servants will form the two witnesses that **YAHUAH** will use in the end-time to show the world that He is the one true Yahuah. These witnesses can be divided into two groups:

The House of Yahudah
- The tribe of Yahudah
- The tribe of Benyamin
- The tribe of Levi

The House of Yahsrael
- The tribe of Yoseph
- The tribe of Manasseh
- The tribe of Reuben
- The tribe of Gad
- The tribe of Asher
- The tribe of Naphtali
- The tribe of Shimeon
- The tribe of Issachar
- The tribe of Zebulun

THE END-TIME TWO WITNESSES WILL BE FILLED WITH THE **SPIRIT OF PROPHECY (Revelation. 1:1-3 & Revelation 19:10)**. THEY WILL HAVE POWER TO DEVOUR THEIR ENEMIES WITH FIRE, SHUT UP HEAVEN THAT IT WON'T RAIN, TURN WATER INTO BLOOD, AND STRIKE THE EARTH WITH PLAGUES, IF ANYONE ATTEMPTS TO STOP THEM **BEFORE** THEY FINISH THEIR TESTIMONY. THEY WILL HAVE AUTHORITY FROM YAHUAH TO NOT ONLY PROPHESY, BUT TO SHOW WONDERS IN THE EARTH AS IT STATES IN **JOEL 2:28-32**. NO ONE WILL BE ABLE TO STOP THEM UNTIL THEIR TESTIMONY IS DONE. THEY (**144,000**) WILL HAVE WITNESSED TO THE ENTIRE 4 CORNERS OF THE EARTH (WHERE THEY ARE SCATTERED) AND WILL FULFILL THE PROMISES OF THE FATHER. BY JUDGMENT TIME, ALL WILL HAVE HEARD; THIS IS WHY THE MOST HIGH WILL PROTECT THEM AND WILL HOLD BACK THE BEAST UNTIL **AFTER** THEIR TESTIMONY IS FINISHED. HE IS A RIGHTEOUS FATHER, AND HOW COULD HE JUDGE THOSE WHO HAVE NOT KNOWN THE TRUTH? ONCE THEIR TESTIMONY IS FINISHED, NO ONE WILL BE WITHOUT EXCUSE WHEN THEY STAND BEFORE THE FATHER! NONE!

Now let's look at the fate of these two (144,000) witnesses, as revealed by Yahonon's (John's) vision. This is what many will not want to hear, but must accept:

Revelation 6:9-11
"9 And when he had opened the fifth seal, I saw **under the altar the souls of them that were slain** for the word of Yahuah, and for the testimony which they held:
10 And they cried with a loud voice, saying, How long, O Most High, set apart and true, do you not judge and **avenge our blood** on them that dwell on the earth?
11 And **white robes** were given to every one of them; and it was said to them, that they should rest yet for a little season, until their fellow servants also and their brothers, that should be killed as they were, should be fulfilled.

REVELATION 11:7-8
7 When they have finished their testimony, the beast that comes up out of the Abyss **will make war with them, and overcome them and kill them**.
8 **And their dead bodies will lie in the street of the great city** which **SPIRITUALLY** is called Sodom and Egypt, where also their Master was crucified.

After the witnesses have finished their testimony before **all** the nations, YAHUAH will allow the Anti-messiyah who had previously come up out of the Abyss (**Revelation 9:11**) to make **war** against them and kill them. At the end of their testimony, **all 144,000 witnesses** (Two Witnesses, Yahudah & Yahsrael) will be martyred for Yahuah:

REVELATION 11:9-10
9 Then those from the peoples, tribes, tongues, and nations will see their dead bodies **three-and-a-half days**, and not allow their dead bodies to be put into graves.
10 And those who dwell on the earth will rejoice over them, **make merry**, and **send gifts to one another**, because these two prophets tormented those who dwell on the earth.

During the time of these Two Witnesses (144,000), their bodies will be left to in the streets for **3 ½ days** after they are killed by the Beast. The world will be so glad to see these two groups of witnesses slain that they will declare a global holiday and rejoice over their deaths. But their defeat is not the end of the story. Read **Revelation 11:11** below.

REVELATION 11:11
11 "Now after the **three-and-a-half days** the breath of life from Yahuah entered them, and **they stood on their feet**, and great fear fell on those who saw them.
12 And they heard a loud voice from heaven saying to them, "**Come up here**." And they ascended to heaven in a cloud, and **their enemies** saw them." This is the physical fulfillment of **Ezekiel Chapter 37**.

Three-and-a-half days after the Beast is allowed to slay the witnesses of the House of Yahudah and the House of Yahsrael (a day for every year they prophesied in the cities of the world), **Yahushua, our Messiyah, is going to return at the 7th trumpet to resurrect them and all the righteous dead,** as numerous Scriptures show (**I Corinthians 15:51-53; I Thessalonians 4:13-17; Matthew 24:31; Revelation 11:15-18**). They will be taken to sing before the throne of the Most High Yahuah, (**Revelation 14:1-5**) and to await the marriage ceremony of the Lamb (**Revelation 19:6-9**).

After the MessiYah establishes His kingdom and begins to rule from Yahrushalom, these witnesses shall be priests of Yahuah and Yahushua, and shall reign with Him a thousand years (**Revelation 20: 4-6**). This is the reward of those from the House of Yahudah and the House of Yahsrael who are called to be the witnesses of **YAHUAH** at the end of the age.

Further Proof Prophesied in Hosea 6:1-4
Hosea 6:1-4
1 Come, and let us return to the Most High: for He has torn, and He will heal us; He has cut, and He will bind us up.
2 After **two days** will He revive **us: in the third day He will raise us up**, and **we shall live in His sight.**
3 Then shall we know, if we follow on to know the Most High: His going forth is prepared as the morning; and He shall come to us as the rain, as the latter and former rain to the earth.
4 O **Ephrayim**, what shall I do to you? O **Yahudah**, what shall I do to you? For your goodness is as a morning cloud, and as the early dew it goes away.

Revelations 11:12
12 And they heard a **great voice** from heaven saying to them, Come up here. **And they ascended up to heaven in a cloud**; and their **enemies** beheld them.

Revelation 11:12 equates to Hosea 6:2

Conclusion: Pre-tribulation dispensationalist **preachers have long misrepresented the scriptural truth**. What they don't get is that the Father reveals His secrets **to His children (Deuteronomy 29: 29/Psalms 147:19-20/ Amos 3:1-3/Amos 2:10-11**).
If everyone is so-called raptured up out of the Earth **before** the tribulation and return of our Hebrew Messiyah, who will be here to witness the blasphemous acts of the **Lawless One** or **Beast** that will eventually kill the two witnesses? So, while Satan has everyone looking for the Two Witnesses, **two literal men**, no one will suspect the 144,000 to be the fulfillers of end-time prophecy.
Yahushua was the first of the first fruits to God. (**1Corinthians 15: 20**). The 144,000 of the tribes of Yahsrael will be the first fruits to God.
Jeremiah 2:3
3 "Yahsrael was holiness to Yahuah and **the firstfruits** of His increase: all that devour him shall be guilty; evil shall come upon them", **says Yahuah.**

REMEMBER THAT YAHUAH REVEALS HIS **HIDDEN TRUTH** TO HIS CHILDREN, His servants!!!!

Be Patient

PREMATURE EXIT: WHERE ARE YOU GOING?
I don't want anyone reading this to think they need to run back to Yahsrael today!! There are those who are ready to pack up, run, and leave right now. There are those who think that we should stay here and try to build up our nation over here in this land, by setting up roots, pooling their money together and making it happen now. Well, actually neither are what we are supposed to be doing at this point. Don't get me wrong. Trying to become a nation is not a bad thing, BUT He has said that whatever the house of Yahsrael tries to do in these lands will NOT prosper (as a nation). So no matter where we try to go, until He restores us as a nation, we will not prosper collectively. What He did say is that after we serve four generations (400 years) among other nations, we will begin to take our exit from our enemies' lands.

According to scripture, we are nearing the end of our 400 years now, so we are getting ready to exit these lands permanently. So what we should be doing is concentrating on returning to His ways as commanded. The rest will be handled because Yahuah has mapped it all out in His Word if we slow down and listen. He has made it clear that "HE" would be the one who would gather the tribes from the four corners of the earth. It's not for us to try to make this happen within our own strength. Hear the words of the Most High concerning this. He has said, "For you shall not go out with haste, nor go by flight: the Most High will go before you; the Power of Yahsrael will be your rear guard" (**Isaiah 52:12**). He shall go out before us leading the way.

The Most High all throughout scripture has promised prosperity to His people Yahsrael when they finally go to possess the land again. He never said that Yahsrael would prosper "**AS A NATION**" in the lands of their captivity. So why are people trying to set up permanent roots in the **lands of their enemies**? Why do they think that we will ever be accepted in these lands by these nations? People have read verses that say, "COME OUT of her My people, so that you will not share in her sins" and they have panicked, thinking that they must pack up and leave to run somewhere right now. But again, I keep repeating this. You cannot take a few verses and run with them.

All scriptures must line up or it's your understanding that is off. When you hear Yahuah's command to wait on him, how do you see that and think you should pack up and run to another place "RIGHT NOW"? Do you really think that "Come out of her verse" means flee the land that you are in? Absolutely not!!! Because he said that "**HE**" **would gather us from ALL** from the four corners of the earth when the time was fulfilled to do so (**Genesis 15:13-15**). Remember that Yahsrael is being oppressed ALL over the earth right now. There is no where to collectively run to. We are being called to **come out** of **the ways of the world** and began to return to his ways and abandon the practices of Babylon.

Here is what he said about what would befall us in captivity. "You shall be only oppressed and spoiled evermore, and **no man shall save you**, and among "THESE NATIONS" shall you find no ease or rest" (**Deuteronomy 28: 16, 29, 65**) we shall be continually <u>Cursed</u> (in the city, and in the field), "**YOU SHALL be defeated before your enemies**, and you shall not prosper in your ways; you shall only be oppressed. So ask yourself, "Where are you going to go?" What land anywhere will take all of us into it?" Where can you flee when he said that we are being oppressed all over the world?" YES, Yahsrael will leave out of this world's system (according to scripture) but He has not physically commanded us to leave today. Hear the command again. "For you shall not go out with haste, nor go by flight: for Yahushua will go before you; and God of Yahsrael will be your rear guard" (**Isaiah 52:12**).

"Do not be afraid, for I am with you; I WILL bring your children from the east and gather you from the west. **Isaiah 43:5**. HE WILL raise a banner for the nations and gather the exiles of Yahsrael; **He will assemble the scattered people of Yahudah from the four quarters of the earth**
(**Isaiah 11:12**). He has made it clear that when the time comes, he would speak to our hearts and allure us to leave. Hear his words, "Therefore, behold, I will draw her, and bring her into the wilderness, and speak comfortably to her"(**Hosea 2:14**). Right now, Yahuah is preparing the way. It is going to be so great that we won't remember the former things that he did for Israel in the first exodus. He plans to get all of the glory for our exit, and not from any of our own efforts.
He said, "Remember you not the former things, neither consider the things of old. Behold, I will do a new thing; now it shall spring forth; shall ye not know it? I WILL even make a way in the wilderness, and rivers in the desert" (**Isaiah 43:18-19**) "For I will take you from among the nations and gather you out of ALL countries, and will bring you into your own land." (**Ezekiel 36: 24, 36**) "Then the nations that are left round about you shall know that I Yahuah has built the ruined places, and planted that which was desolate: I the Yahuah have spoken it, and **I WILL DO IT!**

HIStory or OUR Story   Chapter 15

Isaiah 42: 14-25

14. "**I have long time held My peace**: I have been still, and refrained Myself: now will I **cry** (roar) like a travailing woman; I will destroy and devour at once.
15. I will **make waste** (shrink/make low) mountains and hills, and dry up all their herbs; and I will make the rivers **islands** (coastlands), and I will dry up the pools.
16. And I will bring the **blind** (people lacking perception/lacking awareness/lacking discernment) (by a way that **they knew not**; (a place they never been); I will lead them in paths that they have not known: I will make **darkness** (uncomprehension) light (comprehension) before them, and **crooked things** (things that make no sense) **straight** (plain). These things will I do to them, and not forsake them.
17. They shall be **turned back** (reminded of the past/look back), they shall be greatly **ashamed** (sorry, embarrassed/guilty), that trust in graven **images** (idols), that say to the **molten images** (images made by man's hands), "You are our gods"
18. Hear, you **deaf** (able to hear but not understand); and **look** (focus) you **blind** that you may **see** (comprehend/understand)
19. Who is **blind** but **My Servant** (Yahsrael) (**Isaiah 41:8**)? Or deaf, as **My messenger** (Yahsrael) that I sent? Who is **blind** as he that is **perfect** (innocent/naïve/gullible), and blind as Yahuah's servant?
20. **Seeing many things** (think they know-it-all/ full of revelation), but you **observe not** (don't have correct understanding): **opening the ears** (teaches), but he **hears not** (cannot take instruction himself)
21. Yahuah is well pleased for His righteousness sake; He will **magnify** (intensify/make important) the law, and make it **honorable** (moral/ethical)
22. But this is a people robbed and **spoiled** (plundered/defeated); they are all of them **snared** (trapped/caught up) in **holes** (ditches/unfavorable situations), and they are **hidden** (concealed/kept out of sight) in **prison houses** (state and federal prisons); they are for a **prey** (hunted for food), and none **delivers** (helps/assists/takes out of predicament); for a **spoil** (a possession), and none says **Restore** (repair/reinstate/return to original place or condition)
23. Who among you will **give ear to** (listen to/understand) this? Who will **hearken** (listen) and **hear** (understand) for the time to come?
24. Who gave Yah'kob for a **spoil** (a possession), and Yahsrael to the robbers? Did not Yahuah, He against whom we have sinned? For **they** (Yahsraelites) would not walk in His ways, **neither were they obedient to His law**
25. **Therefore** (this is why) He has poured upon him the fury of His anger, and the **strength of battle** (allowed us to be severely defeated by our enemies): and **it** (our enemies) has **set him on fire** (severely tortured Yahsrael) **round about** (a lot/very much/very many times/all over), yet **he knew not** (Yahsrael did not understand/ did not put dots together): and **it burned him** (Yisrael suffered greatly) **yet he laid it not to heart** (after all of the calamity Yahsrael still did not put two and two together/Yahsrael still does not know why he suffers).

HIStory or OUR Story   **Chapter 15**

Now that we Hebrew Yahsraelites are here, and we know who we are what must we do next? Well the scripture tells us to repent from our law breaking ways, and to keep Yahuah's commandments again. Also **ACCORDING TO YAH'S OWN WORD**, we need to pray towards the east, towards our land, towards the place where He puts His Name while we are in our enemies land, just as Daniel did.

Daniel 6:10 "But when Daniel learned that the law had been signed, he went home and knelt down as usual in his upstairs room, with its windows open toward Yahrushalom. He prayed three times a day, just as he had always done, giving thanks to his God"

1Kings 8:33-53, 1Kings 11:36

World War III and The Final Judgement

Ezekiel Chapter 38

1 And the word of Yahuah came to me saying,
2 "Son of man, set your face toward Gog of the land of Magog, the prince of Rosh, Meshech and Tubal, and prophesy against him
3 And say, 'Thus says Yahuah God, "Behold, I am against you, O Gog, prince of Rosh, Meshech and Tubal.
4 I will turn you about and put hooks into your jaws, and I will bring you out, and all your army, horses and horsemen, all of them splendidly attired, a great company with buckler and shield, all of them wielding swords;
5 Persia, Ethiopia and Put with them, all of them with shield and helmet;
6 Gomer with all its troops; Beth-togarmah from the remote parts of the north with all its troops—many peoples with you.
7 "Be prepared, and prepare yourself, you and all your companies that are assembled about you, and be a guard for them.
8 After many days you will be summoned; in the latter years you will come into the land that is **restored from the sword**, whose inhabitants have been **gathered from many nations** to the mountains of Yisrael which had been a continual waste; but **its people were brought out from the nations**, and they are living safely, **all of them**.
9 You will go up, **you will come like a storm; you will be like a cloud covering the land**, you and all your troops, and **many peoples with you**."
10 'Thus says Yahuah God, "It will come about on that day, that **thoughts will come into your mind** and **you will devise an evil plan**,
11 and you will say, 'I will go up against the land of unwalled villages. I will go against those who are at rest, that live securely, all of them living without walls and having no bars or gates,
12 to capture spoil and to seize plunder, to turn your hand against the waste places which are now inhabited, and against **THE PEOPLE WHO ARE GATHERED OUT OF THE NATIONS**, who have acquired cattle and goods, who live at the center of the world.'
13 Sheba and Dedan and the merchants of Tarshish with all its villages will say to you, 'Have you come to capture spoil? Have you assembled your company to seize plunder, to carry away silver and gold, to take away cattle and goods, to capture great spoil?
14 "Therefore prophesy, son of man, and say to Gog, 'Thus says Yahuah God, "On that day when **My people Yahsrael** are living safely, will you not know *it*?

₁₅ You will come from your place out of <u>the remote parts of the north</u>, you and **many peoples with you,** all of them riding on horses, a great assembly and a mighty army;

₁₆ and you will come up against **My people Yahsrael** like a cloud to cover the land. It shall come about in **the last days** that I will bring you against **My land, so that the nations may know Me** when I am sanctified through you before their eyes, O Gog."

₁₇ **'Thus says Yahuah God,** "Are you the one of whom I spoke in former days through My servants the prophets of Yahsrael, who prophesied in those days **for many years** that I would bring you against them?

₁₈ It will come about on that day, when Gog comes against the land of Yahsrael," declares Yahuah God, "**that My fury will come up in My Face.**"

₁₉ In My zeal and in My blazing wrath I declare that on that day there will surely be a great earthquake in the land of Yahsrael.

₂₀ The fish of the sea, the birds of the heavens, the beasts of the field, all the creeping things that creep on the earth, <u>and all the men who are on the face of the earth</u> **will shake at My presence**; the mountains also will be thrown down, the steep pathways will collapse and every wall will fall to the ground.

₂₁ I will call for a sword against him on all My mountains," declares Yahuah God. "Every man's sword will be against his brother.

₂₂ With **pestilence** and **with blood I will enter into judgment with him**; and **I will rain on him** and on his troops, and on **the many peoples who are with him**, a torrential rain, with **hailstones**, **fire** and **brimstone.**

₂₃ **I will magnify Myself, sanctify Myself, and make Myself known in** the sight of many nations; and they will know that I am Yahuah."

HIStory or OUR Story **Chapter 16**

Joel Chapter 3

1. "For, behold, in those days, and in that time, when I shall **bring again** (bring back) (restore) **the captivity** (captives)(slaves)(war prisoners) of **Yahudah and Yahrushalom**,
2. **I will also gather all nations**, and will bring them down into the valley of **Jehosh'a-phat** (Yah's judgement), and will plead with them there for **My people** and for **My heritage Yahsrael**, whom they have scattered AMONG THE NATIONS and **parted** (divided up) My land.
3. And they have **cast lots** (rolled dice) for My people; and have **given** (traded) a boy for a harlot, and sold a girl for wine that they might drink.
4. Yea, and what have you to do with me, O Tyre, and Zi'don, and all the coasts of Palestine? Will you render Me a **recompense** (repayment)? And if you **recompense** (repay) Me, swiftly and speedily will I return your **recompense** (payment) upon your own head.
5. Because you have taken **My silver** and **My gold**, and have carried into your temples My **goodly pleasant things** (sacred scrolls/Menorah):
6. The children also of Yahudah and the children of Yahrushalom have you sold to the **Grecians** (Greeks/natives to Greece) that you might remove them far from their borders
7. Behold I will raise them out of the place where you have sold them and will return your recompense upon your own head:
8. And I will sell your sons and your daughters into the hand of the children of Yahudah and they shall sell them to the **Sabeans** (present day Iraq/Yemen) to a people far off: for Yahuah has spoken it.
9. Proclaim you this among the **Gentiles** (nations): Prepare for war, wake up **the mighty men** (your strongest men), let all the men of war draw near; let them come up:
10. Beat your **plowshares** (main cutting blade of a plow) into swords and your **pruninghooks** (farm tools) into spears: let the weak say, "I am strong"
11. Assemble yourselves, and come, all you **heathen** (nations) and gather yourselves together round about: there cause your mighty ones to come down, O Yahuah
12. Let the **heathen** (nations) be awakend, and come up to the valley of **Jehosh'a-phat** (Yah's judgement): for there will I sit to judge all the **heathen** (nations) round about.
13. Put you in the **sickle** (blade for cutting fruit or grain), for the **harvest** (process of gathering) is **ripe** (fruit or grain ready to be cut or eaten): come, get you down; for the **press** (big bowl) is full, the vats overflow: for their wickedness is great
14. **Multitudes** (many people), multitudes in the valley of **decision** (judgment): for the day of Yahuah is near in the valley of **decision** (judgment)
15. The sun and moon shall be darkened, and the stars shall withdraw their shining"
16. Yahuah also shall roar out of Zion, and **utter** (shout) His voice from Yahrushalom: and the heavens and the earth shall shake: but Yahuah will be the hope of His people and the strength of the children of Yahsrael

17. "So shall you know that I am Yahuah your **God** (power) dwelling in Zion, My **Holy** (set apart) mountain: then shall Yahrushalom (Jerusalem) be **holy** (set apart) and there shall **no strangers** (people of other nations) pass through her any more

18. And it shall come to pass in that day, that the mountains shall drop down **new** (fresh) wine, and the hills shall flow with milk, and all the rivers of Yahudah shall flow with waters, and a fountain shall come forth of the house of Yahuah, and shall water the valley of Shittim

19. Egypt shall be a **desolation** (ruined)(destroyed) and **E'dom** (modern day Buseirah) shall be a **desolate** (empty) **wilderness** (abandoned/uninhabited) for the violence against the children of Yahudah, because they have shed innocent blood in their land.

20. But Yahudah shall dwell for ever and Yahrushalom from generation to generation

21. For I will **cleanse** (avenge) their blood that I have not yet **cleansed** (avenged): for Yahuah dwells in Zion"

Daniel 7:9 "I beheld till the thrones were cast down, and the **Ancient of Days** (The Most High) did sit, **whose garment was white as snow**, and the **Hair** of His head like the **pure wool**: His throne was like the fiery flame, and His wheels as burning fire"

Ezekiel Chapter 39

1 Therefore, you son of man, prophesy against Gog, and say, Thus says Yahuah God; "Behold, I am against you, O Gog, the chief prince of Meshech and Tubal:
2 And I will turn you back, and leave but the sixth part of you, and will cause you to come up from the north parts, and will bring you upon the mountains of Yahsrael:
3 And I will strike your bow out of your left hand, and will cause your arrows to fall out of your right hand.
4 You shall fall upon the mountains of Yahsrael, you, and all your bands, and the people that is with you: I will give you to the ravenous birds of every sort, and to the beasts of the field to be devoured.
5 You shall fall upon the open field: for I have spoken it, says Yahuah God.
6 And I will send a fire on Magog, and among them that dwell carelessly in the isles: and they shall know that I am Yahuah.
7 So **I will make My Holy Name known** in the midst of **My people Yahsrael**; and **I will not let them pollute My Holy Name anymore**: and the heathen (nations) shall know that I am Yahuah, the Holy One in Yahsrael.
8 Behold, it is come, and it is done, says Yahuah God; **THIS IS THE DAY** whereof I have spoken.
9 And they that dwell in the cities of Yahsrael shall go forward, and shall set on fire and burn the weapons, both the shields and the bucklers, the bows and the arrows, and the handstaves, and the spears, and they shall burn them with fire seven years:
10 So that they shall take no wood out of the field, neither cut down any out of the forests; for they shall burn the weapons with fire: and **THEY SHALL SPOIL THOSE THAT SPOILED THEM, AND ROB THOSE THAT ROBBED THEM**, says Yahuah God.
11 And it shall come to pass in that day, that I will give to Gog a place there of graves in Yahsrael, the valley of the passengers on the east of the sea: and it shall stop the noses of the passengers: and there shall they bury Gog and all his multitude: and they shall call it The valley of Hamongog.
12 And seven months shall the house of Yahsrael be burying of them, that they may cleanse the land.
13 Yea, all the people of the land shall bury them; and it shall be to them a renown the day that I shall be glorified, says Yahuah God.
14 And they shall sever out men of continual employment, passing through the land to bury with the passengers those that remain upon the face of the earth, to cleanse it: after the end of seven months shall they search.
15 And the passengers that pass through the land, when any sees a man's bone, then shall he set up a sign by it, till the buriers have buried it in the valley of Hamongog.

16 And also the name of the city shall be Hamonah. Thus shall they cleanse the land.

17 And, you son of man, thus says Yahuah God; Speak to every feathered fowl, and to every beast of the field, Assemble yourselves, and come; gather yourselves on every side to My sacrifice that I do sacrifice for you, even a great sacrifice upon the mountains of Yahsrael, that you may eat flesh, and drink blood.

18 You shall eat the flesh of the mighty, and drink the blood of the princes of the earth, of rams, of lambs, and of goats, of bullocks, all of them fatlings of Bashan.

19 And you shall eat fat till you be full, and drink blood till you be drunken, of My sacrifice which I have sacrificed for you.

20 Thus you shall be filled at My table with horses and chariots, with mighty men, and with all men of war, says Yahuah God.

21 And I will set my glory among the heathen (nations), and all the heathen (nations) shall see My judgment that I have executed, and My hand that I have laid upon them.

22 So the house of Yahsrael shall know that I am Yahuah their God from that day and forward.

HIStory or OUR Story   Chapter 16

The Judgement to the Nations Who Do Not Know Yahuah's Law

This passage of scripture below is addressed to all the nations, which Yahushua addresses in judgment after He has gathered Yahsrael from the four corners of the earth. As it is written in **Psalms 147:19-20**, the scripture states that "He has not dealt so with any other nation: and as for His judgments they have not known them." It also says that **He NEVER** ruled over the other nations (**Isaiah 63:19**) The scripture says that all the nations worship idols (**Psalms 96:5**) which are not the true and living God. He punishes us for all of our sins, according to His law and the covenant that we Yahsraelites have with Him. But as for the nations that have not truly known Him or His ways He will judge them by the most fundamental law, "**Love your neighbor as yourself**" (**Leviticus 19:18/Matthew 22:39**) which is a basic human standard.

Matthew 25: 31-46

31 When the **Son of man shall come in His glory**, and all the holy angels with him, then shall He sit upon the throne of His glory:
32 And before Him shall be gathered **ALL NATIONS**: and **He shall separate them one from another**, as a shepherd **divides** His sheep from the goats:
33 And He shall set the sheep on His right hand, but the goats on the left.
34 Then shall the King say to them on His right hand, "Come, you blessed of My Father, inherit the kingdom prepared for you **from the foundation of the world**:
35 For I was **hungry**, and you gave me food: I was **thirsty**, and you gave Me drink: **I was a stranger**, and you took me in:
36 **Naked**, and you clothed me: **I was sick**, and you visited me: **I was in prison**, and you came to me."
37 Then shall the righteous answer him, saying, "Master, when did we see You **hungry**, and feed You? or **thirsty**, and gave You **drink**?
38 When did we see You **a stranger**, and take You in? or **naked**, and clothe you?
39 Or when did we see you sick, or **in prison**, and come visit you?"
40 And the King shall answer and say to them, "Verily I say to you, Inasmuch as you have done it to one of the least of **THESE MY BROTHERS**, you have done it to Me".
41 Then shall He say also to them on the left hand, "Depart from Me, you cursed, into everlasting fire, prepared for the devil and his angels:
42 For I was **hungry**, and you gave Me no food: I was **thirsty**, and you gave Me no drink:
43 I was **a stranger**, and you took Me not in: **naked**, and you did not clothe Me: sick, and **in prison**, and **you did not visit Me**."
44 Then shall they also answer Him, saying, "Master, when did we see You **hungry**, or **thirsty**, or a **stranger**, or **naked**, or **sick**, or **in prison**, and **did not come visit** You?"
45 Then shall He answer them, saying, "Verily I say to you, "Inasmuch as you did it not to one of **the least of these**, you did it NOT to Me."
46 And these shall go away into everlasting punishment: but the righteous into life eternal.

The Regeneration

Yahsrael, we must reclaim our righteous minds of our ancestors, our generative minds.

Generative means: capable of production or reproduction.

Our ancestors had their righteous minds taken from them, thus causing us to never receive that righteous mind. We received a degenerative mind.

Degenerative means: symptom) characterized by progressive, often irreversible deterioration, a decline, and loss of function .

We Africans living in America have been viewing the world through a degenerative mind. We have envisioned the world through Degenerative Western eyes instead of Generative Eastern eyes. The generative mind is the way the Original Africans viewed the world for centuries. The Euro-Americans have only been on the scene a little over 6,000 plus years and have been wreaking havoc on the planet ever since. Below is an example of the two different viewpoints on life.

Original African Generate Mind	**Euro-American Degenerate Mind**
Spiritually prosperous, technologically bankrupt	Technologically prosperous, spiritually bankrupt
Social roles are clearly defined	Social roles are easily confused
Everything in the universe is interconnected	Everything in the universe is independent
Seeks harmony with nature	Seeks dominance over nature
Injustice anywhere is injustice everywhere	Injustice over there is not injustice right here
It takes a community to raise a child	Each parent is responsible for his/her own
Embraces the past, tradition is stability	Escapes the past, tradition means stagnation
Violence and war is an obstacle to peace	Violence and war is necessary for peace
All relationships are complimentary	All relationships are competitive
Everyone can win	Everyone cannot win
Community and Family Centered	Self-Centered
Positive music, fashion, arts	Negative music, fashion, arts
The purpose of life is to live	The purpose of life is to win
You work to live	You live to work
A man's word alone can be trusted	A Man's word alone cannot be trusted
There's enough to go around for everyone	Resources are scarce
Money is a means to an end	Money is a means to more money
Spirituality is a social everyday experience	Spirituality is an intellectual concept
Education is for character development	Education is for monetary gain
You help because help is needed	You help in case you one day need help
The bible is a history book	The bible is a religious text
Religion is a culture and way of life	Religion is whatever you choose to believe
Capable of sustaining heaven on earth	Calibrated to create hell on earth

What's mine is yours	What's yours is mine and what's mine is mine
If I win we win, if I lose we lose	If I win you lose, if you win I lose
If I win we won, if you win we won	If you won then I lost

So as you can see there are some vast differences in the two mind sets. The Generative mind is love based. The Degenerative mind is fear based. We must now Re-Generate our minds back to oneness again. We must first seek to understand. Once we understand then we must inner-stand. After we inner-stand then we can over-stand. To overstand is to take information by the horns and be in command of it.

In the Original African phase of life we were healthier and lived much longer. No living creature that had breath had to die because Yahuah had given man every herb bearing seed for food in the original state of man (**Genesis 1:29**).

Another word for regeneration is **rebirth**, from which we get the phrase "born again." To be born again is opposed to, and distinguished from, our first birth, when we were conceived in sin.

Once we are evacuated out of the lands of our enemies, which we are in now, we will be in the wilderness again. And again, Yahuah will reveal His name and laws to **all of us** again first hand; not second hand through a pastor, elder, the Pope, mother, father, friend, monk, but personally.

Jeremiah 31: 29-34

29 "In those days people will no longer say,
   'The parents have eaten sour grapes,
   and the children's teeth are set on edge.'
30 Instead, everyone will die for their own sin; whoever eats sour grapes—their own teeth will be set on edge.
31 "The days are coming," declares Yahuah,
   "when I will make **a New Covenant**
   WITH THE PEOPLE OF YAHSRAEL
   and **with the people of Yahudah**.
32 It will not be like the covenant
   I made with their ancestors
   when I took them by the hand
   to lead them out of Egypt,
   because they broke My covenant,
   though I was a husband to them,"
   declares Yahuah.
33 "This is the covenant I will make **WITH THE PEOPLE OF YAHSRAEL**
   after that time," declares Yahuah.
   "I will put My law in their Minds
   and write it on their hearts.
   I will be their God,
   and they will be My people.
34 NO LONGER WILL THEY TEACH their neighbor,
   or say to one another, 'Know Yahuah,'
   because **THEY WILL ALL KNOW ME,**
   from the least of them to the greatest,"
   declares Yahuah.
   "For I will forgive their wickedness
   and will remember their sins no more."

HIStory or OUR Story Chapter 17

Ezekiel 20: 33-38

33 "As I live, says Yahuah God, surely with a mighty hand, and with a stretched out arm, and with fury poured out, will I rule over you:
34 And I will **bring you out from the people**, and will gather you out of the countries wherein you are scattered, **with a mighty hand**, and **with a stretched out arm**, and **with fury poured out**.
35 And **I will bring you into the wilderness of the people**, and there will I plead with you **FACE TO FACE**.
36 **Like as I pleaded with your fathers** in the wilderness of the land of Egypt, **so will I plead with you**, says Yahuah God.
37 And I will cause you to pass under the rod, and **I will bring you into the bond of the Covenant**:
38 And **I will purge out from among you the rebels**, and them that transgress against Me: I will bring them forth out of the country where they dwell, and **they shall not enter into the land of Yahsrael**: and you shall know that I am Yahuah."

At that point, there will be no question as to whether there is or is not a God. There will be no question as to what to call Him. There will be no question on His law and how to keep it and He will test us once again. Everyone who makes it out of these enemy lands **will not** make it into the kingdom, but only those who are spiritually re-born, which we call 'born again'. They will make it into the kingdom.

John 3: 3,5

3 Yahushua answered and said to him, "Truly, truly, I say to you, Except a man be born again, he cannot see the kingdom of God".
5 Yahushua answered," Truly, truly, I say to you, Except a man be born of water (natural birth) and of the **Spirit** (supernatural birth of fire (Matthew 3:11), He **CANNOT ENTER** into the kingdom of God".

So during this time, Yahuah will plead with everyone **face to face**. There will be no excuse to sin. Not only will we, the Hebrew Yahsraelites, have to keep the **Torah** (law), but so will all of the nations. If they do not, then they will be destroyed with plagues. He will purge out the rebels from among the nations as well. They will have to keep His Sabbaths, Feasts, and Laws. This time of testing and Yahsrael's ruling will be what takes place during the 1,000 year period.

Read Zechariah 14: 16-19

16 And it shall come to pass, that **EVERY ONE THAT IS LEFT OF ALL THE NATIONS** which came against Yahrushalom shall even **GO UP FROM YEAR TO YEAR** to worship the King, Yahuah of hosts, and to **KEEP THE FEAST OF TABERNACLES**
17 And it shall be, that **WHOSEVER** will not come up of all the families of the earth to Yahrushalom to worship the King, Yahuah of hosts, even upon them shall be **no rain**.
18 And **if the family of Egypt go not up,** and **come not**, that have **no rain**; there shall be the **plague**, wherewith Yahuah will **strike the nations** that **COME NOT UP TO KEEP THE FEAST OF TABERNACLES**.
19 This shall be THE PUNISHMENT of Egypt, and **THE PUNISHMENT OF ALL NATIONS** that **COME NOT UP TO KEEP THE FEAST OF TABERNACLES**.

All nations will also keep the same Sabbath in the New Earth

Read Isaiah 66: 22-24

22 For as the NEW HEAVENS and the NEW EARTH, which I will make, shall remain before me, says Yahuah, so shall **your seed** and **your name** remain.
23 And it shall come to pass, that from one NEW MOON TO ANOTHER, and from ONE SABBATH TO ANOTHER, shall **ALL FLESH** come to worship before Me, says Yahuah.
24 And they shall go forth, and look upon **the carcasses of the men that have transgressed** against Me: for their worm shall not die, neither shall their fire be quenched; and they shall be an abhorring to all flesh.

And so shall we ever be with Yahuah.

HIStory or OUR Story   Chapter 17

In the 1,000 year regeneration, Yahsrael will be the ruling nation on the planet with Yahushua at the head. The scriptures says that Yahushua will rule with a **rod** of iron. Yahsrael will be that rod that is in His hand in which He rules the nations. Perceive the following scriptures:

Isaiah 61: 1-9
1 The Spirit of Yahuah God is upon me; because Yahuah has anointed me to preach good tidings to the meek; he has sent me to bind up the brokenhearted, to proclaim **liberty** to the captives, and the opening of the prison to them that are bound;
2 To proclaim the acceptable year of Yahuah, and **the day of vengeance of our God; to comfort all that mourn;**
3 To appoint to them that mourn in Zion, to give to them beauty for ashes, the oil of joy for mourning, the garment of praise for the spirit of heaviness; that they might be called trees of righteousness, the planting of Yahuah that He might be glorified.
4 And they shall build the old ruins, they shall raise up the former desolations, and they shall repair the ruined cities, the desolations of many generations.
5 And **strangers** shall stand and feed **your** flocks, and **the sons of the foreigners** shall be your plowmen and your vinedressers.
6 But **you shall be named the Priests of Yahuah**: men shall call you the Ministers of our God: you shall eat the riches of the Nations, and in their glory shall you boast yourselves.
7 For your shame **you shall have double**; and for confusion they shall rejoice in their portion: therefore **in their land they shall possess the double**: everlasting joy shall be to them.
8 "For I Yahuah love judgment, I hate robbery for burned offering; and I will direct their work in **truth**, and I will make an everlasting covenant with them.
9 And **their seed shall be known among the nations**, and their offspring **among the people**: all that see them **shall acknowledge them**, that **they are** the seed which Yahuah has blessed."

Jeremiah 16: 19-21
    19 O Yahuah, my strength and my stronghold,
      And my refuge in the day of distress,
      To You the **Gentiles**(nations) will come
      From the ends of the earth and say,
      "Our fathers have inherited lies,
      Vanity and things of no profit."
    20 Can man make gods for himself?
      Yet they are not gods!
    21 "Therefore behold, I am going to make them know
      This time I will make them know
      My power and My might;
      And they shall know that My name is YAHUAH."

HIStory or OUR Story   **Chapter 17**

Isaiah 61: 10-14

10 "The **sons of the strangers** will rebuild your walls,
and their kings will serve you.
Though in anger I struck you,
in favor I will show you compassion.
11 Your gates will always stand open,
they will never be shut, day or night,
so that people may bring you the wealth of the nations
their kings led in triumphal procession.
12 For the nation or kingdom that will not serve you will perish;
it will be utterly ruined.
13 "The glory of Lebanon will come to you,
the juniper, the fir and the cypress together,
to adorn My sanctuary;
and I will glorify the place for My feet.
14 The **children of your oppressors** will come bowing before you;
all who despise you will **bow down at your feet**
and will call you the City of Yahuah,
Zion of the Holy One of Yahsrael.
15 "Although you have been forsaken and hated,
with no one traveling through,
I will make you the everlasting pride
and the joy of all generations.
16 You will drink the milk of nations
and be nursed at royal breasts.
Then you will know that I, Yahuah, am your Savior,
your Redeemer, the Mighty One of Yahkob.

HIStory or OUR Story   **Chapter 17**

Acts 1: 6-7

6 So when they had come together, they asked him, "Master, will you at this time **RESTORE THE KINGDOM TO YAHSRAEL?**"
7 He said to them, "It is not for you to know times or seasons that the Father has fixed by His own authority"

Revelation 12: 5

5 "And **she** (Yahsrael) brought forth and a **man child** (Christ) who was **to rule all the nations** with a **rod** of iron: and her child was caught up to God and to His throne"

The question becomes who or what is this rod of iron? What is this rod in his hand? The answer is Yahsrael. See the below scripture.

Ezekiel 37: 16-19

16 "Moreover, you son of man, take you **one rod**, and write upon it, For Yahudah, and for the children of Yahsrael his companions: then take another **rod**, and write upon it, For Yosef, the stick of Ephrayim and for all the house of Yahsrael his companions:
17 And **join them one to another into one rod**; and **they shall become one** in your hand.
18 And when the children of your people shall speak to you, saying, "Will you not show us what you mean by these?
19 Say to them, Thus says Yahuah God; Behold, I will take **the rod of Yoseph**, which is in the hand of Ephrayim, and the tribes of Yahsrael his fellows, and will put them with him, even with the **rod of Yahudah**, and make **THEM ONE ROD**, and **they shall be one** in My hand.
20 When the sticks on which you write are in your hand before their eyes
21 Then say to them, Thus says Yahuah God: Behold, I will take **the people of Yahsrael** from the nations among which they have gone, and will **GATHER THEM FROM ALL AROUND**, and bring them to their **OWN LAND**."

Micah 6: 9

9 "Yahuah's voice cries to the city, and the man of wisdom shall consider Your name: "Listen to the rod, and Who has appointed it."

Revelation 2: 26-27

26 "And he that overcomes, and keeps My works to the end, to him will I GIVE POWER OVER THE NATIONS:
27 And he shall rule them with a **rod of iron**; as the vessels of a potter shall they be broken to pieces: even as I received of My Father."

HIStory or OUR Story   **Chapter 18**

A Letter To Men

Gentlemen, if you're lucky enough to find a woman who will pick you up when you fall, notice when something is wrong, accept you just the way you are, and still love you for everything you're not, you don't let that woman go for nothing or anyone. You hold on to her while loving, respecting, honoring, valuing, treasuring, admiring, caring, guiding, protecting, but most importantly being faithful till the very end, no matter what because finding such a woman is the most difficult thing nowadays.
If you love the woman you're with you better prove it because if you don't; they might not believe it. For **love is not a noun to be defined, but a verb to be acted upon.**

Gentlemen, touch a woman's MIND and you get her INTEREST. Touch a woman's HEART, and you get her LOVE. Touch a woman's SOUL and you get PASSION beyond your wildest dreams. Touch ALL THREE and you have found your SOUL-MATE for life. Gentlemen if you truly love the woman you're with, you don't need to unbutton her shirt to have a better view of her heart. **Touch her heart**, not her body. **Steal her attention**, not her virginity, and make her smile, don't waste her tears.

Gentlemen, if you're out there going after the looks of these basic brainless females nowadays, you're misguided. Yes, you love the way she's looking now, but are you going to love her the same way when her breasts start sagging? When she no longer has teeth and needs dentures? When her hair starts falling and turning grey, or better yet, when that '*big backyard*' you love turns into a sack of wrinkled meat with cellulite? Are you going to be there for her then, or just walk away like the majority of **so-called** men do these days and replace her? If so, is that what you call love? My friend, you're delusional and have no idea of what love is if all you're doing is falling for and chasing the **outward appearance** of a woman. **A real man doesn't chase women, HE LEADS THEM.** Learn the difference between LOVE and LUST. Next time, try falling in love with her inner beauty, mind, character, faithfulness, ability to hold down a home, job or school. The physical beauty of a woman fades away as she gets older, but her soul becomes wiser and her passion to love becomes stronger: Charm is deceptive, and beauty is fleeting; but a woman who fears Yahuah is to be praised, **Proverbs 31:30.**
Gentlemen, try finding a woman with a brain, they all have a vagina.
And if you are in a relationship, remember do not discuss your relationship issues with your family, friends, or others. Whatever you do, **do not seek relationship counsel under someone else's covers.** If you want something to last forever, **you treat it differently**. You shield it and protect it. You never abuse it. You don't expose it to the elements. You **don't treat it as common or ordinary**. If it ever becomes tarnished, you lovingly polish it until it shines like new. It becomes special because you have made it so in your mind and heart, and it grows more beautiful and precious as time goes by. Treat your spouse and your marriage likewise and your marriage will last forever. **LOVE is not about how much you say 'I love you', but how much you can prove that it's true.** And women do not want a "*Real Nigga*", they want a "**Real Man**". So let's cease from using this **vulgar** term **taught to us by our slave-masters** and passed down. If you allow someone to call you a '*nigga*', then you are still a slave. If you call one of your own a '*nigga*', you are an Uncle Tom. Do not sag your pants. Slave masters had male slaves do it so they would know they **DON'T WEAR THE PANTS!!** If you forget everything that I've said, do not forget this: **love is not a noun to be defined, but a verb to be acted upon.**

A Letter To Women

Ladies, real women don't label themselves as "Dimes", "Barbies", or "Bad Bitches", because real men don't carry **loose change**, play with **dolls** or turn a **dog** into their wife. **A real man will be more interested in opening your mind before he attempts to open your legs**. Put some clothes on. Why do you want to be 'eye candy' when you can be someone's soul food?

If you're not being treated with love and respect, check your price tag. Perhaps you have marked yourself down. It's YOU who tell people what you're worth, by what you accept. **Get off the clearance rack and get behind the glass where they keep the valuables! DARE TO BE RARE!** Bottom line: Value yourself more! If you don't, no one else will. Also, if you have to keep wondering where you stand with someone, maybe it's time you stop standing and start walking. Don't blame people for disappointing you, blame yourself for expecting too much from them. Dare to be rare. To blend in blend out. Don't be able to match shoes and purses and not be able to match your baby daddy, what until marriage.

Open your mind before you open your legs. A 'husband' is not just a title. Husband is not just the ability to make a wife pregnant. Husband means great responsibility. Husband means house band; the band that binds the house together. A godly husband is a Priest, a Provider and a Protector. As a Priest, a husband subjects himself to Christ and opens the Word and leads his family to Christ through daily family worship at the family altar. As a Provider, the husband works hard to ensure that the family is well fed, nourished and decently dressed. As a Protector, the husband shelters his family from physical harm, emotional and spiritual attacks. A godly husband, the man of the house will stand up for his marriage and defend his wife and children, and fight for his family at all costs.

HIStory or OUR Story Chapter 20

A Love Letter to the Righteous From Dr. Paula King

Dear Righteous Ambassadors,

I love you! Let's stay in love always. You are the light bearers of the world. You are ambassadors of the Truth. You represent the best and brightest, the most brilliant minds on the planet earth. I am writing this love letter to encourage you to stay in love. Let the law of love and the law of kindness dominate and define your personal style and your interpersonal relationships. Yah has endowed you with much truth. As you continue to grow in wisdom and knowledge, let us always remember to operate in the spirit of love and patience toward one another. We must resist the tendency for "knowledge to puff up" or fill us with pride and remember that "charity/love edifies" (love builds up) – **1 Corinthians 8:1**.

Historically, as a people, we have endured the ruthless injustice of slavery, disparate and disadvantaged circumstances and countless tragedies, horrors and atrocities. Others have indeed received therapy or counseling for much less! However members of the diaspora haven't been so fortunate. No doctor has ever attended to the emotional and psychological lacerations, wounds, avulsions and abrasions sustained over the course of our history. We had to lean on that age old proverb "physician, heal thyself"! The degree of injury and imbalance is immense! Hence, we are co-facilitators of our own healing. Therefore, love, compassion and patience are prerequisites for our interpersonal relations with each other.

We must remember that in this trajectory called "life", as we have our individual awakenings and continue to recover from the emotional and psychological traumas of our past, we are in various stages of healing and recovery.

Moreover, we are in various stages of rehabilitation from our collective miseducation and misunderstanding. One of my favorite albums, from several years ago, is "The Miseducation of Lauryn Hill" by Lauryn Hill. Sadly, Lauryn wasn't the only one that was miseducated. Summarily, we have all been miseducated to varying degrees—every last one of us!

At one time or another, we each have been lulled to sleep and have had our own pre-ordained date with destiny and spiritual awakening. In the words of author Neville Goddard, **"we sleep collectively, but we awaken individually"**. **Everyone doesn't wake up when we wake up; just like in real life**. It is a process. So, as we shake off the spirit of slumber and sleep and experience awakenings and ascension of consciousness, let us be ever so loving and supportive of other Ambassadors as they, too, find their way to righteousness and truth.

HIStory or OUR Story   **Chapter 20**

On that note, I often hear enlightened members of the diaspora, who now have knowledge of the truth, mock, belittle and deride other members of the diaspora who have not fully come into the truth yet. We must do better. In the infamous words of Lauryn Hill,"how you gon' win when you ain't right within". We are called to a higher standard. We are commanded to love one another. Yahushua commands us in

John 13:34, "A new commandment I give to you, That you love one another; as I have loved you, that you also love one another."

As those that honor and abide by the Torah i.e. law of Yahuah, we must remember that Love IS the fulfilling of the law! "Love works no ill to his neighbor: therefore love is the fulfilling of the law." (**Romans 13:10**). For all the law is fulfilled in one word, even in this; You shall love your neighbor as yourself" (**Galatians 5:14**).

Therefore, if you encounter members of the diaspora who are still in the infancy of their spiritual walk in Westernized Christian tradition or some other spiritual/philosophical orientation, be loving and patient with them. Don't disparage your brothers and sisters. Let us not forget. "There, but for the grace of God, go I"; meaning without Yah's grace I could be in the same situation or worse.

Let's keep it real. The grand majority of us were not born into families who knew or taught the full scope of Hebraic traditions and culture. Most of us started our journeys indoctrinated in the teachings of the traditional Western Christian church or Islam, or Buddhism or some other spiritual/philosophical path. Now that you've emerged from the darkness of ignorance and miseducation into the marvelous light of knowledge and understanding, don't hold those that are unaware and less fortunate than you in derision. Let the "light" of your enlightenment be a lamp to the path of other righteous brothers and sisters, as they awaken and discover the truth also.

Bottom line: We, too, were once enshrouded with ignorance as it relates to our Hebraic heritage and culture. At one point in time, we were exactly where many of our family members, friends and associates now find themselves. I cannot emphasize enough, please refrain from ridiculing your brother or sister for not knowing what you think they ought to know. I say this because this issue is a **serious problem** in our community. They don't know what they don't know. So, don't criticize your brothers and sisters. Instead, help them. Encourage your brothers and sisters along the way.

Be patient. **Remember that education often occurs in gradations and phases**. Most educational models reflect this fact by having "grades" (1_{st} grade, 2_{nd} grade, 3_{rd} grade, etc.) or other classifications (freshman, sophomore, junior, senior, etc.). Even upon graduation, we graduate at different levels (Summa Cum Laude, Magna Cum Laude, and Cum Laude). Moreover, we all learn at different paces and in different ways. Please respect that everyone's awakening and the time table involved will be unique. Again, it's only by Yah's grace that we have been refined from the dross of our previous miseducation and sin (transgression of the law i.e. **I John 3:4**).

So, let's stay in love. Love is the healing balm. Love is the highest vibrational force in the universe. Think about it. Love is **THE ONLY** emotion that God declares as equivalent to Himself. **1 John 4:8** states that "**God is love**". The scriptures go on to proclaim in **1 John 4:10-11** "Herein is love, not that we loved God, but that He loved us, and sent His Son to be the propitiation for our sins. **<u>Beloved, if God so loved us, we ought also to love one another.</u>** "And this commandment have we from Him, That he who loves God loves his brother also (**1 John 4:21**)

I Corinthians 13: 1-7 delivers a powerful exposition on Love.

I Corinthians 13 (New Living Translation)

1 If I could speak all the languages of earth and of angels, but didn't **LOVE** others, I would only be a noisy gong or a clanging cymbal.
2 If I had the gift of prophecy, and if I understood all of God's secret plans and possessed all knowledge, and if I had such faith that I could move mountains, but didn't **LOVE** others, I would be nothing.
3 If I gave everything I have to the poor and even sacrificed my body, I could boast about it; but if I didn't **LOVE** others, I would have gained nothing.
4 **LOVE** is patient and kind. **LOVE** is not jealous or boastful or proud or rude.
5 It does not demand its own way. It is not irritable, and it keeps no record of being wronged.
6 It does not rejoice about injustice but rejoices whenever the truth wins out.
7 **LOVE NEVER GIVES UP**, never loses faith, is always hopeful, and endures through every circumstance."

HIStory or OUR Story   **Chapter 20**

In closing, I love you, my Hebrew brothers and sisters! Continue in the faith and let's stay in love always—Doctor's orders! ☺

Continued blessings to you for a healing and prosperous journey,

Dr. Paula King, M.D., Professor of Health Science

HIStory or OUR Story

THE TRUTH

The Truth is not always clear and on the surface
Most of the time it's buried deep and done on purpose
Scoffed at, down trodden, treated and called worthless
But in the end the work and effort, is all worth it
The Truth isn't popular, it can hurt and offend
Reveal the best of a person, or the worse in a friend
It can open your eyes to Lies lurking and sin
Show us how our people just go to church and pretend
First John two four may go against tradition
Since the one who says, "I know Him, is likely to be a Christian
But doesn't regard His commands, listen, because this is wisdom
The scripture says he is a liar and the truth isn't in him
It's one thing to be blind, but to cover your eyes
To read it line after line and still utter the lies
There's no excuse, the truth would be what you despise
In conclusion you're a deceiver and a lover of lies
Fear Yahuah and keep his commands, they are commands not suggestions
Open the Bible and read your history, and find the answers to all of your questions
So-called black Negro of North America, know thyself
You are the peculiar treasure chosen of the Most High and you've been hidden at the back of the shelf
You are here because your forefathers didn't follow the Most High's Laws
You were brought here for punishment and to be destroyed without pause
But now your Father's calling you home from this bondage saying, "Come out of her My people"
Leave vain man-made traditions and days, Islam and Christianity most deceitful
It is written, "You shall know the truth and the truth shall make you free"
You don't even know who you are, yet you claim you've been free since 1863
If a man tells you that you have freedom of choice go through, either door number one or door number two
He gave you your options meaning he already pre-selected your choice so it doesn't matter what you do
90% of everything you've been taught and told, I'm sorry to say has been a lie
But you were taught by the oppressed and the oppressors of your oppressors in whom you unknowingly rely
You are the Hebrew Yahsrael, the set apart people of the book
Read the scriptures with a renewed mind, all you have to do is open up the book and your eyes and just LOOK!

HIStory or OUR Story

REFERENCES:

1. The Original King James Bible
2. http://www.marytruth.com/home/constantine-cover-up-and-sun-worship#sthash.ActsoIsd.dpuf
3. Dr. Paula King
4. Dr. Cindy Trimm - quote"If your context is wrong your conclusion is wrong"
5. Dr. Bobby E. Wright
6. Dr. Martin Luther King- "quote from Letter in Birmingham Jail about Injustice anywhere"
7. Dr. Julia Hare- (quote from Black Family Speech)
8. Muhammad Ali - (You my Enemy Speech)
9. Malcolm X- "Grass Roots Speech"
10. Leo Muhammad
11. Kim Torah - Quotes from "2 Witnesses Explained"
12. Smithsonian Institute
13. http://www.stewartsynopsis.com/washitaw.htm
14. http://www.avengingtheancestors.com/releases/wedidit.htm (http://www.avengingtheancestors.com/releases/wedidit.htm)
15. Images of Public Domain
16. The Jewish Encyclopedia
17. The Encyclopedia Judaica (1972): The Universal Jewish Encyclopedia: The Universal Jewish
18. Encyclopedia: http://guardianlv.com/2014/05/what-jesus-really-looked-like-prepare-to-be-shocked-video/#zSzm8KiTYowQPBe3.99
19. http://www.eyewitnesstohistory.com/jewishtemple.htm)
20. (http://www.ohchr.org/EN/ProfessionalInterest/Pages/Vienna.aspx (http://www.ohchr.org/EN/ProfessionalInterest/Pages/Vienna.aspx))
21. (http://www.stewartsynopsis.com/washitaw.htm (http://www.stewartsynopsis.com/washitaw.htm))
22. (The Encyclopedia Judaica (1972): The Universal Jewish Encyclopedia: The Universal Jewish Encyclopedia:
23. (http://en.wikipedia.org/wiki/Primacy_of_the_Bishop_of_Rome (http://en.wikipedia.org/wiki/Primacy_of_the_Bishop_of_Rome))
24. (http://www.timeanddate.com/calendar/december-solstice-customs.html (http://www.timeanddate.com/calendar/december-solstice-customs.html))
25. (http://www.timeanddate.com/calendar/december-solstice-customs.html (http://www.timeanddate.com/calendar/december-solstice-customs.html))
26. http://www.timeanddate.com/calendar/december-solstice-customs.html
27. (http://www.timeanddate.com/calendar/december-solstice-customs.html () ")
http://www.bibletruth.cc/Easter.htm
28. (The New Book of Knowledge)
29. (http://www.avengingtheancestors.com/releases/wedidit.htm (http://www.avengingtheancestors.com/releases/wedidit.htm))
30. (http://www.avengingtheancestors.com/releases/wedidit.htm (http://www.avengingtheancestors.com/releases/wedidit.htm))

HIStory or OUR Story

31. New King James Version (NKJV)
32. New American Standard Version (NASV)
33. Hebrew Roots Bible
34. Dre Akil - "Slave Mentality" quote
35. Hilenna Model
36. Dr. Martin Luther King "Burning House" Speech
37. Malcolm X- Unity Rally Speech in Harlem, NY 1963
38. Lauryn Hill
39. Neville Goddard
40. http://raceandhistory.com/historicalviews/ancientamerica.htm)
41. James Scott Trimm

I hope that you enjoyed the numerous illustrations put in this book. I formatted this book to cater to the reader who is a visually-dominant learner. With this truth, I hope you research it thoroughly because there is so much more truth than what I have revealed to you. One book could not contain it. My hope is that you equip yourselves with this truth and spread it because the so called 'black people' in America are suffering from an identity crisis. We are missing a common bond. We have NO COMMUNITIES! Community broken down, by its morphology, (a linguistics term meaning 'the form and structure of words') is common-unity. We have been divided according to the Jim Crow laws, Willie Lynch letter, etc. We have no unity. We don't look for common ground with one another. We look for differences . So, we lack 'common ground' and 'unity'. We are devoid of community.

We search for unity in all things, but where we should. We used to find unity in the fact that we all shared a common condition. Nowadays, our oppressors have allowed some of us to have improved conditions that are better than others in the struggle, causing us to divide further. We are like 'crabs in a barrel'. We pull those down who are trying to ascend from our condition. The reason is, we are afraid that if those 'fortunate few', or 'talented tenth' rise above us, they will snub us.

The so called 'blacks' in America are **looking for unity** and a **sense of belonging** in all kinds of organizations, except for unity in **Yahsrael or in the name of our God, Yahuah**.

All these organizations have a common ground which have unifying ingredients, for example:
Gangs -
Bloods: Initiation process (beat-in/kill), **hand symbols, terminology, colors** (red) and **creed**
Crips: Initiation process (beat-in), **hand symbols, terminology, colors** (blue) and **creed**
ViceLords: Initiation process (beat in), **hand symbols, terminology, colors** (gold, black and red) and **creed**
Folk Nation: Initiation process (beat-in), **hand symbols, terminology, colors** (blue and black) and **creed**

The four gangs above are mainstream gangs, but there are many other black gangs. See below.

Almighty Black P. Stone Nation, Almighty Vice Lord Nation, Four Corner Hustlers, Black Disciples, Black Guerilla Family, Black Mafia Family, Black P. Stones (Jungles), Bounty Hunter Bloods, Double II Set, Nine Trey Gangsters, Pirus, Sex Money Murda, United Blood Nation, East Nashville Crips, Du Roc Crips, Grape Street Watts Crips, Rollin 30's Harlem Crips, Rollin 60's Neighborhood Crips, Venice Shoreline Crips, D.C. Blacks, Gangster Disciples, OutLaw Gangster Disciples, Hidden Valley Kings, KUMI 415, Mickey Cobras, People Nation, Philadelphia Black Mafia, Zoe Pound Gang, etc.

We also have petty divisions such as East Coast, West Coast, North, South **seeking territory** in our enemies' land. We claim hoods, blocks and streets, which only exist in our minds because these things truly belong to the cities, which belong to the states, which belong to the United States--all of which are owned by Europe, our original oppressors.
And these gangs are all unified by hand symbols, terminology, colors and creeds.

IN GREEK LIFE
Some mainstream male fraternity unifying traits are:
Alphas: Initiation process (MIP/Pledging), **symbols, terminology, bylaws, colors** (black&gold), and **creed**
Kappas: Initiation process (MIP/Pledging), **symbols, terminology, bylaws, colors** (red &white) and **creed**
Omegas: Initiation process (MIP/Pledging), **symbols, terminology, bylaws, colors** (purple & gold) and **creed**

Some mainstream female sorority unifying traits are:
Deltas: Initiation process (MIP/Pledging), **symbols, terminology, bylaws, colors** (red and white) and **creed**
AKAs: Initiation process (MIP/Pledging), **symbols, terminology, bylaws, colors** (pink and green) and **creed**
Zeta Phi Beta: Initiation process (MIP/Pledging), **symbols, terminology, bylaws, colors** (royal blue and white) and **creed**

These organizations have secret proceedings and secret knowledge that you only learn if you are a member.

With Yahuah's law, it's meant to be known and practiced by everyone openly. Nothing is to be said or done in secret. **John 18:20 "Yahushua (Christ) answered him,** "I spoke OPENLY to THE WORLD; I always taught in the synagogue, and in the temple, where the Jews always gather: and IN SECRET have I said nothing"

We run to **European Church Denominations** that were established before we came to America looking for truth, unity and a sense of belonging. I mention European denominations because they were **ALL** established by Europeans, and we were not even allowed to participate in them when they were established.

We are all really seeking two things: Unity and Community. We had that in Yahuah's laws and the only way to return to true Nation building is getting back to Kingdom life. Yahuah's laws distinguish us from this wicked world, but unify us as a nation. It is our knowledge and understanding in the sight of the nations. **Read: Deuteronomy 4:5-8, Esther 3:8**
5Behold, I have taught you STATUTES and JUDGMENTS, even as Yahuah my God commanded me, that you should do so in the land where you go to possess it.
6 Keep therefore and DO THEM; for THIS IS YOUR WISDOM AND UNDERSTANDING in the sight of the nations, which shall hear all these statutes, and say, Surely this GREAT NATION is a WISE and UNDERSTANDING PEOPLE
7 For what nation is there so great, who has God so near to them, as Yahuah our God is in all things that we call upon Him for?
8 And what nation is there so great, that HAS STATUES AND JUDGMENTS SO RIGHTEOUS as ALL THIS LAW, which I set before you this day?

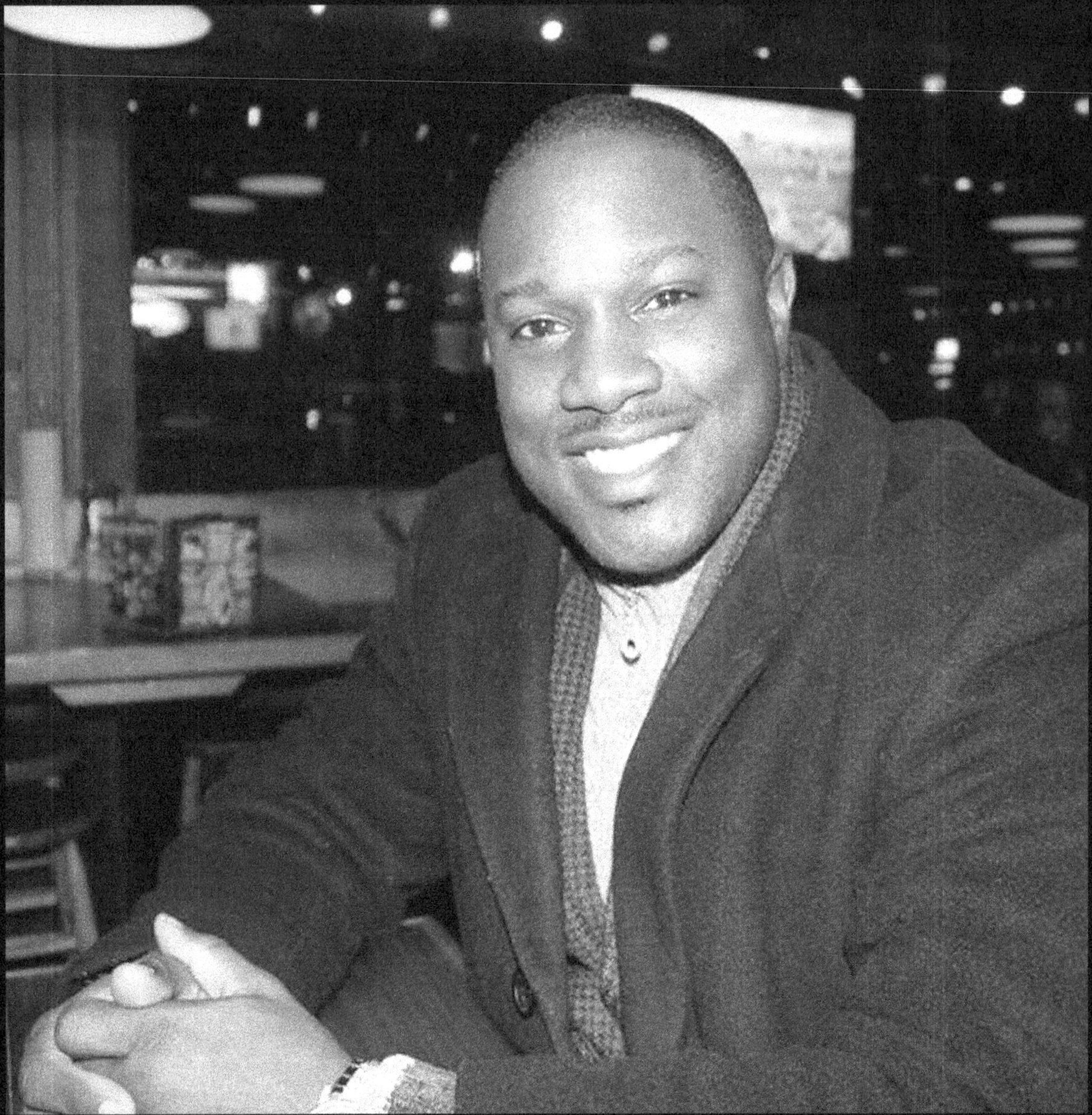

They say "If you want to hide something from black people, then put it in a book." And I say they have been somewhat successful, because they have fed us so many lies and contradictions that we no longer wanted to read. I am here to put the Truth in a book and cause us to read and become conscious again. The eyes are useless when the mind is blind. Read this and heal your injured mind.

What's Written is Written

ISBN 978-1-4116-8691-5

www.ingramcontent.com/pod-product-compliance
Lightning Source LLC
Chambersburg PA
CBHW081222170426
43198CB00017B/2688